The Spoils of World War II

The Spoils of World War II

The American Military's Role in the Stealing of Europe's Treasures

KENNETH D. ALFORD

A Birch Lane Press Book
PUBLISHED BY CAROL PUBLISHING GROUP

A Birch Lane Press Book
Published by Carol Publishing Group
Birch Lane Press is a registered trademark of Carol Communications, Inc.
Editorial Offices: 600 Madison Avenue, New York, N.Y. 10022
Sales & Distribution Offices: 120 Enterprise Avenue, Secaucus, N.J. 07094
In Canada: Canadian Manda Group, P.O. Box 920 Station U, Toronto, Ontario M8Z 5P9
Queries regarding rights and permissions should be addressed to Carol Publishing Group, 600 Madison Avenue, New York, N.Y. 10022

Carol Publishing Group books are available at special discounts for bulk purchases, sales promotions, fund-raising, or educational purposes. Special editions can be created to specifications. For details contact: Special Sales Department, Carol Publishing Group, 120 Enterprise Avenue, Secaucus, N.J. 07094

Design by Mher Raffi Nercessian

Manufactured in the United States of America

10 9 8 7 6 5 4 3 2 1

Library of Congress Cataloging-in-Publication Data

Alford, Kenneth D.
    The spoils of World War II : the American military's role in stealing Europe's treasures / by Kenneth D. Alford.
        p.   cm.
    "A Birch Lane Press book."
    ISBN 1-55972-237-1
    1. World War, 1939-1945—Art and the war.   2. Art thefts—Europe—History—20th century.   3. Art treasures in war—Europe.
I. Title.
D810.A7A37   1994
709'.4'09044—dc20   94-12608
                                                     CIP

Contents

v

Contents

(Illustrations follow page 84)

Introduction

Everybody sends home souvenirs through the Army Post Office, whose sign over the door reads "The best loot in the world passes through these doors."
—*Company History: 603 Graves Registration Company*

In 1980, QUITE BY CHANCE, I read a misfiled document at the MacArthur Archives in Norfolk, Virginia, concerning U.S. soldiers filching valuables from civilian homes in Japan. Since it was written at the division level, the document did not mention looting, but described the confiscation of jewelry and art under military orders.

Later, at the National Archives in Washington, D.C., I requested the Joint Chiefs of Staff directive for removing such valuables. The archivist was convinced I had read about this in a novel. (Later I discovered that the answer to my inquiry was Military Law 53.) During our conversation I asked what had become of the Nazi gold the U.S. Army recovered from Merkers, Germany, a small village in Thüringia about two miles from the former East German border. He did not know, but after further conversation told me that the Center of Military History in Washington had a folder about the recovery of the Merkers gold.

I arranged a visit to the center. They were very helpful and gave me a folder to review, which provided much information about the gold at Merkers, including a reference to the Bretton Woods Conference's Resolution VI, authorizing the gold's seizure.

Beginning with the *New York Times* index for 1945, I began researching. In addition to Bretton Woods information, I found a newspaper story about a Hungarian train loaded with treasures that was seized by the Americans at Badgastein, Austria. This, in turn, led me to explore the *Foreign Relations Series of the United States,* which I borrowed from the Virginia State Library and Archives. These volumes contain a summary of Department of State foreign relations activities and a decimal number relating to documents stored in the National Archives. I learned of gold seized from Italy, Hungary, and other European countries. I went to the National Archives armed with decimal numbers and requested this record group, which consisted of two large cartloads of documents. In two days of research I found little information about the gold seizure, but I identified the army units involved in the capture of it. Within these thousands of documents was one reference to a Hungarian Gold Train, with a file number of S4.8002/2.

Much later, at the U.S. Military Archives, I uncovered some additional intriguing information in the after-action reports. Material concerning the Hungarian Gold Train had been removed from all pertinent folders. Each folder contained a checkout card, written in pencil, and now illegible except for the name Midkiff, a former archives employee who had died in 1972. A search through other material pointed to the Foreign Exchange Depository.

I continued to write for information and visit the Military Archives about two days each month, making good progress but finding nothing about the mysterious train. I wrote more letters and spot-checked U.S. Army records for Austria, since the train had been captured there.

I doggedly continued, requesting in writing folder number S4.8002/2—the number I'd discovered during my research in the summer of 1982. Several months later the assistant chief, Archives Division, phoned me, saying he had my letter but that the folder was somewhere in one of several thousand boxes and that my request was unreasonable. Furthermore, he continued, the boxes were covered with a layer of fine dust, which I already knew because I had searched some of the boxes with a handkerchief over my nose in order to breathe. I offered to go through the boxes with the help of my son, who was home from college. The assistant chief thought we would madly search through all of the boxes for the single folder, but I asked him to look in box 1000 first. Based on the file sequence in that box, we would know whether to search in boxes 1–1000 or go to boxes greater than 1000. Then I would look into box 500 to narrow the search down to 500 boxes. By halving the range of boxes each time, the tenth or eleventh box would contain the folder I wanted. This is the process—called a binary search—that a computer uses to search large data files.

About an hour later the assistant chief called back saying he had the folder I wanted. It contained a typed checkout card showing that the Judge Advocate General's Office in the Pentagon had removed the files in September 1966. That same afternoon, the archives informed me that they had all of the Hungarian Gold Train material in one box for my review. Eureka!

Through the Retired Activities Division, I located Captain Howard A. Mackenzie, who had been the property control officer of the Hungarian Gold Train treasure. When I later interviewed him at his home in Alexandria, Virginia, he mentioned the court-martial of several guards who had stolen valuables from a warehouse in Salzburg, Austria.

Excited by this new information, I wrote to different departments in the Army, and requested information about this incident and an index of court-martial subjects. I was told, however, that I could not review any index, because that might involve an invasion of privacy of innocent individuals. At this point I almost gave up hope.

Weeks later I was having lunch at the Western Sizzlin Steak House in Richmond, Virginia, when I happened to notice that on the restaurant wall were several shelves holding fifty large volumes of court-martial reports, part of the decor. I was so startled that I rudely lunged over an occupied table and began flipping through the books, which contained court-martial reviews for the 1950s, 1960s, and 1970s. The restaurant manager said he had bought ten linear feet of books from Fort Lee during a sale and agreed to loan me one of the books. I then copied the cover of the book and two pages of court-martial cases and mailed them, along with a cover letter describing how I had obtained the material, to the Clerk of Court of the U.S Army Judiciary. I was subsequently invited to visit its law school library in Charlottesville, Virginia, and to use its indexes and facilities. Much later I received the court-martial records I had been seeking from the U.S. Army Judiciary.

After thirteen years of meticulous research, I have uncovered the truth that the U.S. Army, after defeating the German army, proceeded to pillage the German nation. Enlisted men, officers, WAACs, and nurses united in a festive treasure hunt that began in the ruined, deserted city of Aachen and ranged across Germany into Austria and Czechoslovakia. Looting was so widespread that it was regarded as soldierly sport. After forty-nine years the American general public still has little knowledge of this reality.

All the occupying forces looted, and the army made it easy. Looting was done without shame or hesitation and was not regarded as stealing. Bankers, clergymen—persons who were normally honest—did not hesitate to dip into an unlimited treasure trove. There were no effective rules to control the game. The army permitted personnel to mail home captured enemy equipment provided that there was no "military need" for it. Technically, soldiers were forbidden to mail home items taken from German homes and public buildings. The ruling was admirable but rarely enforced. An occasional commanding officer attempted to apply the law, but even in respectable outfits it was possible for an enlisted man to have an officer censor his package without inspecting it, or even let it go after inspecting it. An officer's signature on a parcel was only as honest or dishonest as he was, and officers' personal baggage was not even examined.

Especially, there was the bold, unmitigated theft of motorcycles, pistols, rifles, knives, cameras, and binoculars, as these were the items most desired by the average soldier. Many of these items were expensive and beautiful, the best in the world. Once in the possession of an American, a camera, pistol, or pair of binoculars might change hands twenty times before reaching the United States. The guns included military Lugers, finely crafted civilian pistols, beautiful shotguns, and superb hunting rifles. Also into the mail pouch went priceless collections of antique ornamental swords.

Destroyed vacated towns were the most fruitful hunting grounds. The conquering American would pop through a hole in the side of a house and survey the ruins. Whatever he wanted he took. Eager hands were waiting to relieve him of his prize; if he was wounded, he was almost certain to lose the booty to ambulance drivers, medics, or hospital attendants.

If a home was still intact, the G.I. would open the door and spend the night. Sometimes he left the house undamaged, but most likely he would throw cigarette butts on the rugs, slash draperies, slam a chair into a mirror, and sleep in a fine bed wearing a filthy uniform and muddy combat boots. The next morning he would fill his pockets and pack whatever he liked. In many instances, G.I.s ordered families out of their homes with less than thirty minutes' notice and commandeered the residences. The abuse of occupied dwellings by Americans was at best vandalistic and at worst downright criminal. Expensive carpets were burned by cigarettes, furniture was thrown out into the rain, partitions were knocked out, walls were disfigured with crude draw-ings—usually obscene—and valuables were stolen.

Enlisted men, officers, and nurses mailed home complete sets of silver and china, vases, linen, paintings, ornaments, jewelry, clocks and watches, crystalware, bedding, toys, books, and an incredible assort-ment of household bric-a-brac. The sheer stupidity of some of the looting is exemplified by the treatment of rare books. One rotund army captain, though he couldn't read a single line of German, stole from the bookcases in his room random volumes from priceless leather-bound sets of Goethe, Schiller, and Rousseau and mailed them home, unaware that by breaking up sets he had made the books less valuable.

Looting became an art. Soldiers stationed themselves outside military government offices and intercepted civilians bringing in weapons and other items. U.S. tactical units posted contraband lists that included automobiles and jewelry, and military government detach-ments would "enforce" the lists by "requisitioning" items for high-ranking U.S. officers. Officers specialized in the appropriation of fine German automobiles. A colonel would simply drive an automobile out of a family garage, paint it olive drab, and register it at headquarters as his own property. The retreating German army had confiscated many bicycles and automobiles, but U.S. troops took the rest.[1]

The sackers of Germany also invaded museums, libraries, and other public buildings. Many U.S. medical and dental officers were talented ransackers, who seized medical instruments from hospitals. If a micro-scope was too difficult to ship home, one merely removed the precision lenses and shipped them. Universities, town halls, libraries, hotels, and businesses were thoroughly pillaged, their contents added to the mail sacks. The only limit to one's daily looting was the size of the sack.

By the end of the war, stories were circulating that the Americans and Russians were as bad as, if not worse than, the Germans when it came to looting. In occupied Berlin the standing joke was that the only difference between an American soldier and a Russian soldier was that the American took a bath.

As an example of the kinds of things that were "requisitioned" after the war, on May 1, 1990, the front page of the *New York Times* featured a story headlined "Germans to Get Priceless Gospels Lost in '45." The treasure referred to included nine items, the most valuable of which was an illuminated illustrated manuscript of the Four Gospels, encased in a jeweled-encrusted gold-and-silver binding, dated ninth century. Also included were a rock-crystal reliquary shaped like a fish that, it was claimed, held a lock of hair from the Virgin Mary and another reliquary of silver, gold, ivory, and precious stones bearing the likeness of Germany's first elected king, Henry I of Saxony. The treasure, valued at over $15 million, had been stored in a mine shaft near Quedlinberg, Germany, during World War II and had disappeared from there shortly after the American occupation. We now know that the Quedlinberg treasure was stolen by an American officer and taken to his home in Texas.

Throughout history, wartime looting—particularly the theft of cultural treasures—has been met with a certain unspoken acceptance. Looting was often a final psychological assault mounted against an already bloodied and beaten opponent. The plunder's public display made victory more tangible. Napoleon surely had this in mind when he brought the Quadriga Gate from Berlin's *Brandenburger Tor* to Paris, where it was paraded before mobs of cheering Frenchmen. With Bonaparte's defeat in 1814, the gate was returned to Berlin and greeted by the Germans with equal fanfare.

Up until the late nineteenth century, British sailors augmented their pay with booty confiscated from enemy ships and ports. U.S. Civil War history is replete with stories depicting soldiers from both sides ransacking entire estates. Wholesale theft has been recorded for as long as wars have been fought. Nevertheless, the magnitude of the looting which took place in World War II surpassed everything done in past wars and has never been thoroughly chronicled. *The Spoils of World War II* attempts to correct this oversight by exposing the widespread thievery commited by the American conquerers of Germany in their lust for quick riches.

The Spoils of World War II

1

Spilling the Beans

MOST OF THIS BOOK would not have been written had it not been for one spring weekend in 1946. James P. O'Donnell, chief Berlin correspondent of *Newsweek,* met with Captains Edith Standen and Everett P. Lesley at the vast Wiesbaden Collection Point to discuss a story regarding a bust of the Egyptian queen Nefertiti. Wiesbaden housed thousands of valuable paintings, tapestries, and other art objects that had formerly been displayed in various city, state, and federal museums and were now under the jurisdiction of the U.S. Army. The most prized item in the collection was the statue of Queen Nefertiti, and O'Donnell was there to write a story concerning the sculpture. Monuments, Fine Art and Archival (MFA&A) officers Standen and Lesley showed the accumulated treasures to O'Donnell and filled him in on the background of Nefertiti. This celebrated bust, the most beautiful piece of all Egyptian sculptures, had been one of the greatest works in the Berlin Museum.

"Afterward," wrote Lesley, "while we were sitting in Edith's office over a drink, to O'Donnell's query of 'D'you know any other good stories floating around?' we said, 'Yes,' and spilled the beans."[1] The "beans" was the fact that these and other MFA&A officers had previously requested that the army investigate the Kronberg House of Hesse robbery of fine jewels, the Büdingen affair, and other cases involving art stolen by army officers.

The facts had been compiled and investigations had been made, but the army stalled until a few days later, in June, a story was published in

3

"Periscope," a department of *Newsweek*. The story began, "Someone may try to hush it up but...." And then the hunt was on for the missing $3 million in Kronberg jewelry. On June 24, "Periscope" mentioned that "a second case involved looting of castle Büdingen, less than fifty miles from Kronberg Castle. Still missing are seven pictures, including a Rubens valued at $100,000."

Upon reading these articles General Lucius Clay, the military governor and commander in chief of the European Command, demanded, with great indignation, an audience with both O'Donnell and Lesley. First, meeting in Berlin with the twenty-nine-year-old O'Donnell, Clay wrote:

> I advised O'Donnell that in no instances had any recommendation for investigation from MFA&A been held up in any way. I further advised O'Donnell that there was no behind the scenes dispute or hushing up of any looting cases. O'Donnell was familiar in a general way with the facts and stated that he knew the story to be factually incorrect.[2]

At the conclusion of the meeting, General Clay presented O'Donnell with a report and demanded that *Newsweek* use that information to print a denial concerning the Büdingen cover-up.

Lesley writes that he was in Amsterdam at this time, lecturing and living on herring and gin. The captain was qualified to instruct, as he was a graduate of Stanford University with a master of fine arts degree from Princeton. Upon his return to Berlin he received a telephone message to report to General Clay at once. He dutifully reported and supplied the general with a well-researched dossier concerning the accusation of looting. Reading the dossier, Clay grew exceedingly angry. As Lesley reported, "The interview was protracted, sultry and painful. The general accused me of every possible infraction of every possible article of war and with *tutti gli strumenti* told me after an hour and a half that I would have to produce or get tried. He was, in short, very nasty and altogether vindictive."[3] Clay demanded a retraction or positive proof from Lesley.

Immediately afterward, because of considerable shenanigans on the part of the army, the tables were turned, and to his complete surprise Lesley found himself subject to court-martial for not completely substantiating Clay's request for recanting the material contained in the dossier! The court martial had been requested by the general himself.[4]

Limping and forlorn, Lesley met with O'Donnell, and after six stiff drinks O'Donnell promised that "if Clay actually tried to court-martial Lesley there would emanate from the Press Camp a blast that would blow him back from Dahlem to Des Moines where he came from." Unfortunately, it was just whiskey talking, because both men, intimidated by Clay's position of authority, backed off from the issue and remained silent. Later, however, O'Donnell would became a journalistic thorn in the side of General Clay, who tried hard to maintain the fiction of Four Power unity and harmony in occupied Germany.

What possible circumstances could have so agitated Clay? During the war years, Clay, as deputy director of war mobilization, had been in charge of administering procurement for war materiel of an 8-million-man army. He had accomplished this job without the hint of a single scandal. Clay was such a perfectionist that he could not accept any insinuation of impropriety. Now, in preserving his reputation, he had every intention of covering up the fact that in the past year the total number of paintings missing in the Büdingen affair had grown to more than 140. In addition, Clay's own distinguished MFA&A officer, Captain Norman T. Byrne, was being investigated for embezzlement, larceny, and bribery in occupied Berlin.

Now, more than forty-eight years later, after thirteen years of research, this shameful cover-up and others can be brought to light. The following pages will acquaint the reader with more of these long-kept wartime secrets.

2

The Hungarian Gold Train

For centuries Central Europe had been dominated by the German and Austro-Hungarian Empire. After Austria fell to the Prussians in 1866, Hungary gained independence, while foreign, naval, and military affairs were controlled by joint ministries. Their relationship continued until the end of World War I. By losing this war, the Austro-Hungarian regime found their nation carved into four separate countries: Austria, Hungary, Czechoslovakia, and Yugoslavia. In addition, Italy and Romania acquired land from the Austro-Hungarian government. From that day forth the Hungarians felt politically and morally obligated to regain territories lost as a result of the Versailles Treaty. This obligation was focused not only on the Hungarian heartland but also upon Hungarians living outside the arbitrarily fixed frontiers.

This aspiration to restore the "wrongdoings" of the Versailles Treaty was also shared by the German nation. In 1938, Germany, under the leadership of Adolf Hitler, began plans for the restoration of its pre–World War I territory by making blatant demands at Munich for Germany's need and "right" to expand into the Slavic lands in search of *Lebensraum*. Sir Neville Chamberlain of England and Edouard Daladier of France yielded to Hitler's flagrant demands. As a result Czechoslovakia ceased to exist. This former northern territory of Hungary was sliced up between Germany, Poland, and Hungary.

The Hungarians gained additional territories in the south during the spring of 1941. Because of Hungary's collaboration with the

Germans in the invasion of Yugoslavia and Greece, Germany returned all the former Hungarian territories under Yugoslavian rule to Hungary. The German invasion of Greece was aimed at preventing the British from establishing an air base that would jeopardize Germany's successful invasion of Russia. Then, however, the Hungarians received a telegram from London informing them that should they associate themselves with the Germans in the war, regardless of their motives, the British would declare war on Hungary and immediately start bombing their territory. The British were, however, well aware that Hungary's affiliation with Germany was not for Germany's sake, but solely for Hungary's own national aims.

Reviewing the telegram, Count Pál Teleki, premier of Hungary, meditated once more upon the reasons for making the reappropriation of the former territories mandatory. The feeble and troubled premier reread Britain's threat to bomb Budapest and other Hungarian cities. He reconsidered the national obligation to agree on aims fervently desired by the constitutional regime since 1919 and saw clearly that there was no possibility of recanting his decision to support Germany in the war. Germany, in fact, had begun its military action independently and could occupy the former Hungarian territories alone. Teleki reasoned that Germany would probably seize the Hungarian railway system, resulting in most unfavorable political repercussions for his party.

On the other hand, the premier was deeply disturbed by a premonition of disaster in the final outcome of the war. Caught in a dilemma, with no way out, tormented by these tumultuous events, and suffering from overwork and insomnia, he visited his incurably ill wife in the hospital, after which he returned home, took a pistol from a drawer, and put a bullet through his brain.

After his suicide, the Hungarian army engaged in its first combat by invading Yugoslavia on April 6, 1941; carrying out a limited invasion in the region between the Danube and Tiza rivers, it regained its longed-for former territories.

After this joint military venture, the Hungarians formed an alliance with Germany and furnished thirteen divisions to fight against the Russians on the Eastern Front. This relationship continued until early 1944, when it became apparent that the Russians were going to invade Hungary and the Allies were going to win the war. They then began to negotiate secretly with Russia for a separate peace. Hitler discovered these negotiations and immediately ordered the dashing Otto Skorzeny to seize the Citadel of Budapest and capture Admiral Miklós Horthy and his cabinet members. (The Führer had faith in Skorzeny as a result of his resourceful rescue of Benito Mussolini from carabinieri guards in a mountain hotel, where the ex-dictator had been incarcerated by the Allied Italian government.)

When the Hungarians signed a peace agreement with the Russians on October 11, 1944, the Germans, under Skorzeny's command, attacked with SS tanks and airborne troops. Skorzeny captured Horthy and his cabinet, and within the hour Budapest radio proclaimed the new Hungarian-Nazi regime. The Germans took over the functions of the Hungarian government and appointed Ferenc Szalasi the premier of Hungary. He organized his own cabinet under the direction of Heinrich Himmler, an action which would cause ill-fated Hungary, even at this late stage of the war, to continue to bleed for Hitler. Most tragically, Adolf Eichmann—working under the directions of Himmler—would within a few months murder 300,000 Hungarian Jews—75 percent of the Jewish population in Hungary—as part of the methodical plan for the destruction of European Jewry. Up to then, because of the alliance with Germany, Hungarian Jews had escaped the horrors of the concentration camps.

As gigantic Russian forces encircled Budapest, the property of the now murdered Jews, under Adolf Eichmann's orders, was loaded onto a train on December 15, 1944. The property had been seized by Hungarian Nazis and, later, by Gestapo agents used to assist them in collecting the valuables. As the train rolled out of Budapest the aim of its new owners was to stay ahead of the advancing Russian army. Heading westward through farmlands, vineyards, and orchards, the train set out on a precarious journey. Its mission: to snatch the treasures of ancient Hungarian towns, as well as the gold deposits of a number of small Hungarian banks.

Other property belonging to rich Hungarian Gentiles was voluntarily loaded onto the train to avoid seizure by the advancing Russian army. Many of the Hungarians who voluntarily packed their belongings on the train followed behind in cars, buses, or other trains.

The train took on a priceless cargo when it stopped at Györ, exactly halfway between Budapest and Vienna. Here the train was loaded with approximately one hundred paintings by the great masters, owned by the Municipal Museum of Györ. The outside of the cases was labeled "*Varozi* Museum Györ/Property of the town of Györ."

Dr. Arpad Toldi, minister of finance, was the train commander, responsible for its contents and destination. After the treasure was loaded at Györ, the train now consisted of fifty-two railroad cars, of which twenty-nine were freight cars containing items of great value. The cars were sealed, locked with large padlocks, and guarded by Hungarian soldiers and gendarmes. Comprising the rest of the train were the large steam engine, the coal car, the dining car, the galley, passenger cars, and sleeper cars for the fifty-two guards and approximately one hundred men, women, and children who had managed to arrange passage.

By the end of March the train had been on its tiring journey for over three months and had covered little more than one hundred miles. The whole train smelled of bouillabaisse made from giant catfish caught in the Danube. After five years of intense warfare, soap was no longer available in everyday life, and as a result, the train crew's skin had taken on a smutty coloration from the constant smoke rising from the coal-fired steam engine. Their clothing fared no better. The galley was crammed with cabbage, pork, smoked sausage, chickens, ducks, and geese. Mineral water, white and red wine, espresso, and Tokay, a dessert wine, rounded out the cook's supplies. The essentials were not difficult to obtain, since the small farms through which the train passed had a bountiful supply of food and there were plenty of gold coins on the train to barter with. Gold, unlike paper money, could be traded for anything.

The freight cars were heavy-duty, top-notch cars, the best that could be found at this late stage of the war. The markings on the outside of the cars indicated varying points of origin: Dresden 191307, Germany l533, Mav Hungary G127260, France 207557, FS Italia FC 1132599, and so on. They contained cases of gold, sixty chests of lavish jewelry, and chests of the finest collections of Meissen, Dresden, and Chinese ivory figurines. There were over five thousand handwoven Persian rugs, exceptional works of art, five large trunks full of stamps, over three hundred complete sets of classical silverware, and twenty-eight large boxes of mink and sealskin furs. Other personal effects of the murdered victims included American dollars, Swiss francs, gold coins, small bags of gold dust, watches, rings, Bibles, skis, musical instruments, cameras, typewriters, and—for some unknown reason—a solitary box of coal. One freight car contained diamonds; assigned to it was a special three-man guard detail.

On March 30, 1945, at Brennberg, Hungary, the German commanders made an agreement with the Hungarian government to allow the train into Germany, take custody of the valuables, and protect escorts and family members as long as the war's circumstances demanded. After hostilities, the agreement stated, the Hungarian nationals and contents of the train would be returned to Hungary. In reality, this accord was of little value; George Patton's Third Army would soon storm in from the northeast, followed by Alexander Patch's Seventh Army from the southeast, Mark Clark's Fifth Army from the south through Italy, and the Russians through Hungary from the east. No longer was the German army able to save itself, let alone the passengers and cargo of a train. Its offer of protection was worthless.

During the trip from Budapest to Brennberg, ten robbery attempts were made—nine by the SS and one by Nazi-Hungarian troops. In all but one instance the Hungarians on board were successful in protecting the cargo. During the one successful robbery, the Germans stole five hundred chrome watches, ignoring items of much greater value. The retreating SS troops were easily identified by their death's-head (*Totenkopf*) cap badges; the Nazi-Hungarian soldiers sported the hated swastika, with a variation: Each end of the swastika's arms ended in an arrowpoint. This modified version was known as the Arrow Cross.

Initially, the gold bars were located in one railroad car and the silver bars in another, but after the repeated robbery attempts and several U.S. air attacks, the gold and silver were redistributed among other railroad cars to prevent their total destruction in case of a direct hit by a bomb.

At the Brennberg railroad station, greed had begun to set in. Dr. Arpad Toldi and his immediate staff began to loot the contents of the train. Boxes, trunks, and other containers were opened and the gold, silver, jewelry, and diamonds removed. The plan was to remove the diamonds from their settings, then smelt the gold and silver jewelry into bars. The gold bars would be most acceptable in Switzerland. If they remained as jewelry, the Swiss or other neutral countries would shy away from it as being SS loot. Unfortunately for Dr. Toldi, the rapidly advancing Russian armies began shelling Brennberg with artillery, preventing the smelting operation from taking place. The items that had been removed from the train were quickly packed up and brought back on board. During this activity at the station, considerable looting by civilians took place. Prior to the departure of the train from Brennberg, Toldi loaded two trucks with fifty cases of gold and diamonds and fled from Brennberg, presumably headed for Switzerland.[1] Dr. Avar Laszlo, the mayor of Ziertz, Hungary, who was a passenger on the train, was then ordered by the ministry of the interior to take command. Russian infantry was only six miles away as the train left Brennberg.

Count Josef V. Markovits had left Budapest after most of his relatives had been killed there during the Russian assault. He arrived in Brennberg just prior to the train's departure and jammed his possessions aboard. He was told that the train's destination was Hallein, located about ten miles south of Salzburg, Austria. The slow-moving train left Brennberg and continued west into another remnant of the great Austro-Hungarian Empire, through Vienna, and Linz, and then southwest through Salzburg.

Markovits, with his young wife, small child, and nanny, continued their journey to Hallein in his automobile. On the journey across northern Austria, the car was appropriated by the retreating Sixth German SS Panzer army. This once proud Afrika Korps had fought under the command of Field Marshal Erwin Rommel. The troops who had stormed North Africa with a deadly array of 88-mm guns, Goliath PzKpfw VI Tiger tanks, and highly mechanized units were reduced to stealing cars from old men. These masters of audacity and deception had had their defenses stripped to the bone; they stole farm animals and carts in their evacuation from the ever-advancing Russians. Markovits and his family mingled with the retreating horde and continued onward by bus and train, arriving in Salzburg after nine days of travel. In November 1945, he would try to reclaim his belongings, as we shall see in a later chapter.

At the Salzburg train station, Markovits observed that Salzburg was bustling with activity as automobiles, motorcycles, and trucks roared through the streets. In one incident, three large SS vehicles collided, and seven people were killed. Markovits noted that one of the vehicles was a prison van which appeared to contain high-ranking Nazis who had been arrested. Wehrmacht troops, SS, high-ranking Nazis, and state officials were seen everywhere. Whole trainloads of SS materials were being loaded onto various trains for unknown destinations. Hundreds of trucks, buses, and cars from Italy, Czechoslovakia, Hungary, and France were abandoned near the train station by the retreating Germans. Stripped of tires, glass, and batteries, the gasoline siphoned out, hundreds of cars had been stacked two and three on top of each other below the train trestle adjoining the station.

As Markovits and his family waited for a train to nearby Hallein, he viewed this scene and thought of the fate of his own car. He tried to keep his wife and nanny shielded from hearing the ghastly rumors that were circulating, the most frightening of which was the story that the Russians had started a large sausage factory in Budapest and were using Hungarian human flesh for meat. These reports were not without effect; fleeing families caustically joked that they were avoiding being stuffed into sausage casings. Although many atrocities did take place, of course, many were invented by Joseph Goebbels's waning propaganda machine, which damned the Russians as barbarians who would rape, plunder, and destroy art and science without discrimination. These exaggerations added hundreds of thousands of displaced persons (DPs) to the masses fleeing toward the relative safety of the advancing Americans.

Markovits and his family arrived in Hallein after an hour's journey from Salzburg. The train was not there, and after a five-day delay, Markovits was informed that the train had not stopped at Hallein but instead had continued down the rail line away from the fast-advancing American army. The Russians were no longer in the chase for the Hungarian Gold Train.

The young count traveled south and caught up with the train in the village of Hopfgarten, Austria, where it had arrived on April 15, 1945. Markovits was allowed to examine his luggage, which had been located in a freight car marked Deutsch-Kassell 55438. The Markovitses were told that the plan was to continue the flight through Innsbruck, St. Anton, Feldkirch, and on into Switzerland. Contact had been made with the Swiss, who were more than happy to accept the contents of the train. They made the same guarantees that had been made by the German command at Brennberg. Unlike the Germans, however, the Swiss could back up their promises. Ironically, they had been the international bankers for the Nazi regime but now saw an opportunity to made a quick profit from the Hungarians.

As the Hungarian Gold Train remained in Hopfgarten, Markovits and his entourage caught a passenger train for the journey to the venerable winter resort of St. Anton, from which they would continue to Switzerland. The train was packed with hundreds of French and Hungarian collaborators, anxiously hoping to find refuge across the Swiss border.

From Salzburg traveling southwest, Markovits could not fathom that the malignant atmosphere of most of Europe, with its wrecked cities, devastated farmlands, demolished transportation facilities and public utilities, with its starvation, ashes, rubble, and death, was conspicuously absent in the Tyrol. It was as if the specter of war had ignored this province of picturesque and striking steep Alpine mountains, had hopscotched across the beautiful valleys. As the train approached the Swiss border, Markovits was lulled into a sense of security. It was common knowledge that the Allies would not bomb targets close to the Swiss border. An incident that happened early in the war had killed several Swiss at a border railway station, and the publicity from the attack had caused much embarrassment to the Allies. Afterward, they made a point of staying well away from the border.

Suddenly, however, Markovits became ill and was taken from the train and transported to a hospital in the border town of Feldkirch, Austria. Markovits, along with his wife and child and the child's nanny, would remain there for several months.

On April 21, 1945, the Hungarian Gold Train began making final preparations for its 150-mile dash from Hopfgarten to Switzerland. The Americans were unaware of the train and its contents but were still conducting war against the Third Reich, which meant that they would shoot practically anything that moved. The transportation system was a prime target for the U.S. Army Air Corps. This area of Austria was the target area for the 450th Bombardment Group of the Fifteenth Air Force, stationed in northern Italy.

On April 21st the 450th bombed and destroyed the railroad bridge in the small village of Brixlegg, and before it could be repaired, the U.S. Seventh Army had joined with the U.S. Fifth Army from Italy at the Brenner Pass. Austria was cut in two by the Allies, and the escape route to Switzerland was blocked. As the train began to backtrack from Brixlegg, the Hungarians removed fifty-four cases of gold (7,937 pounds) and two cases of diamonds from the train and buried them between Brixlegg and the more or less safety of the nearby Tauern Tunnel. The train then steamed into the tunnel to protect it from the constant threat of Allied bombing attacks.

During this time, the Allies had made their final move against Fortress Europe, beginning in Normandy with the D day attack of June 6, 1944. Five months later, 3 million Allied troops were in France preparing to smash the West Wall, or "Siegfried Line," and explode through Germany. It was then, however, that the Germans made a last desperate move, the massive counterattack in the Ardennes. This counterattack, the Battle of the Bulge, would be the last in the west. After a long, hard month of bitter fighting, the Ardennes offensive failed, and the U.S. Army penetrated the West Wall into Germany. In March 1945, the U.S. Army crossed the Rhine for the first time and dashed across Germany into Austria and Czechoslovakia. The war ended in Europe on May 8, 1945. The cost of winning the war was spelled out in the 125,670 crosses and Stars of David stuck in the soil of fifty-four U.S. cemeteries in Europe.

On May 16, 1945, THE 3D INFANTRY DIVISION, 15th Regiment, A Company, commanded by Lieutenant Joseph A. Mercer, entered the Tauern Tunnel, sixty miles south of Salzburg. To their astonishment, they discovered a partially concealed train crammed with gold and other valuables. Presumably the train was hiding in expectation of the forthcoming repairs in Brixlegg and the eventual escape into Switzerland. The kitchen waste and human filth that had accumulated in the tunnel was sickening. The decision was quickly made to move the train from the tunnel to avoid the risk of disease to the crew and its captors. The train chugged from the darkened tunnel and pushed on to the small market town of Werfen, fifty miles north of the Tauern Tunnel.

There the train was jointly guarded by the Hungarian guards and soldiers of the 3d infantry Division. A round-the-clock guard detail was assigned to protect it. The cars containing gold and diamonds were posted with double security, and the complete area was declared off-limits to unauthorized personnel. The families remained on the train and continued, despite hardships, with their daily routine of living.

Because of the widespread destruction of the railway system, the train remained in Werfen until July 18, 1945. The army then abandoned the steam locomotive at Werfen and connected an army locomotive to the train for the last thirty miles of its precarious journey. The train finally left the rail siding in Werfen under the tight security of both the 101st Airborne and Hungarian guards, bound for the Stuberkaserne army barracks located on 51 Klessheimer Allee in the Marglan suburb of Salzburg. This military camp had been renamed Camp Truscott by the Americans.

Hitler had intended for his Third Reich to last for a thousand years; consequently his military bases were built to last. Unlike the American military camps, built of flimsy construction material during the early 1940s, the German bases were built of large granite blocks, with ceramic baths and iron veranda doors. The Stuberkaserne was built in this style. A large granite fence with a spiked iron rod crest surrounded the camp. The mess hall, barracks, garages, and warehouses were made from granite. Most windows were French veranda style and made with iron frames. This base and its counterparts, the other German military bases in Austria and Germany, were appropriated by the Allies. At Stuberkaserne a large steel gate was rolled open, and the train entered the rail siding.

In charge of overall security during unloading was Major John F. Back, commander of the highly esteemed but off-the-record Target Force, and four enlisted men under him. Back was a G-2 executive officer, and during hostilities, his Target Force had been assigned to the Supreme Headquarters, Allied Expeditionary Forces (SHAEF). Among its target objectives were synthetic oil and rubber, designs for rockets, Luftwaffe jets, secret-writing chemicals, and top German rocket development scientists such as Wernher von Braun. Back had been sent by SHAEF because an adjacent warehouse contained a large quantity of tungsten, a valuable ingredient in the production of lightweight hardened steel. The major was there primarily to protect this previous shipment of the valuable metal and to scrutinize the contents of the Hungarian Gold Train for material that might be of interest to Target Force.

As the unloading began, Dr. Avar Laszlo, who had taken over as train master after Dr. Arpad Toldi's exit at Brennberg, delivered to Major Back two black suitcases packed in a canvas rucksack, apparently a getaway bag. The valuables were not included with the material in the train but were in the possession of Laszlo. The suitcases contained diamonds, jewelry, and currency that had been stolen from the many parcels in the train.

During the unloading, it was noted that practically all of the containers had been broken into and then reclosed by nailing boards across the containers. Seven parcels, numbered V1 through V7, were sealed with sealing wax and displayed the names of the owners on the outside. These were culled out by Major Back and Colonel Homer K. Heller from the contents of the train during the four days of unloading. Parcel V1 contained currency that included $44,639 in U.S. bills. Included in this stash were six $1,000 bills and two $500 bills. Also found were a packet of diamonds and two lots of gold jewelry. Parcels V2 through V6 contained jewelry, diamonds, rings, and watches, but V7, a canvas bag, contained only diamonds. During the examination of an old steel box, after removing old rags and envelopes, the two men found many papers written in Hungarian. The papers were lists of the owners of the train's contents and were separated and left in the warehouse with Colonel Heller for possible future use in determining ownership. It was never made clear what later happened to packages

V1–V7, nor did the papers of ownership ever surface.

It took four days for two U.S. Army trucks to move the valuables from the train to the ground floor of a former Wehrmacht warehouse, one hundred yards away. The cargo included 850 chests of silverware, 5,000 handwoven Persian rugs, alarm clocks, watches, cameras, bolts of cloth, underwear, topcoats, typewriters, chinaware, stamp collections, coin collections, cases of diamonds, cases of gold coins, and large amounts of currency. The warehouse was selected because it was considered to be a fire-resistant, dry, burglarproof building. Assigned as guards during the four days of unloading were soldiers of G Company, 242d Infantry Regiment, 42d Division.

After unloading, and to their complete surprise, the Hungarian guards were disarmed and sent to a POW camp. Their wives and children were separated and sent to Riederburg, Austria, a displacement camp for homeless people.

The unloading was completed on August 29, 1945. The 1945 estimated value of the contents of the train was $206 million—which would translate to several billion dollars today. The fate of this treasure was now in the hands of the Americans, especially Major General Harry J. Collins, as we shall see in a later chapter.

3

The Büdingen Affair

THE REPORT THAT GENERAL LUCIUS CLAY had given to Jim O'Donnell, chief Berlin correspondent for *Newsweek* during the summer of 1946, stated that in April 1945, a first lieutenant was placed in custody of art objects in the Büdingen Castle. The owner of the castle was Prince Otto Ysenburg, who later was arrested for his participation in the Nazi party. Six of the art objects taken to the castle had disappeared, and suspicion pointed toward the lieutenant. After investigating the case, the inspector general's office recommended a general court-martial, but a subsequent pretrial investigation recommended that the charges be dismissed.

Clay's report further stated that the lieutenant was ordered arrested by a lieutenant colonel who had become intimately acquainted with Princess Felicitas, the wife of Otto Ysenburg. The report also claimed that the suspected officer was of a minor rank and that documents concerning the case were not classified secret, although they would remain classified as confidential.

O'Donnell surmised that the document Clay had furnished him was a continuation of the cover-up, but he did not react to the information, since there were no named sources in the report. All documents concerning the case were removed from the MFA&A files under orders from Clay. The documents were not returned.[1]

What happened at Büdingen?

Long before the dust had settled on the European battlefields, the

U.S. Army had planned the difficult task of occupying and governing war-torn Germany. The leaders and troops of military government units were called upon to deal with complex challenges and tasks beyond the traditional combat role of soldiers. The majority of these units proved their value both in and out of combat. They demonstrated their competence to manage a major occupation in the national interest of a conquered people. Relatively few units contained members who were downright crooked, but the actions of a handful of individuals far overshadowed the competency of others. A unit with one such unconscionable member established control of Büdingen.

On March 31, 1945, following the combat fighting of the 26th Infantry Division, Lieutenants Sinclair Robinson and Robert K. Bryant arrived in Büdingen with the 2d Military Government Regiment, XIX Corps, to establish military control of the province of Büdingen, which contained the small town of Büdingen and 101 villages. Lieutenant Bryant was the commander of the attachment, and thirty-five-year-old Robinson held the concurrent positions of legal officer, safety officer, finance officer, public health officer, prosecutor, and MFA&A officer. One of Robinson's first acts was to call on Prince Otto Ysenburg at Büdingen Castle. The castle, surrounded by seventeen thousand acres of forest and meadows, had been in the family since A.D. 1250. It contained a large collection of antique guns, and according to military law these guns, though antiques, were to be seized by the U.S. military and stored in a secure place.

During these early days of April, Prince Ysenburg visited the Military Government office each day to inquire about his collection and to offer his services as a translator. During these visits, Robinson asked the prince if he knew where any valuable paintings were stored. Ysenburg replied that he did not know of any, but that surely his cousin Count Solms, who lived in Laubach, would know because he was a director of the Städel Museum (Städelsches Kunstinstitut und Städtische Galerie), located in Frankfurt. Two days later they made the thirty-mile northern trip to Laubach in Robinson's confiscated German Opel automobile.

At Laubach, on April 17, they met with Count Solms. He told them that he did not know the location of any stored art, but that Dr. Albert Rapp, professor and curator of the Städel, might know of some art storage areas. Rapp just happened to be at Count Solms's house, and the count introduced Robinson and Ysenburg to Dr. Rapp. During an ensuing conversation, Rapp told them that he had received permission from the Military Government in Frankfurt to travel by bicycle in order to check on some artworks that had been stored in Amorbach, a small town about sixty-five miles south of Büdingen. Robinson told Professor Rapp that there was no reason for him to take his bicycle because he would take him in his car to Amorbach; together they would inspect the artwork. The paintings had been moved there on July 29, 1944, to avoid constant bombing by the Allies. Fortunately, these works had been removed just in time, because the Städel Museum had been completely destroyed by incendiary and high-explosive bombs.

Prior to leaving Laubach, Robinson was shown several valuable paintings that had been stored there. Dr. Rapp readily accepted Robinson's offer of transportation, so from Laubach they drove back in the little Opel to Büdingen, where Rapp stayed overnight at the castle. Early the next morning the three men drove the two-hour trip to Amorbach, which was not under Robinson's jurisdiction. Upon arrival at the castle, they found it occupied by U.S. troops. Following the now standard procedure, the former German occupants of the castle had been given two hours to vacate, as the structure was to be used to house American troops. Robinson and Rapp found that the storage rooms had been broken into and many items of value were missing.

Rapp ran from room to room talking incoherently and surveying the damage. Cases and boxes were broken open, the contents strewn about. Fragile objects such as small statues lay in fragments on the floor, and paintings were damaged, several having been cut free from their mountings, with only the empty frame remaining.

Prior to the arrival of Robinson and his party, the castle had been sacked by members of the 45th Company, 2756 Engineer Construction Battalion. John Bodner, Jr., New York City, had himself managed to relieve the repository of a thirteenth-century illuminated manuscript, a Napoleonic courier's briefcase, twenty-five Japanese shadowgraphs, two casts of Egyptian cylinders, one small treasure chest, a small jewel box, and five medieval documents on papyrus. Bodner later stated that he had grabbed the boxes containing these valuables at random:

> There were other boxes there I could have gotten and I didn't take them—there were so many trying to take things, but I sent the valuables I took home one at a time. The officer told us that if we got caught sending it he would be fined $70. We knew we were not supposed to steal valuable things like that; still, if a fellow can get it he takes it. Some fellows were going

around smashing things just for spite. When I went into the storage room you couldn't move in there there were so many fellows in the place. They broke open the crates and took out the things. It went on for a day or two.[2]

This aftermath of mob looting is what Lieutenant Robinson, Professor Rapp, and Prince Ysenburg encountered when they entered the unguarded storage room at the Amorbach Castle. Rapp, completely bewildered, murmured that the room still contained many valuable objects. Robinson then posted an Off Limits sign at the entrance of the repository and suggested that he get a truck and take the valuables back to Büdingen, where they could be protected. Considering that soldiers had unimpeded access to the unlocked and unguarded castle, Rapp concurred. Robinson arranged to borrow a truck from an army unit in Amorbach and, with the help of a local officer and some soldiers, loaded it with the most valuable remaining paintings selected by Professor Rapp. The rooms were without electricity, and Rapp had to use a single flashlight to make his selections.

Rapp began making a list of the paintings as they were loaded, but Robinson said that they were in a hurry and that there would be plenty of time to compile a listing in Büdingen and send that back to Amorbach. Grateful for Robinson's help and not wanting to irritate him, Rapp complied, and they began to load the truck loosely, hurriedly, and without any packing material. Nineteen valuable but unframed paintings were loaded into Robinson's tiny Opel, along with Rubens's *Pan and Nymphs,* which was in a hand-carved gilded wooden frame. Robinson suggested that the painting be removed from the frame, but Rapp explained that the frame had been made expressly for this one painting and that it also was most valuable. As the Rubens was loaded, a gold flake was nicked from the frame and Rapp picked it up and put it into his pocket. When Robinson got into the car, he was unable to see out of the back window, so some of the paintings were taken back to the truck.

They drove away from Amorbach with fifty-five paintings, Rapp riding in the truck with the driver and Ysenburg riding with Robinson. During the trip Robinson asked Ysenburg about the value of the paintings in the backseat, and Ysenburg put his hand on the Rubens and told Robinson that Rapp had said the painting was worth $200,000. For a lieutenant making $200 a month, that one painting equaled a lifetime of income. Robinson then questioned Ysenburg concerning any assets he might himself have in any foreign countries. The lieutenant offered to sell some of the paintings from Ysenburg's castle and deposit the proceeds to the credit of Ysenburg in New York. Robinson explained that while Ysenburg's marks would become worthless he could get dollars for the paintings. Uncomfortable with this line of conversation, Prince Ysenburg changed the subject.

About that time they noticed that the truck was no longer following them, so they turned around and went back and discovered that the truck had two flat tires. While changing one of the tires, Rapp noticed that the glass covering Joos van Cleve's *Two Saints* had broken. To prevent further damage, Rapp removed the painting from the frame and gave it to Robinson to carry in the Opel.

The valuable cargo arrived at the Büdingen Castle around five in the afternoon. Ysenburg got out of the car and went inside to the large kitchen and told his relatives, Princess Ingrid Wittgenstein; Prince Huberthus and his wife, Princess Magdalene of Prussia; and Ysenburg's wife, Princess Felicitas, that a large truckload of valuable art was in the courtyard and that he needed their assistance in unloading the valuables. Aided by the truck driver, the royal bluebloods unloaded the truck and stored the paintings in a large archive room in the castle.

While the truck was being unloaded, Robinson remarked that he had to "go and get something" and drove off. He proceeded to the large white house that he shared with Lieutenant Bryant and unloaded several paintings from his car. As one of the young "housekeepers," Jeannene Pouillon, looked on, Robinson gave her coworker, twenty-year-old Martha Morbé, *Pan and Nymphs* and Joos van Cleve's *Two Saints* to take upstairs to an unused kitchen in his apartment. Morbé noticed the signature "P. P. Rubens" in the center of the bottom frame of one of the paintings. Robinson then took a key and locked the room. Miss Pouillon, twenty-five-years-old, later described two of the other paintings:

> One was the portrait of a military dress, seventeenth century, in ancient clothes and a long curly white wig, and across his chest was a sash. I believe that the clothing was black and white. The second painting represented a lady dressed in a veil with long blond hair and wearing a garland of flowers. I believe that this lady was in a semi-reclining position. I believe it was supposed to be an allegory of Spring.[3]

After about fifteen minutes Robinson returned to the castle and took the remaining paintings from his car into the castle. Ysenburg then fetched a bottle of wine for the truck driver and drew him a map. The driver immediately returned to Amorbach to avoid driving in the dark.

The paintings from the truck were all stored in the archive room, and as the party looked the paintings over, Rapp explained something about each painting. The prince and Rapp laughed a little because Robinson had no interest in the paintings as art and asked only questions concerning their value. He showed a particular interest in a landscape by Claes Berchem and also in Max Liebermann's *Orphan House in Amsterdam*. In what Princess Felicitas Ysenburg took as a joke, Robinson said, "If you ever come to America, you will see that picture in my drawing room."[4] As they continued to view the paintings Robinson told Rapp that he was a collector and that he had a shopping list of artists that had been given to him by a friend who was an art dealer in America. He showed Rapp the list, and it contained only the most exalted names, such as Rembrandt and other great masters. Rapp told him that to acquire such paintings on the open market would be impossible. Rapp then realized that Robinson was not asking questions because he was interested in paintings but purely out of greed, and he began to feel most uneasy about the situation. After Robinson left, Rapp suddenly noticed that the Rubens and a few other paintings were missing. Ysenburg then told Rapp about the suspicious conversation that he had had with Robinson during the trip from Amorbach.

Robinson returned to his quarters to eat his customary 7:00 P.M supper. Prior to the meal, Robinson took Lieutenant Bryant, who shared the house with him, upstairs and opened the door to the unused kitchen and revealed his collection of art. To this collection, Robinson had added a considerable amount of silverware bearing a royal crest. He had told Miss Pouillon that the silverware had been "loaned" to him by Prince Dieter.

Three days later, on the morning of April 20, Robinson returned to the Büdingen Castle with a jeep and a trailer. He asked Prince Ysenburg for the key to the archive room and, along with Ysenburg's sister-in-law, Casimir, went to the room, where he opened the door and removed four paintings and put them in the trailer. Prince Ysenburg was then told by Robinson to get into the jeep and help him with the paintings. Afterward the two rode over to Robinson's apartment. The two young "housekeepers" were there, and one of then unlocked the door while

Ysenburg helped take the paintings upstairs to the unused kitchen. While moving Liebermann's *Orphan House in Amsterdam*, Robinson told Ysenburg, "You will see that painting in my room in New York when you visit me." That evening Rapp returned to the castle and was told of the removal of the paintings. He inventoried all of the paintings and noted that six were missing, including Berchem's *Motiv aus Tivoli*, Rubens's *Pan and Nymphs*, Liebermann's *Orphan House in Amsterdam*, Van Cleve's *Primitive*, Constant Troyon's *Landscape With Cattle*, and Canaletto's *Venetian Vedoubt*.

A few days later Lieutenant Robinson made a trip with Dr. Rapp and Prince Ysenburg to Bad Wildungen for the purpose of inspecting properties of the Städel Museum. Because of Robinson's confiscation, Rapp was rather reluctant to make the ninety-mile trip north. The building housing the paintings was known as the Bunger and was a one-story building located just off the main street of Bad Wildungen. Rapp was relieved upon arrival to find that the building was well guarded and that the key was in the possession of a U.S. Army captain. Upon observing the security of the building, Rapp did not request entry, thinking that Robinson might take more of the paintings. As a result, no property was removed from the repository—this time.

The status quo was maintained until May 21, when Lieutenant Colonel James F. Wood took over Büdingen Castle as a command post for the 978th Field Artillery Battalion, XIX Corps. At the same time, the Counter Intelligence Corps arrested Prince Ysenburg for Nazi affiliations. Ysenburg was taken to an internment camp at Schwarzenborn. Shortly afterward Robinson alleged that Wood had become involved in an affair with Princess Felicitas Ysenburg and that the two of them had conspired against him.

When Colonel Wood took over Büdingen Castle, he was told by the residents about the missing paintings. On June 25 he sent a car to Laubach and had Rapp brought back to Büdingen. On orders from Wood, Dr. Rapp wrote a complete report concerning the activity surrounding the missing paintings. Wood turned over Rapp's statement to the proper authorities and requested that the matter be investigated by the Criminal Investigation Section of the 518th Military Police Battalion. (Dr. Rapp also filed a request with Robinson stating that he was entitled to a signed receipt for six missing paintings. Rapp was careful not to accuse the American officer of thievery, but wanted a signed statement that the paintings were in Robinson's possession.) Rapp filed the report with the Military Government, but when

Robinson got wind of it, he refused to accept it as written. He had the report returned to Dr. Rapp and ordered Rapp to remove the last sentence, which stated that some of the paintings had been *taken into custody* by the Military Government while others were stored in the Büdingen Castle. Rapp changed the report as directed by Robinson to state that the paintings were *under the control* of the Military Government. Understandably, Rapp feared that if he pushed the issue, serious harm could come to him and the Ysenburg family, and as of now he presumed that the paintings were still in Büdingen.

On June 13, as the heat was turned on, Robinson took his Opel convertible and a three-quarter-ton truck (weapons carrier) and left Büdingen to go fetch a load of champagne. The pickup point for the champagne was in the Wiesbaden area, but Robinson's trip ticket was issued for Liège, Belgium. Robinson led the driver to pick up the load, then disappeared and did not return with the champagne. Where Robinson went and what he did is unproven, but by now the Americans knew that Belgium was a good place to sell stolen paintings and other cultural objects. It is possible that Robinson returned to Bad Wild-ungen, where a few days later the priceless *Lieber Sapientiae* with the *Hilderbrandslied* pages and the *Willehalm* manuscripts were discovered missing.

On June 29, Criminal Investigation Division (CID) agent George W. Harer drove to the crowded Schwarzenborn internment camp and obtained a statement from Prince Ysenburg concerning the missing paintings. Harer got a statement from Robinson's "housekeepers," traveling to Belgium for Martha Morbé and to France for Jeannene Pouillon. (Shortly before his investigation, both young women were abruptly accused of being prostitutes for the German army, had their papers revoked, and were run out of the country for aiding and abetting the enemy.)

Colonel Wood had Robinson arrested on July 4 and transferred him to nearby Friedberg for incarceration. After the arrest, Bryant accompanied Wood and his men as they searched Robinson's apart-ment. They tore down the locked door to the unused kitchen but did not find the paintings in question. They also searched Robinson's office and placed guards outside the Military Government office building and would not allow anyone access to the building until noon the following day. Wood told Bryant that Robinson was worthless, a fifth-rate lawyer, and a disgrace to the American uniform. The silverware that Robinson had taken, telling his "housekeeper" that it had been "loaned to him" by

Prince Dieter (an Ysenburg brother-in-law, who also lived in the castle), was recovered and returned to the Ysenburgs' castle, whence it had been stolen.

The following day, Wood telephoned Bryant and told him to prefer charges against Robinson. Under pressure, Bryant refused to comply and stated that he knew nothing of the case and did not think that it was justifable to bring charges against Robinson. As a result, Robinson only remained under arrest for one day and then returned to Büdingen and his duties as an MFA&A officer.

On Saturday, July 7, Robinson began an odd journey that took him to nearby Frankfurt. Traveling with Lieutenant Leonard H. Harrison, they picked up Lieutenant Hans Witten, a friend of Harrison's in Frankfurt. Witten was fluent in German, and they continued on to what was left of the Städel Museum, now only a small administrative office. The museum was under the military control of Lieutenant Julius H. Buchman, MFA&A officer. Without contacting anyone in authority, the three men entered the building and stated that they were looking for Dr. Rapp and paintings looted from the Louvre in Paris by Hermann Göring. Unable to locate Rapp, they ransacked the remaining file cabinets. One of the men then drove to the home of Doris Schmidt, an employee of the Städel. She was not at home, so they left a message for her to go to the Städel upon her return. Miss Schmidt returned home at six P.M and, upon instructions from her mother, rode her bicycle to the Städel Museum. Entering the museum, she noticed that the file cabinets and desk drawers had all been emptied and that the contents were lying on the floor. She was then approached by Robinson and his party.

In a very harsh tone Robinson asked if she was Doris Schmidt. Responding affirmatively in English, she told the men that they should contact Lieutenant Buchman and added that they had no right to create such a mess. Lying, Robinson informed her that they were from the U.S. Secret Service and had jurisdiction over any local military government detachments or any criminal investigations divisions. Witten had located the report that had been submitted to the Städel by Rapp concerning the removal of property from Amorbach to Büdingen. He then gave this report and another containing the complete inventory of items sent to Amorbach to Schmidt and told her to type a duplicate copy for them. Schmidt protested that she could not type such a large volume and that she could not allow them to take the only copy. Robinson continued to lie, telling her that they were on a secret mission involving thirty stolen paintings that belonged to the Städel and had surfaced in Düsseldorf.

Believing this story, she agreed to type them a short summary of Dr. Rapp's report concerning Robinson's activities centering around the trip from Amorbach to Büdingen and the missing art. She also agreed to type the reports in their entirety later on and said they would be ready for Robinson on Monday. Back in the car, Robinson held up the summary report and, to impress his two fellow officers, crowed, "I think this proves me innocent." As Robinson drove off, Doris Schmidt climbed onto her bicycle, nursing a gigantic headache and thinking surely she would be arrested at any moment. She had a premonition that the only argument that the Städel had for the return of their paintings was the inventory list that she had kept Robinson from taking with him. She wrote, "I had the feeling that I arrived just in the right moment."[5]

The following day, a Sunday morning, Robinson and Lieutenant Juan J. Beotegui carried the summary report from Büdingen to Laubach. Robinson stopped at the castle that was serving as the home of Dr. Rapp and sent someone upstairs to tell the ailing Dr. Rapp that he was urgently needed by two men. He dressed himself unsteadily and went down into the courtyard. There Robinson ordered Rapp into his car, and the three men drove through several back roads and into a wooded area. Getting out of the car, Rapp noticed that Robinson was heavily armed. Hostilities had ceased more than two months ago, and not a shot had been fired in anger during this time.

Robinson was wearing a Colt .45 and was carrying a carbine with a sling of bullets over his shoulder. He and Rapp walked down a footpath into the woods as the other lieutenant remained in the car. Robinson told Rapp to sit down on a tree trunk opposite him. Handling the carbine in a threatening manner, Robinson told Rapp that he, a German, had accused him, an American army officer, of being a thief and that he would see to it that Rapp was put in jail for his lying. Rapp replied that this was untrue and that he had only requested a receipt for the paintings taken by Robinson. The lieutenant then told Rapp that "the general" had called the accusations "ridiculous" and would set aside the investigative proceedings against him. Lying, Robinson said that Colonel Wood had been relieved of his command and was on his way back to America. Robinson further stated that he would remain in Büdingen for another three years and demanded that Rapp give him an oral report. He produced a pencil and paper and told Rapp to start talking.

Facing the muzzle of a carbine, Rapp began to try to recall the incidents connected to the missing paintings. Rapp began by telling Robinson how they had brought Rubens's *Pan and Nymphs* to his car, but Robinson denied ever seeing the painting. The amazed Rapp told him that he must remember as Rapp reached into his pocket and removed a gold flake that had been nicked from the frame by the car door during loading. As he seized the gold flake, Robinson retorted that "this is the most ridiculous thing I have ever heard. You were too nervous to notice anything correctly."[6] As Rapp continued talking, Robinson would stop him at critical points and refused to write down many of the details. Robinson wrote what he pleased and refused to let Rapp read the report or give him a copy.[7]

Robinson was well aware that he was in trouble with U.S. military authorities and through hook or crook had obtained more documents that were highly damaging to his character. One of these was a statement obtained from Princess Ingrid of Sayn-Wittgenstein by CID agent George W. Harer on July 6. The statement positively identified Robinson in the courtyard of the Büdingen Castle, with the four paintings in the trailer attached to a jeep that he was driving. The statement revealed that the princess had stood by the trailer, observed the paintings, and asked Robinson what he was going to do with them and that he had replied that he was going to "hang them up and they would look nice." The details are not known, but with great speed on July 9, Robinson and Beotegui drove to the Kreus Wertheim Castle, Main-Franken, and obtained from Princess Ingrid a statement contradicting the sworn statement that she had made to Harer just three days earlier.

Robinson continued his vengeance. With the help of Colonel Wood, Prince Ysenburg had been released from prison in less than a month, a contradictory action if, as Robinson claimed, Wood was indeed having an affair with the princess. On July 13, Robinson sent his interpreter for Ysenburg. In the administration building of the Military Government, Robinson sat alone with Prince Ysenburg. Nervously, Robinson voiced the opinion that the men from the CID had put words into his mouth or that Ysenburg had made the written statement to them because he held Robinson responsible for his internment. Robinson further stated that Ysenburg had only made the statement to shorten his stay. Ysenburg responded by saying that his relationship with Robinson had nothing to do with his internment and that he had been jailed because of his Nazi party relations. Robinson ignored this statement, saying that he wanted Ysenburg to make a new, shorter statement that all the things written down about him had been said out of ill feeling for him.

Robinson continued by claiming that he controlled the assets of Ysenburg and hoped to have a good future working with him. For example, he claimed he had already released fifty thousand marks from the frozen assets of Ysenburg's estate, but could just as easily confiscate his complete fortune, since he had been arrested as a Nazi official. Robinson then said, "I know Wood from earlier days and you can rest assured I have a friend with a much higher rank than Colonel Wood."[8] Ysenburg refused to dictate Robinson's requested retraction, and with that Robinson told Ysenburg that not much faith would be put in the word of a German.

During this time, Robinson had a German gunsmith named Weiss make him several rifles and a shotgun.

Under constant pressure from Colonel Wood, investigators continued looking into the case, an intensified investigation being conducted during the period of August 22 to August 29, 1945, by Lieutenant Colonel Charles A. McLean, the assistant inspector general (I.G.) of the XXIII Corps.

On August 23, Lieutenant Robert K. Bryant was questioned by the I.G., and during his testimony Bryant stated that he could not remember certain events. The I.G. asked Bryant to pull his own records and check out certain dates. Bryant left the room to obtain the requested information and after a few minutes returned and stated, "It seems they didn't keep the records up. After a certain time they destroyed the records." Bryant "could not remember," and the records had been destroyed: how convenient. Bryant further denied that he had ever seen any paintings in the kitchen of his and Robinson's shared quarters.

Later, Ysenburg was interrogated by the I.G. in the presence of Robinson at the Military Headquarters Detachment in Büdingen. During the session, Robinson, in an effort to discredit Rapp, made several comments that Rapp was irrational, confused, and stupid. Ysenburg defended Rapp and said that he considered him to be a very clever man. Robinson then introduced the four-page report signed by Rapp that he had obtained under duress on July 8. Reading perhaps the biggest lie in the report, a statement that Rapp, not Prince Ysenburg, had ridden in the car from Amorbach with Robinson, Robinson pointedly asked Ysenburg if he wished to change his testimony. Not to be discredited, Ysenburg under oath responded, "It isn't true. I rode with Lieutenant Robinson and I am more sure about that than any of the other testimony."[9]

Lieutenant Sinclair Robinson was then taken to Bad Homburg, Germany, on August 28 for more questioning. At the beginning of Robinson's testimony, he was cautioned that perjury was punishable under the Articles of War. Immediately, Robinson lied by saying, "Sir, I have a request. Could I see the statement as to what has been going on? I haven't the slightest idea what has been going on." All questions relating to the missing paintings, visiting the Städel Museum, intimidating Dr. Rapp, and the trip to Liège were answered by "I am sorry, sir. I cannot answer that under the twenty-fourth Article of War." Robinson was in essence acting as a civilian pleading the Fifth Amendment to avoid self-incrimination. There were three exceptions during the testimony. One, when asked if he had removed the paintings from Büdingen, Robinson answered, "Sir, I most assuredly did not." The second was when, questioned about his trip with Dr. Rapp to Bad Wildungen, he answered, "Sir, this is very embarrassing. I do not wish to answer any questions or make any statement at this time." And finally, for some erratic reason Robinson, under oath, said that he was having a gun made for General Walter Bedell (Beetle) Smith, chief of staff for General Eisenhower.

At the conclusion of various testimonies, McLean wrote the following:

> In view of the lack of any desire on the part of Lieutenant Robinson to explain away the allegations and his avoiding answering any questions that connect him with any activities concerning Dr. Rapp and Prince Ysenberg; and in view of the testimony available from witnesses whose credibility there is no reason to doubt, it can only be concluded that the allegations have some basis in truth.

McLean's report recommended that Robinson be tried by general court-martial for larceny of the paintings and the misuse of government transportation.

The documents supporting this case were turned over to Lieutenant Colonel C. J. Merrill, a pretrial investigating officer. On October 17, 1945, he wrote:

> I have investigated the inclosed charges against Lieutenant Sinclair Robinson. In the presence of Robinson, I have examined all available witnesses and documents. Robinson after being carefully warned by me said he did not desire to make a statement. Recommend that the charges be dismissed. In arriving at my conclusion, I have considered not only the nature of the offenses, but likewise considered the age of Robinson, his military service and the necessity of preserving the manpower of the Nation.

After all was considered, Merrill only had the sworn testimony of three Germans and two "prostitutes"—not in opposing the word of an American officer but in opposing his actions to avail himself of the privilege against self-incrimination by remaining silent.

Not surprisingly, something even more remarkable happened—134 paintings that had been stored in Bad Wildungen plus the valuable manuscripts, *Lieber Sapientiae (Hildebrandslied)* and *Willehalm Codex* vanished. The *Hildebrandslied* (Song of Hildebrand) was a heroic poem in High German, written in A.D. 800.

In the fall of 1945 the manuscripts were sold to a New York book dealer. On February 16 and 23, 1962, ten of the twenty-five missing paintings were put on auction by Christie's in London. On August 7, 1963, and again in 1984, a private owner sold one of the missing Städel paintings to a New York art dealer.

Surely in 1946, Jim O'Donnell was not presented by General Lucius Clay with the above story when the general demanded that *Newsweek* print a denial concerning the Büdingen cover-up? Now we understand why the high command did not want Robinson investigated. Some high-ranking officer was out to make a killing in looted art, but who was it? Was this individual responsible in 1965 for the destruction of the 110,000 investigative files of the CID?

Norman T. Byrne, Hollywood, California

4

The Occupation of Berlin

ALTHOUGH HOSTILITIES HAD ENDED on May 8 and the division of Germany and the four zones of Berlin had been established the previous year at the Yalta Conference, the American occupation of Berlin was no easy matter. The Russians balked at allowing Military Government Detachment A1A1 access into Berlin. Although Eisenhower had stated that he had stopped advancing at the Elbe in order to save American lives by not occupying land that would be returned, the Americans had in reality invaded Thüringen and Saxony. These two provinces were in the preestablished Russian Zone of Occupation and were a source of concern to the Soviets. The Russian command finally agreed to the occupation of Berlin by U.S. troops, provided that the Americans vacate the provinces of Thüringen and Saxony. Finally, on July 4, 1945, an exchange was made, and the Russians received 16,400 square miles of rich and fertile land in exchange for 185 square miles of bombed-out rubble in the western sector of Berlin. And into this seeming wasteland stumbled Norman T. Byrne of Hollywood, California.

One unit stands head and shoulders above all others in the molding of Europe into the unified democracy of today. That noncombat unit was Military Government Detachment A1A1. It was to be the crèmè de la crèmè of military government units as it trudged onto Omaha Beach, on June 10, 1944, with Cherbourg, France, as its first operational assignment. The A1A1 was chosen to be the military presence of the United States in Berlin. It consisted of 150 officers and 200 enlisted men, all well educated, all chosen for the job by Colonel Frank L.

33

Howley. During the occupation, this fine line of noncombat troops guarded the freedom of Western Europe, and only through the leadership of Colonel Howley, commander of the A1A1, could such action have taken place. The best example of his predominance is shown in his insistence in 1948 that Berlin not be abandoned by the U.S. military. Due mainly to his influence during this period of the Cold War, the Berlin Airlift began, and the U.S. maintained a presence in Berlin. This single action of Howley's is largly responsible today for a unified Germany.

Unfortunately, not everyone in the A1A1 had Howley's fortitude and moral uprightness. (One particularly rotten apple in the A1A1 barrel was Captain Norman T. Byrne, Monuments, Fine Art and Archival officer, who is discussed in the next chapter.) Most MFA&A officers felt it was their duty to prevent art from being a pawn in the barbaric chess game of war; they deeply felt that art should be a universal medium in the search for mutual respect and understanding. They felt that great works of beauty could be used as symbols of hope to establish a new and better era in human relations. They had agreed to take part in this phase of the war only because of their professional interest and deep commitment. Two of these highly commited types were Captain Calvin Sutliff Hathaway and Captain Doda Conrad, who were assigned to Berlin under the command of General Eisenhower's Supreme Headquarters. They reported to Colonel Mason Hammond, who was, prior to the war, a professor at Harvard University. They were all there to protect the artwork of Berlin, most of which lay buried beneath the bombed-out ruins.

During the war, Berlin, like many German cities, had built large *Flakturms* to protect the local population. These bombproof shelters were also used to store the most valuable of art treasures and archival materials. In Berlin six of these massive shelters were built in 1941 after the first Allied bombing attack. *Flakturms* were also built at Humboldthain, Friederichshain, and on the grounds of the Berlin Zoo. Each site contained two large air defense towers, one for observation (*Leitturm*) and the other for antiaircraft fire (*Geschützturm*) and both connected by an underground cable passageway. The largest shelter, known as G Tower, was located in the Berlin Zoo. G Tower covered almost a complete city block and was as tall as a thirteen-story building. The reinforced concrete walls were eight feet thick, and the building was heavily fortified. Housed in the Friederichshain Tower were the famous Pergamum sculptures, parts of the huge sacrificial altar built by King Eumenes II of Hellenes around 180 B.C. Other works of art included the Gold Treasure of Priam, a huge collection of gold and silver bracelets, necklaces, earrings, amulets, ornaments, and precious jewels, all excavated by the German archaeologist Heinrich Schliemann in 1872 on the site of the ancient city of Troy.

Entirely self-contained, G Tower, like the other Berlin *Flakturms,* had its own water and power supply and could accommodate fifteen thousand people during Allied bombing attacks. The complex was so well stocked with supplies and ammunition that the German army believed that no matter what happened to the rest of Berlin, the zoo tower could hold out for a year if need be.[1]

In April 1945, with their capital's inner city razed by bombing and under imminent attack by the Russian army, the Germans began moving the art from the six *Flakturms.* The bulk of the treasures of Kaiser Friedrich Museum, the National Gallery, and the Egyptian Department were stored in the Friederichshain Tower. These items had originally been stored in the zoo tower, but the tower had been designated battle headquarters for the defense of Berlin, so the National Gallery art was then transferred. The local transfer was done because Hitler had long forbade the evacuation of the most valuable items for fear that such a step would be taken as a sign of defeatism. But as the Russians closed in, the works were shipped out on trucks, barges, and streetcars from the *Flakturm* to the Kaiseroda and Ransbach mines. On trucks originally designed for the transport of tanks were placed the most important collections of Prussian castles and museum pieces, removed on April 6 and April 7. This last shipment contained the bust of Nefertiti and nine thousand boxes of other valuables. The Pergamum Altar had to remain behind because of a lack of shipping space, but the contents of the libraries, archives, and scientific museums of Berlin had largely been evacuated, widely dispersed, and in many instances simply stored without crating.

The State Art Library (*Kunstbibliothek*) beautifully crated 170 cases containing the Ornamental Engravings Collection, illustrated books of ancient and modern periods, and the Lipperheide Library of Costumes. Two million or so books from the Prussian State Library were loaded loosely into barges and shipped to Magdeburg, where they were stacked in great piles in the Schönebeck salt mine. The collection of the Museum of Prehistoric and Early History (*Vor und Frühgeschichte*) and the Museum of Ethnology (*Völkekunde*) were to a large extent crated and stored in the Grasleben and Schönebeck mines. The other valuable cargo was shipped to the Grasleben Mine near Helmstedt and to a mine near Schönebeck, where, during the later years of the war, extensive underground storage places were established.

The *Flakturms* survived direct bomb and artillery hits during the Battle of Berlin, and the remaining contents were turned over to the Russian army. The contents of the Friederichshain Tower also survived bombings during the fierce battle for Berlin. On May 2 this *Flakturm* was surrendered to the Russians. The doors to the compartments containing the most valuable art objects were locked and the keys given to three German museum guards. On May 4 one of the guards, Herr Eichhorn, returned to the *Flakturm* and found the museum rooms in perfect order and locked. The Russian guard also allowed another museum employee, Herr Kiau, to enter the building, and Kiau also verified the secure condition of the museum rooms. Kiau returned the following day and found entry to the compartments on the first and second floors forbidden. The strong door on the third floor had been forced open, and he saw German civilians looting. Russian soldiers forced him to leave the *Flakturm*. The following day, May 6, Kiau and his wife returned to the tower and found the first and second floors partially consumed by fire. Because of the damage, he was unable to inspect the most valuable art objects on the third floor.

Twelve days later, on May 18, 1945, a huge fire consumed the floors containing a very large number of museum pieces. The cause of the fires was never officially determined, but it is believed that the first fire was set to cover the looting by German civilians. The second fire was most probably due to the carelessness of a Russian guard. The Russians, lacking flashlights, would twist paper into a tight bundle, light it, and use this crude torch to illuminate the interior of a building. As the paper burned down they would extinguish it by dropping the torch and stamping on the flames. This practice perhaps set off some ammunition or other inflammable material, permitting the rapid destruction of the interior of the Friederichshain Flakturm.[2] Many valuable art objects, including Schliemann's Gold Treasure of Priam, were considered destroyed. Nothing remained of the valuables except a deep bed of ashes in which were found bits of china and sculpture.[3] The ashes would later be sifted by both the local populace and the occupying Americans in an attempt to recover some of the items that survived the fire.

On July 4, 1945, the A1A1, under the command of Colonel Frank

L. Howley, became the authority for the American Zone in the isolated island of Berlin. Accompanying Howley's detachment were 100 trucks, 136 enlisted men, and 85 officers. One of the officers was thirty-eight-year-old Calvin Sutliff Hathaway, a graduate of Harvard University, who had been employed by Cooper Union Museum in New York City from 1933 until his enlistment in the U.S. Army in 1942. Commissioned a second lieutenant, he served in the capacity of an MFA&A officer for the duration of the war. Hathaway was in the first echelon of U.S. MFA&A officers, and he entered Berlin on July 10, 1945. From that day forth, he had an extraordinary fascination bordering on an obsession for the treasure that had been stored in the Friederichshain Flakturm. He would maintain this early preoccupation until his death in 1974.

Captain Hathaway visited the *Flakturm* upon his arrival in Berlin, never missing an opportunity to show new MFA&A officers the wonders of the place. On August 10, Captain Doda Conrad wrote:

Captain Hathaway was anxious to show me the *Flakturm*. We left the jeep at a convenient distance and leisurely went on a stroll through the grounds. A Polish conscript with a rifle and one eye received us with genuine Slavic hospitality, offered us to come right in and showed us around with grand gestures....The guard had a generous disposition and a cigarette appetite and would yield to the temptation of a U.S. Army flashlight....Calvin and I walked away with a certain number of objects, heavy enough to necessitate the jeep driver's help, including a large relief (marble), early Italian in perfect condition, a Renaissance horse (bronze), several terra-cotta heads (Greek), Meissen fragments, and a bronze Aphrodite, a personal gift from the one-eyed host.

The officer further wrote that they could drive a two-and-a-half-ton truck into the *Flakturm* and carry out whatever they wanted.

On other trips, Hathaway observed the Polish guard, full of enthusiasm, trading undamaged "naked women" to American soldiers for cigarettes. He recognized the small statues from illustrated catalogues of the Kaiser Friedrich Museum. Many items were trodden underfoot by groups of visiting military personnel with no respect for what they were destroying. Hathaway, with an instinct for preservation, again took many items from the Friederichshain Flakturm. These included some of Michelozzo's early-fifteenth-century polychromed terra-cotta pieces and two Riccio bronzes. Most of the art objects collected by Hathaway were shipped to the Wiesbaden Collection

Point, but a few of the small "naked women" remained with the MFA&A officers.

There was more to this city than ruined museums, for the largest, most open, and most international black market in Europe was located in the famous Tiergarten in the center of Berlin. Crowds of soldiers and civilians gathered there daily for legal and illegal trade. Fortunes could be made with a minimum of effort. As one soldier put it, "Any damn fool can make a fortune without even trying." Berliners went to the Tiergarten carrying jewelry and household goods, hoping to exchange them for food, cigarettes, and foreign currency. Russian soldiers took suitcases of money containing four years' back pay, looking to purchase cameras, clothing, and—especially—watches. The German marks they carried, just printed by the Russian army, were burning a hole in their collective pockets. They had to spend the money before being sent back to Russia or find themselves stuck with a suitcase of worthless currency.

Armed with insatiable appetites for consumer goods, the gullible Russian nouveau riches were great customers for the Americans, who would arrive with their pockets bulging with goodies for sale. A carton of cigarettes or a pound of coffee would fetch $100, a bar of soap or chocolate $5, and a small container of K rations $20. Watches went for as much as $1,000. Cheap Mickey Mouse watches, originally purchased by G.I.s for $3.95, were snatched up by the wide-eyed Russians for $500 apiece. After selling such a timepiece to a Russian soldier, one G.I. crowed, "I'll buy a car with this dough back in the States."

The black market was so profitable for Americans that U.S. Postal money orders purchased by G.I.s in Berlin alone during July of 1945 exceeded $4 million. The total amount disbursed for pay and allowances during this month was less than $1 million.

By now the only German males left in Berlin were boys under sixteen and men over sixty, who numbered about 500,000. Most of the young German men would not be returning from the terrible war. The women numbered more than 2 million. Many of these were young, unattached German girls. The girls and women were a sight for sore eyes to war-weary, lonely G.I.s.

The young Berlin women had little choice but to hustle the local military personnel. Hunger, fear, and the needs of their children and parents made sexual promiscuity a necessity in order to survive in a desperate situation in which 65 percent of newborn babies were dying within the first week after birth. Also, a steady boyfriend with military rank was another way to avoid gang rape by the Russian conquerers, which was quite common in the early days of occupation. All of this necessary carnality took place under the aegis of the most childish regulations ever devised by a conquering army: the Nonfraternization Policy.

This policy as written stipulated that it was against U.S. military law to visit German homes, drink with Germans, shake hands with them, play games or sports with them, attend social events with them, or accompany them to taverns, theaters, hotels, or elsewhere. This short-lived policy led to astonishing legal interpretations, such as the famous "copulation without conversation is not fraternization." The girls winked and smiled at the Americans and sometimes, as they walked through the Tiergarten, would rub their fannies and with a wicked smile say, *"Verboten."* It was a hot summer in Berlin, and this behavior did nothing to help lower the average G.I.'s temperature.

The gap between a moralizing general and an American soldier with healthy sexual instincts was perhaps best demostrated by the following drivel written by General Lucius Clay:

> An early order prohibiting fraternization prevented the normal boy-meets-girl process and the soldier who could not be kept away from the opposite sex was forced to meet German girls in dark halls and alleys and under cover of darkness. Obviously only the lowest type of girl, the tramp, would meet with soldiers in such conditions.[4]

It was appropriate for General Dwight Eisenhower to have sex with Kay Summersby, his young English chauffeur, and for General George Patton to have an affair with his American niece. Adultery was not a violation of military regs for them, but for a German woman to have sex for bread with a young, single American soldier caused men like General Clay to label her a tramp. It was a hard truth that a G.I. who violated military policy was subject to court-martial, but many were willing to gamble for a little romance. This double-standard struggle for sex had been addressed during the war by Bill Mauldin in his popular cartoon series "Willie and Joe." Mauldin had been chastised by General Patton for the observation, but pulling rank for choice sexual partners by officers was a fact during World War II and is older than history itself. Fortunately, the Nonfraternization Policy lasted only a month longer than the first summer of occupation, as hush-hush German-American sexual relations continued, destroying to a degree both the German and the American respect for army authority.

5

The Early Raids

A versatile soldier of fortune who is a Phi Beta Kappa with two
master's degrees.
—*Army commendation ribbon presentation to
Captain Norman T. Byrne, June 17, 1946*

B ERLIN WAS AN IDEAL PLACE for a Hollywood resident and full-time
scoundrel like Captain Norman T. Byrne. Chief of the American
Military Government, Fine Art Section, in Berlin, he was responsible
for a great deal of cultural mistrust that existed between the Russians
and Americans during the Cold War. The forty-five-year-old Byrne was
one of the first Americans to enter Berlin in July 1945. An early
member of the A1A1, he was immediately appointed as a representative
to the Russian Berlin District Headquarters. Although this was a
prestigious position, he quickly gained the reputation of being a lazy,
heavy-drinking womanizer. Berlin was an ideal haven for a man with
Byrne's bohemian predilections; destiny had surely placed him in
occupied Europe.

The five-foot-nine-inch, 190-pound Byrne was a Protestant and
married, with no children. After earning degrees from Harvard and the
University of California, he had been a professor of anthropology at
Los Angeles City College. Prior to the war he had traveled for three
years in Europe and was a war correspondent for the *New York Post* in
1937, covering the Spanish Civil War. He spoke and wrote Spanish and
French and could speak some Chinese. His U.S. military record
included an enlistment with the marines during World War I, when he
served in China, the Philippines, and Hawaii. He was discharged as a

corporal. After World War II broke out, he was inducted into military service on November 13, 1942. Commissioned a second lieutenant on May 6, 1943, he served with the British during the Normandy and northern France campaigns and joined the A1A1 while it was headquartered in Paris. He was promoted to captain on December 12, 1945, while under the command of General Clay.

Byrne's duty as MFA&A officer was to protect cultural buildings from fire, weather, damage, and looting and to preserve all works of art, monuments, archives, and valuable documents in the American Zone of Berlin. It was Byrne's responsibility to establish a collection center and to amass and inventory paintings and other fine-art objects. He was to remove these valuables from bombed-out buildings, unsatisfactory storage areas, and private collections. He was to restrict the movement of all cultural objects, recover and report looted objects, and "freeze" these in the central collection point until a liaison could be worked out with the British, French, and Russians for further restitution of the valuables. The Magazinbau of the Ethnological Museum, located in the upper-class neighborhood of Dahlem, was chosen as the collection center by the Americans. The legal control document regarding the collection and preservation of the items was U.S. Military Law 52.

Byrne had an important and responsible job, with contents of the most famous musuems in Europe under his supervision and control. This task required several Americans and a large German staff. The German staff came under the heading of "Revival of Civilian Administration." This meant that not one German employee could be, or ever could have been, a member of the Nazi party or any of its affiliates. Byrne did not have the background or desire to function as an MFA&A officer, but fortunately Captain Calvin Hathaway and Lieutenant Doda Conrad of the SHAEF staff were assigned to Berlin, and both men had a great interest in the preservation of art. Deplorably, Colonel Howley refused to work directly with these two dedicated men and forced them to work through Byrne concerning any recommendations they had in regard to MFA&A functions in Berlin.

Eleven days after entering Berlin, Byrne found the ideal secretaries for his ambitions. Margarete Loesche, thirty-three years old and married, was a small, dark-complexioned woman who wore her hair cut short, which was unusual in Europe at that time. Loesche began with the normal routines of office work, plus translating for Captain Byrne. On the same day, July 11, 1945, Helga von Corvin, a twenty-nine-year-

old attractive single woman, began working for Byrne after an interview with Lieutenant Colonel Daniel J. Horney. What was most
unusual and completely against U.S. policy was that Corvin had been a
member of the Nazi party; this information was recorded on her
Fragebogen. This was a questionnaire with 131 questions that left
nothing to chance; it was designed by U.S. Customs and questioned
potential employees about their every action during the Nazi era. Its
completion was required of every German seeking any kind of job.

On July 15, after four days on the job, Loesche went with Byrne to
the former home of Baron Kurt von Behr and confiscated a wood
carving of unknown origin, for which he gave a receipt to the
housekeeper. (The baron and his devoted English wife had just
committed a most elegant suicide by drinking vintage champagne laced
with cyanide. Theirs were only two of the many suicides that took place
in Germany at the end of the war.) A few days later Corvin went in a
truck with Byrne to a bombed-out building. The cellar of the building
contained a considerable quantity of wine. She and Byrne spent several
hours loading the truck with bottles, and Byrne took most of them to
his apartment; about a fourth of the haul was taken to a Major Smith's
apartment and unloaded. Byrne gave Corvin four bottles for her efforts
in the theft.

On August 10, 1945, Lieutenant Conrad had been inspecting the
condition of several libraries, and as he was walking back to his office,
the rainy mist that had plagued the cold city for the past month
intensified into a steady rain. To get out of the rain, Conrad went into a
bookstore and art gallery called Gerd Rosen, located on the Kurfürstendamm in the British Zone. Conrad later commented:

One of the saleswomen, rather insultingly I thought, offered
me one of the "à la Brueghel" canvases with the temptation
"This is by a pupil of Raphael." I took the painting in my hand
and discovered plain and radiant the Goudstikker label on the
back of it! There were six small paintings, and all of them had
identical marks of origin.

As Conrad was inspecting these paintings that had been looted
from Holland, he noticed Byrne and the dark-haired Margarete Loesche
discussing the problem of getting authorization to sell pornographic
German paintings. Conrad interrupted the conversation and showed
the paintings to Byrne. They had been offered for sale and had been

consigned by Emil Linden, the director of the Schantung Trading Company, which was 214 Kurfürstendamm, next door. Linden's paintings were removed from the shop and taken first to Byrne's apartment and then to the Magazinbau. Byrne obtained permission from the British to search Gerd Rosen and Mr. Linden's apartment. Byrne and Loesche searched through several suitcases and various cabinets and then ransacked the apartment. They removed the Bronzino, a large handwritten book of biblical interpretations. The book was bound in leather and was most valuable. Byrne also removed three more paintings from Linden's apartment. The paintings seized from the Gerd Rosen gallery and belonging to Mr. Linden were from the famous Goudstikker Collection acquired principally by Hermann Göring and valued then at $40,000.

All of the files from the Schantung Trading Company were taken by Byrne and Conrad and stored in the MFA&A storage room at the Magazinbau. Byrne took the book to his apartment and put it on his bookshelf. The following day, while going through these files searching for clues to more missing paintings from the Goudstikker collection, Byrne found a Dürer copper-plated engraving representing a horse. The horse immediately caught Byrne's attention, and he removed the eight-by-eleven-inch copper etching from the file and took it home with him.

The removed etching was Albrecht Dürer's *Big Horse*, valued at $100,000 in 1945. Etching is a plate-making process. Rather than working directly on paper or canvas, Dürer had created this work on a plate of copper and reproduced many identical prints on paper. The plate on which the design was created, called the etched plate, was what Byrne had stolen. The following day, the complete file of the Schantung Trading Company mysteriously and completely disappeared from the MFA&A storage room. The files were never recovered.

One of the first to visit Byrne's office was Joseph Emiel Steylaerts, a Belgian citizen. Reading the want ads in 1942 advertising the many well-paying jobs in Germany, Steylaerts, like many Europeans, had left home and worked at several lucrative jobs in Berlin. During this time he had purchased four paintings valued at $45,000 from the art dealer Fritz Weber. After reading in the paper that the Allies had voided all art transactions since 1933, Steylaerts visited Byrne to ask about the status of his acquired paintings. Byrne stated that the paintings would be assessed by the Military Government and, accompanied by military police, went to Steylaerts's apartment and removed the paintings from the walls. Steylaerts later asked Byrne for a job in the recovery of stolen art, but Byrne declined the offer. The four paintings were taken to Byrne's apartment. A few days later Byrne told Steylaerts to come see him at home. At Byrne's apartment Steylaerts noticed his paintings and, with nothing to lose, asked Byrne which painting he liked the most. Byrne replied, "The Teniers." Steylaerts then gave it to him as a present, which Byrne accepted. A few days later the three remaining paintings were delivered by car back to Steylaerts's apartment. Byrne was now the owner of David Teniers's *Smoker*. Byrne's job responsibility required that he turn the painting over to a U.S. collection center, after which it would be returned to the country of origin, in this case Holland.

Later, Byrne was tipped off by Joseph Steylaerts that Fritz Weber and several associates had taken many valuable paintings from the houses of several high-ranking Nazis. Weber had been in the art business since 1909, working primarily in the Alsace-Lorraine area. According to Steylaerts, they had taken cases containing porcelain, prayer rolls, and clerical garments that were the property of Haj Amīn al-Husaynī, the grand mufti of Jerusalem, a staunch ally of the Nazis and former next-door neighbor of Weber. On the morning of September 1, 1945, Byrne, Loesche, and five military police searched Weber's apartment; they then took three oil paintings. These were Nicolas Verkoje's *Alderman, Ten Hof* and a fifteenth-century Gothic *Ascension*. The three paintings, valued at $2,500, were taken and stored in Byrne's apartment, but were later taken to the Magazinbau. A garage used by Weber was then searched, and six cases were confiscated. One contained a three-foot-high standing "Old Vienna" flower vase, another a chess set of ivory carvings, another a painting, *Old-Furestenberg*, and three contained Meissen porcelain. The remaining three cases contained valuables that Weber had collected for himself during the past twelve years. Also taken from the garage were the religious objects of the grand mufti. The painting from the garage was stored in the Magazinbau with the three paintings from Weber's home. The remainder of Weber's valuables, including the grand mufti's property, disappeared and has never been recovered. Byrne gave Weber a receipt for the three paintings but did not issue any receipts for the other items taken. After that raid, Steylaerts was put on the Military Government payroll and began to work for Byrne as an informer.

Meanwhile, Steylaerts, the official spy and informer of Byrne, had been investigating black market activity and notified him that Bero Berow and several other Bulgarians were involved in the purchase and sale of paintings. They were living in the British Zone of Occupation, so Byrne notified British authorities and accompanied them on the raid of the Bulgarian's apartment during the first week of September. Byrne and his soldiers entered the apartment and found only Mrs. Kaete Berow at home. Byrne opened the doors of a large cabinet and started going through it, removing Mrs. Berow's clothing and shoes. The frightened woman told him that the clothes belonged to her family, but Byrne accused her of lying and continued to help himself to the loot. He then went to a dressing table with a mirrored door and opened it, taking Mrs. Berow's hairbrush and other personal items. He then took a large bag that the Berows had used to carry food and stuffed it with a fur jacket, a radio, a pair of boots, several pairs of stockings, cameras, soap, cigarettes, leather goods, and other personal items that he fancied.

No pictures were found, but foodstuffs, an American army overcoat, several typewriters, a painted church window, and a wood carving were confiscated by the Allied military. The items were carried down to the street and, after a brief conversation between the men, were divided between the British and Byrne, with Byrne taking a majority of the property to his apartment. Margarete Loesche and Helga von Corvin had been in on the raid, and a few weeks later Byrne gave Loesche a pair of shoes, the typewriter, the fur jacket, a pair of boots, and the handbag that had been taken during the raid on the Bulgarians. The property had belonged to Kaete Berow.

The British, adding insult to injury, came back and arrested Bero Berow for having the American army overcoat. He remained in jail until he was tried and acquitted by a British military court.

From the beginning, Byrne had spent considerable time with Margarete Loesche in her apartment. During the Christmas holidays of 1945, he met Herta Waschow, a close friend of Margarete Loesche. One evening Waschow said that she was in desperate need of money, and to her surprise Byrne handed her five thousand marks and three cartons of American cigarettes. This was the beginning of many shady deals the two would be involved in. For several more weeks the thirty-year-old Waschow sold cigarettes on the black market for Byrne. There was no shortage of cigarettes for the two, because Byrne was receiving three parcels of goods shipped from the United States each week. By now he had tired of Margarete Loesche, who was five months pregnant with his baby. He needed a new lover, so on February 5, 1946, he hired Waschow and put her on the Military Government payroll at a monthly salary of fifty dollars, the going price for a secretary then in Berlin. Waschow had previously worked in a textile factory and had no office skills.

In the spring of 1946 there was a sudden urgent order to confiscate all antique arms in Germany. A general search of all museums, castles, and private collections was made by various military agencies throughout Germany. On the morning of May 10, 1946, Military Police sergeant Charles L. Wood noticed several swords, spikes, and coats of arms in an antique shop on Gneisenaustrasse. These weapons' existence, now subject to seizure under Military Law 52, were immediately reported to Norman Byrne. Wood took Byrne to the antique shop, along with Byrne's new constant companion, Herta Waschow. As they were removing the antiques, the store owner told the party that he had purchased the items from a Mrs. Gertrud Quiadkowski and furnished Byrne with the address.

Upon leaving the store, the party of three proceeded a few blocks away to Mrs. Quiadkowski's apartment at 22 Hallesches Ufer. Finding no one at home, they forced the front door open and found many valuables in the four-room apartment that had sustained considerable interior bomb damage from the recent hostilities. Upon viewing the apartment, Byrne conjectured that the valuables were stolen and should be seized according to Military Law 52, but at this time he did not have a truck with which to remove the booty. He told Wood to station a twenty-four-hour guard in the apartment until he could return.

The next morning, a Sunday, Byrne returned with his car, a small three-quarter-ton truck, and Herta Waschow. With the help of the six military policemen who were guarding the apartment, they systematically went through each room, taking anything of value and loading the truck. One bedroom contained a large rug wrapped in brown paper. One of the MPs tore back one corner of the paper, revealing a valuable Persian rug. During the loading Waschow made a list of the items that were being seized. From a night table Waschow removed some silk stockings; underneath them was a large collection of gold watches, silver ornaments, and other jewelry. As Waschow started to collect the valuables, one of the MPs moved in and proclaimed that these were not MFA&A objects. He thereupon confiscated the items and said that he would take them back to headquarters. The MP officer in charge then took one pair of the silk stockings, along with a cigarette case and fountain pen, and gave them to Waschow as a present. Byrne told the loading crew of MPs that if they wanted some souvenirs from Berlin to ask him and if the items were not too valuable they could have them. From time to time an MP would show Byrne an ashtray or other small item, and he would give his consent for them to keep the item.

After stripping the rooms, Byrne and company noticed several small night tables, bureaus, and a wardrobe containing small locked drawers. These were forced open, and one contained a small piece of jade. On the way out Byrne noticed a desk with a locked side door. After considerable effort and damage the door was forced open. The compartment contained a large, valuable stamp collection. Again the MPs suggested they take the stamp collection, but quoting Law 52, Byrne said the stamp collection was to be taken by him. While flipping through the eight-inch-high stack of stamps, He murmured that the collection was worth well over fifty thousand dollars. Byrne had the three-quarter-ton truck loaded with the Persian rug and other valuables, then hand-carried the stamps as the truck delivered its cargo to his apartment. The MPs proceeded with the gold jewelry back to headquarters and locked Mrs. Quiadkowski's goods in a safe deposit box for safekeeping. On the return trip they decided that the commandeering of the souvenirs was stealing, so the small items of value were impounded along with the jewelry.

When MPs demanded a receipt for the stamp collection taken by Byrne, he refused to comply with their request. The MPs persisted and told Byrne to come along to precinct headquarters with them. Carrying the stamps, he went to the station. There the MPs called their colonel and explained the situation. They put Byrne on the phone, and he told the colonel that he would have to catalog the stamps and then he would issue a receipt. Bryne then left the station with the stamps tucked under his arm and, needless to say, never issued a receipt for the confiscated items.

Notified by her niece of the theft of her property, Mrs. Quiadkowski, a fifty-four-year-old widow, immediately returned to her Berlin apartment. Unable to gain entrance, she stayed with a neighbor while she contacted the local detachment of military police. Upon her demand they returned her gold jewelry and two days later returned her house key. She explained that these valuables had been collected by her late husband during the past seventy years and were her personal property. The MPs gave her Captain Byrne's military address. After she spoke with Byrne, a truckload of valuables was returned to her apartment, but the most valuable items, including the stamp collection and the Persian rug, were missing. The rug was valued at more than one thousand dollars.

6

The Kaminsky Affair

D URING THESE ARDUOUS DAYS of black market activity, Alexander Kaminsky's art shop, at 3 Teltowerdamm, Zehlendorf, was sort of a safe haven for Berliners. The shop was a consignment shop where customers could bring in the better works of art, and if the items were accepted, Kaminsky's competent staff would appraise them and mark them for sale. The customer would receive a receipt and, when the item was sold, would collect the appraised value minus a 15 percent commission kept by Kaminsky. Count Kaminsky, a prominent Russian colonel, had established this reputable shop in the American Zone of Berlin, and he was doing quite well until he met Captain Norman Byrne. Kaminsky was marketing an incredible $200,000 worth of merchandise a month.

Kaminsky first met Byrne in October 1945, when Byrne came by and placed a Military Law 52 poster in the window of his shop. Then, just before Christmas, Byrne came by and introduced himself to Kaminsky and in an overbearing manner said, "You deal in diamonds." Kaminsky did not deny the accusation and stated that he had a right to deal with diamonds. Byrne angrily ordered all customers out and closed the shop until it could be audited by military personnel to ensure that it did not violate Military Law 52.

Apparently, Kaminsky had developed a good relationship with several high-ranking military personnel and had entertained many of them at his apartment as dinner guests. He had sold Colonel Sigmund Fisher, judge advocate general, a number of items that the American had sent to his wife. The elderly, gray-haired Fisher had been so

48

impressed with the items that he had presented Kaminsky with a gift. Kaminsky had also developed a rapport with Colonel Daniel J. Horney, so to demonstrate his political clout to Captain Byrne, Kaminsky reported this incident to the colonel, who allowed him to promptly reopen his shop. Colonel Horney's secretary came to the shop and assured Kaminsky that from now on civilians would audit his transactions and not disturb his customers. Kaminsky let Captain Byrne know that he was well connected with the higher brass, but shortly something would happen that would place Kaminsky on the wrong side of Byrne.

It all began with a valuable painting that had been removed from the bombproof Friedrichshain Flakturm. Paintings from the Kaiser Friedrich Museum had been stored in the *Flakturm,* which was now in the American Occupation Zone. The *Flakturm* had survived many Allied bombings and the furious assault on Berlin by the Russians, but after the war the bombproof structure was accidentally destroyed by the fire mentioned earlier. Many valuable paintings were believed to have been destroyed in the fire. One of these was Albrecht Bouts's *Saint Augustin the Donor and Saint John the Baptist.*

On February 5, 1946, Dr. Wilhelm August Luz, a commissioned art agent for the art shop of Kaminsky, stopped by the apartment of Dr. Winkler, curator of paintings for the Berlin Museum, and had with him *Saint Augustin the Donor and Saint John the Baptist.* He left the painting with Dr. Winkler and asked him for his expert opinion on the merits of this important painting. Winkler was amazed that the painting from the Kaiser Friedrich Museum was still in existence. Luz had, in a matter-of-fact manner, stated that a Russian had saved the painting from the blaze in the Friedrichshain Flakturm and had reasoned that it was his lawful trophy to sell. This view had also been shared by the Russian Kommandature of Berlin. After all was said and done, the painting had been purchased by Kaminsky for $2,500 from Soviet captain Ewdokimow, the brother-in-law of the Russian general Kommandature of Berlin. Kaminsky's shop was also an ideal outlet for Soviet black market items.

Because of the scarcity of housing in Berlin, Winkler's apartment was situated in one of the rooms of the vast Magazinbau. As he strolled through the building to his office, Winkler could not help telling his associate, Irene Kühnel-Kunze, about the Bouts painting. Both worked for MFA&A and the Occupation Military Government United States, or OMGUS. This was the parent organization of the MFA&A in Berlin and other German states under the control of the American occupation.

Kühnel-Kunze reported the existence of the Bouts painting to her boss, Captain Calvin S. Hathaway, who in turn reported it to Byrne.

On February 9, Byrne went immediately to Winkler's apartment and moved the Bouts painting to one of the rooms under his control in the same building. The following day, he and Herta Waschow, without any military police, went to 2 Berlinstrasse, Kaminsky's apartment, and seized various items from the U.S. Post Exchange: a carton of silk stockings, ten pounds of chocolate, a gold watch, jewelry belonging to Kaminsky's daughter, and a large sum of currency. To make this worse, he had Kaminsky help them load the car. He then told Kaminsky to get into the car, as he was under arrest for the purchase of the Bouts painting. As he was being driven to prison, Kaminsky asked Byrne why, if he was trying to be unlawful, would he have sent his representative to a reputable museum in the Magazinbau to check the painting out? When Byrne claimed that he would see to it that he was released, Kaminsky replied heatedly, "No, thanks, I'll see to it myself." After he dropped Kaminsky off, Byrne took the carload of valuables to his apartment.

With that, Mrs. Kaminsky immediately went to the Soviet general in the Russian Zone and arranged for the release of her husband. After his release, Kaminsky notified the Russian Kommandature in writing that Byrne had obtained the painting. This created a furor, and Kühnel-Kunze and Winkler were ordered to appear before the Russians for interrogation concerning the Bouts incident. Holding a letter written in Russian with an attached photograph of the Bouts painting, the Russians demanded that Kühnel-Kunze and Winkler deliver the painting to them within three days, since it was the legally acquired property of Kaminsky. During the interrogation the Russians told them that in order to watch over German interests, they should report incidents of the Kaminsky nature to the Soviet authorities instead of the U.S. military. Kühnel-Kunze and Winkler were unable to produce the painting; the menacing Russians, in order to send a message to other Germans, had Kühnel-Kunze fired from her job, which they could do, based on the governing agreements of the Four Powers in Berlin.

By now the Russians were beginning to suspect Byrne's motives. They knew that Mrs. Waschow was on both the U.S. military's and Kaminsky's payroll and that she was purchasing and selling valuables from that shop for Captain Byrne and that, furthermore, he was up to his ears in black market activities. Because of Byrne's escapades the Russians, during one of their Kommandature meetings, had presented a list of crimes for which Byrne had been responsible. Their protest was not taken seriously because the Russian reciting the charges repeatedly referred to instances where the American soldiers had "bitten" old women. There was such a roar of laughter from the American representatives that it was never clarified whether the Russian meant to say "beaten."

The following Sunday, Kaminsky was told by a German policeman that there was a phone call for him at the local police station. He went down to the station, and waiting for him was Byrne, who again drove him to prison in his personal car. On the way to prison, Byrne asked Kaminsky why he had gone to the Russian Kommandature with the story of the painting. Kaminsky said it was his duty and asked Byrne if they could be friends. At this, Byrne replied, "If you had done this better," and rubbed his fingers across his thumb, indicating a payoff. Following this latest arrest, Byrne and Waschow returned to Kaminsky's apartment, and Byrne demanded that the sick Mrs. Kaminsky vacate the apartment immediately and forbade her to take any furniture or clothing with her. He was taking over the apartment in its entirety as a gift to Herta Waschow. Only after pleas from her neighbors was Mrs. Kaminsky's apartment not taken over, but she soon suffered a nervous breakdown and had to be committed to a sanitarium.

On March 4, Kaminsky's lawyer presented proof that Kaminsky and his family were Soviet citizens, and he was released from jail and turned over to the Soviets. At that time he was told that because he was denied the jurisdiction of a U.S. court he could not conduct business in the American Zone. In taking this action, the American court system felt that they were ridding their zone of a notorious black marketer who had been protected too long by a myriad of affiliations in Berlin. After Kaminsky was turned over to the Russians, he was appointed director of a Soviet Berlin officers' club. His shop had been closed on February 11 but was reopened on March 12, 1946. It was officially reopened by Horst Ehrke, property control officer of OMGUS, but it was truly under the "management" of Waschow and Byrne.

Byrne granted Waschow a position within Kaminsky's large art shop. The young woman was supposed to monitor transactions at Kaminsky's and act as a go-between for Byrne in his duties as an MFA&A officer in fulfilling Military Government Law 52. In addition, she was to watch out for items from the black market. Byrne told Mr. Ehrke that he should have a constant "eye" in the shop and that that eye would be the eye of the law and that, furthermore, he had selected a lady to be that eye, and he introduced Waschow. Byrne stated that she had quasi-supervision of the complete shop, including Ehrke. As soon as she took over, Waschow felt the need to compensate herself with more money, so she paid herself an additional $125 a month plus, at the insistence of Byrne, a monthly bonus of $250 a month. Waschow was thus earning $425 a month, a fortune in 1946 in war-torn Berlin. Byrne himself, with housing allowance and overseas pay, was only making $241.50 a month. The other employees at Kaminsky's shop were earning $100 a month.

Customers would bring valuable items into the shop, and on items that she wanted for herself or Byrne, Waschow would render appraisals well below fair value. Occasionally a customer would balk and start to leave the shop with the item, but Waschow would demand that he or she leave the item or endure a jeep's coming around to pick up the item without paying anything for it. She would then purchase the item or mark it at its real value and pocket the difference. Several managers questioned her procedures, but Waschow would threaten, "I'll tell Captain Byrne all about this and he will have you arrested."

As an employee of the U.S. Military Government and Kaminsky, Waschow felt that it was her responsibility to confiscate select items for Byrne and his friends. She was spending considerable time in Byrne's apartment, and without asking Byrne, she would take valuables that she considered ugly to the shop and exchange them for more beautiful pieces. Broken items that Byrne had accumulated were taken to the shop and sold by her. She later stated that she operated "only by having good connections, and people were rather anxious to buy them."[1]

The amoral Waschow even sold a few items that belonged to her husband. As items came in, valuables worth thousands of dollars would be sent down to the basement, where a large collection was being accumulated. On Sundays, Byrne and Waschow would go into the basement and pack pieces into large wooden crates. Byrne shipped ten crates to the United States. For packing material Byrne used large Nazi flags, the type used during the war for rallies in Berlin.

Large collections of expensive Meissen, Hochst, Frankenthal, and Nymphenburg potteries were selected and purchased. The items were taken to Byrne's apartment, where they were sorted out, with a considerable amount of Meissen selected for Colonel Harold Mercer. Mercer had already returned to the States, but Byrne was helping the colonel add to his collection. (Meissen was the first European porcelain of Chinese quality, originally produced in Dresden in 1710. Its pieces were consistently stamped on the bottom with blue crossed swords, the "Meissen mark," and their motifs included the red dragon, the onion, and the vine leaf. Still in production today, Meissen is expensive and in great demand.)

One large collection for Mercer was purchased by Byrne for $1,325. Others were purchased and resold at Kaminsky's shop, with Byrne pocketing the profits. With these profits the resourceful Waschow purchased $1,000 worth of additional Meissen valuables. For herself she purchased $250 worth of champagne glasses and some tableware. She then began to sell many of the items that Byrne had seized under Military Law 52. Byrne had an ideal setup: he had a license to steal and a legitimate place to sell the stolen property, all under his control.

Other Americans who made large purchases at Kaminsky's were Lieutenants Bergmann, Chipchin, Sokoloff, Hinrichsen, Miller, Waysy, and Gittler, Mr. Ifstepsky, and E. M. Alfred Lehrberger, who had a dress shop in New York.

One item of interest purchased by Byrne from Kaminsky's shop was a $30 riding crop that he gave to Colonel Frank L. Howley as a gift.

7

Concealing the Nest Eggs

B<small>YRNE HAD BEEN LIVING</small> at 10A Biesalskistrasse ever since his apartment had been requisitioned by the U.S. authorities on July 15, 1945, from the Hubing family. The apartment was crammed with items that he had stolen since he had arrived in Berlin. In early May 1946, Byrne moved across the street into a larger apartment at number 11 Biesalskistrasse. The apartment was to be vacated by Major Paddock, an officer who was returning to the States, and Byrne needed the extra space for his loot. The elderly Otto Lummitzsch and his wife, owners and also occupants, watched in amazement as hundreds of exceptionally beautiful and valuable works of art were moved into Byrne's new location. Admirers of fine art, they remembered later two priceless Dutch paintings, one of them representing the bust of a distinguished young lady, the other a full-sized painting representing a Dutch girl in peasant costume with a wide red skirt, plus an unframed fifteenth-century painting, two antique Chinese engravings, four cases of Meissen china, an antique Vienna-porcelain vase, an antique Chinese vase, a large collection of antique Chinese statuettes, and several genuine Persian rugs. On June 6, Byrne removed several items from his apartment and took them to the Magazinbau. One item was Mrs. Quiadkowski's valuable handmade Persian rug, but her four sets of Rosenthal china remained in his apartment.

On June 7, Byrne met in his apartment for about thirty minutes with Herta Waschow and Helga von Corvin. He told them that he was on his way to the United States for a rest-and-recreation leave (R & R), which was normal for soldiers who had been in Europe for several years. He told the two that Herbert Stuart Leonard, the current MFA&A officer for OMGUS, would assume his duties during his absence. Byrne told Waschow to go through the items in his apartment and ship the valuable ones to Colonel Harold Mercer, who had been discharged from service on May 9, 1946. Byrne left the apartment with five thousand dollars in cash and a large number of gold Danish, Belgian, and French coins in his possession. After leaving Waschow, and on his way to the airport, Byrne stopped by for a short visit to see Margarete Loesche, the mother of his baby daughter. Loesche had left her job in May to have the baby. By now she had obtained a divorce and had reassumed her maiden name of Biester. From the Berlin Airport Byrne flew to Le Havre, France, where he waited for a ship for twenty-five days and finally arrived in New York on July 11.

On June 12, 13, and 14, Waschow, with the help of Mr. Karl Zoch, an elderly employee of Kaminsky's, examined the contents of Byrne's apartment and packed valuables into seven boxes. In each box Waschow placed little slips of paper containing her address, and she told Mr. Zoch that she was hoping that Byrne would send her a Christmas package. A considerable amount of loot that Waschow was packing, including the Meissen porcelains taken from Weber's garage, had been stored in the upstairs hall, just outside the door. As the elderly Zoch watched part of the packing, Waschow said to him, "You cannot imagine in what an awkward situation Captain Byrne has brought me. I am having a lot of trouble and now I am left to face the music." If Byrne intended to return to Berlin, why was Waschow left to "face the music"? Why did Waschow pack the slips of paper with her name and address in each box?

She addressed each box to Harold Mercer, 75 Ralph Ave., White Plains, N.Y.

The seven boxes had been inspected, and censored forms had been made out by Major Paddock, who was sharing the apartment with Byrne. Interestingly enough, the return address on the boxes was that of Paddock. The major mailed six of the boxes, but one box was too large for the postal system, so it was stored in the Magazinbau, room 5. Immediately thereafter, the major left for the United States to be discharged from the army.

Byrne had told Helga von Corvin that after Waschow was finished, she should pick up the rest of his things, including his bed linen, and store them in the Magazinbau, room 5, where he kept his personal belongings. Byrne had had a special padlock installed on the door so that he could control access to the room. He had also told her to stay busy at the office by finishing the writing of the history of the MFA&A activities in Berlin.

Corvin would not get the chance. On June 17 she was called into Lieutenant Arnow's office. In front of him was her *Fragebogen*. He told her that she was fired immediately for her participation in the Nazi party. Corvin telephoned Herbert Stuart Leonard for advice, and he told her to come over and he would talk with her. Leonard could not help her get her job back, but told her to get "denazified" as soon as possible in order to become reemployed. Although she was fired, she was allowed to meet with her replacement and two men dispatched by the motor pool. The four of them loaded Byrne's belongings and stored them in the Magazinbau. Corvin removed a looted radio for her use and, with a padlock and key supplied by Byrne, locked Byrne's almost empty apartment. The key remained with Corvin, and she was jailed for a short term because of her affilation with the Nazi party.

On June 7, when Norman Byrne left Berlin, life was a bed of roses, and he was a rich man. Unfortunately, Jim O'Donnell wrote his story for *Newsweek*, prompting the Department of Defense in Washington to order the Berlin Criminal Investigation Division to conduct a top-secret investigation concerning art looting in Berlin by U.S. military personnel.

The American civilian investigators began to look into the affairs of more than five hundred Germans dealing in art. In a short space, fifty officers and high-ranking American civilians were suspected of being generally involved in black market art. It did not take long for Byrne's name to surface to the top of this list. On July 20, 1946, working as a team, CID agents Lester A. Kolste and Niklos A. Strauch, 11th CID, picked up the trail of Captain Norman T. Byrne. Their first contact was Dr. Wilhelm Luz, the Kaminsky employee. This contact led them to Byrne's apartment and then subsequently to Byrne's office at the Magazinbau and the unmailed box with Harold Mercer's name and address. The box contained six valuable porcelain items. It was removed and sent to CID Headquarters. Following various leads, the CID agents interrogated Herta Waschow. Following the interrogation, Waschow contacted Kaminsky and sent him $2,500, asking him not to notify the public prosecutor. The scorned Margarete Loesche was most informative and gave the agents the complete story concerning Byrne's eleven months of looting in Berlin. The agents determined that Byrne had left Germany with Teniers's *Smoker* and Durer's *Big Horse*. They knew that these two paintings were worth a fortune and that Byrne had also mailed more valuables to the United States.

On August 4, Kolste and Strauch boarded a military airlift transport flight to Washington. There, with the help of the CID, they solicited the aid of customs officials in New York to accompany them on a raid of Harold Mercer's home in White Plains. Mercer had recently been discharged from the army and was currently employed selling cars. Of great interest to them was the fact that his father was an art dealer.

On August 9, at 3:00 P.M, the two agents and James D. Carroll of the Customs Bureau called on the startled Mercer. The retired officer told the investigators that five boxes had arrived at his home on July 15 and were still there. He said that Byrne had come by for a week's visit and had been there when the boxes arrived. Together they had inspected the boxes, and Byrne had also shown Mercer and his wife some paintings that he had in his possession, telling them that they were very valuable. The agents and customs officer were amazed at the vast quantity of porcelain in the Mercers' home. Byrne had left Mercer a fowarding address in Los Angeles and had asked him to keep the boxes until he returned from California.

The boxes contained fifty-two pieces of valuable Meissen porcelain and one box of German stamps. The five boxes were confiscated by the customs officer and shipped to Bremerhaven, Germany, where they were later picked up and returned to Berlin by CID agent Kolste. Waschow had packed seven boxes. One remained in Byrne's office in Berlin. What happened to the missing box remains a mystery. Later, under oath, Herta Waschow would testify that a box was missing, but no one paid any attention.

Tracking the address left with the Mercers, the agents took a military plane to California. Following leads from Los Angeles collected by the Sixth Army provost marshal, the agents flew to San Francisco. At four o'clock in the afternoon of August 12, 1946, agents Kolste and Strauch were waiting in the San Francisco Municipal Airport to arrest Captain Byrne as he stepped off the airplane from L.A. This was a stopover for Byrne, who, after spending a few days in Los Angeles, was on his way to New York, where he had made arrangements for a divorce from his wife. Although neither of the men knew Byrne, they had a good description of the forty-eight-year-old captain and knew that his uniform contained a rare World War I patch on his right shoulder and farther down on the same sleeve were three V-shaped, World War I chevrons. Recognizing these badges, the agents walked up and, to the astonishment of Byrne, told him that they had orders to take him to the nearby Presidio of San Francisco, Sixth Army Headquarters. Both men displayed their CID badges and arrest orders to Byrne and, with his luggage under their watchful eyes, walked him and a female companion to a cab. In the taxi, Byrne asked what this was all about. Informed that a couple of paintings in Berlin were missing, Byrne replied that he had them with him at the moment. Not wanting to discuss the case in front of the woman, the agents remained silent.

At that late hour, there was no one at the provost marshal's office, so the four of them rode into downtown San Francisco and checked into a hotel around 7:00 P.M.They checked into two rooms, with Byrne and his lady friend checking into the same room. The agents told Byrne that he could have a few minutes with his friend but that they would return and talk to him alone. They came back in fifteen minutes, and Byrne was alone. The agents immediately warned him of his rights under the Twenty-fourth Article of War. Strauch then began to search Byrne's military B-fold bag. Expecting two but finding three paintings in a briefcase in the outside pocket of the bag, the agents did a double take. Noticing their astonishment, Byrne said, "That's the Pechstein, I purchased that watercolor in Berlin." Strauch then went downstairs and deposited the watercolor, Dürer's *Big Horse,* and Teniers's *Smoker* in the hotel safe.

After removing the three paintings, the two agents told Byrne that they were going to eat and advised the captain to get some food also. They had been told in Berlin that Byrne was a heavy drinker, and they advised him not to drink anything yet, because they had several questions that they had to clear up. They told Byrne that he was an officer and a gentleman and that they would treat him as such, but if he decided to go someplace to please put a note in their hotel box. They also informed him that he was under arrest and had been put in their custody and that his current travel orders were null and void.

The agents went to a nearby restaurant, while Byrne went to Solari's and had several martinis. After eating, the agents returned to the hotel and went to Byrne's small room. Again advising him of his rights, Kolste began by telling Byrne what they knew of the case based on information obtained from various sources in Berlin. A three-year veteran, Kolste also knew enough to begin to develop a written statement as they talked. The interrogation took place as Kolste sat in a chair next to a writing table and Byrne sat in the remaining upholstered chair, with Strauch lying on the bed. As Byrne told his story, which began with his bringing the paintings of great value to the United States to show to some friends and on and on with more lies, the resounding voice soon put the fatigued Strauch into a deep sleep as Kolste continued to write. Byrne had an excellent mind for details, and he accurately cited all of the names, dates, and addresses concerning the past year's activities from memory.

Around midnight Strauch was awakened by Kolste, who then proceeded to read the very clear, detailed seven-page statement out loud for the benefit of Byrne and Strauch. After that, Byrne read it, made a few corrections, and signed the statement, and Strauch, in noticing how fast he had signed, commented that it was a very odd signature. The statement was a full confession admitting the confiscation of porcelain from Weber, the acceptance of *The Smoker* from Steylaerts, the confiscation of property from Emil Linden and Gertrud Quiadkowski, and his activity in the Kaminsky affair. The confession contained almost every nasty deed commited by Byrne while in Berlin. It even contained additional information concerning a blue ten-place setting and centerpiece of Meissen china that had been taken from the basement of the Rathaus Nikolskie and given to Colonel Mercer prior to his departure from Berlin.

Byrne talked freely, was very polite, and continued to behave himself and never once gave the agents any trouble. Again, the agents had been told that when Byrne drank excessively he was difficult to handle, so they made a point of keeping him away from alcohol.

It is interesting to note that during this time Herbert Stuart Leonard, who had taken over Byrne's responsibilities back in Berlin, wrote a letter to Calvin Hathaway, on August 13, 1946. It contained the following passage: "Would your museum [Cooper Union Museum] want a rather large publication in some ten volumes of drawings in the National Gallery, the work being that of German nineteenth-century artists? If so, I am prepared to forward that as a small gift."

Of course Leonard had no authority to give away the valuables of the Berlin museum.

On August 26, the agents and Byrne returned to Berlin, where Byrne was turned over to his commanding officer and restricted to Andrews Barracks for six weeks. Then the "fox in the henhouse" was returned to his old job as MFA&A officer. While awaiting trial, Byrne continued his close relationship with Herta Waschow, Margarete Loesche, and Helga von Corvin in spite of the fact that they were material witnesses in the court-martial case. Even during questioning by the trial judge, Byrne would have his chauffeur drive the women back and forth in his personal car. This caused the judge to recommend that Byrne be confined during the investigation. This recommendation was ignored.

While awaiting trial, Byrne talked quite freely with various investigating authorities and stated that the actions taken against him were done in order to ignore potential related matters concerning other high-ranking officers. He told Lieutenant Colonel John P. MacNeil, an investigative officer, in the presence of his counsel, that the porcelain collected by Fritz Weber and later seized by him was actually the fraudulently collected goods of Lieutenant Colonel Daniel J. Horney. Byrne was insinuating that he had seized the looted property of other high-ranking officers and that he was being investigated so that they could get even with him and recover their looted valuables. Byrne also told the investigating officer that his trip to the United States was strictly for R & R, and he had had no intention of requesting a discharge while in the United States. There are several reasons to suspect that Byrne did not intend to return to Germany. One of them was Waschow's action in packing her return address in the boxes mailed to Mercer.

During the last week in January, Byrne, Waschow, and an army buddy went to the Magazinbau, to room 5. Captain Byrne asked about the Persian rug that had been taken from Mrs. Quiadkowski's apartment and was informed that it had been removed by the CID. The freewheeling Byrne had gone there to get rid of this incriminating evidence. The day before the trial began was Byrne's birthday, and the untroubled suspect gave a big party at his house on 15 Schweizerstrasse. The party was attended by Waschow, and he told his anxious guest not to worry, that he would beat the charges filed against him. During the party, Waschow received a telephone call from CID agent Kolste, who told her to be at the trial the following day to testify against Byrne. The phone call was placed to Byrne's residence because for several days the Berlin police had been unable to locate Waschow.

The trial began on February 6, 1947, and on that day Byrne was finally restricted to his apartment on Schweitzerstrasse, the officers' mess, the PX, and courtroom number 320 at McNair Barracks, formerly the SS's Adolf Hitler Kaserne, all in Berlin. He was charged with seventeen counts of embezzlement and larceny. The accusers in the original charges were Colonel Frank L. Howley, Byrne's commanding officer, and Captain Albert W. Stockell, assistant staff judge advocate.

This accusation was normal operating procedure for a court-martial, and the trial began as all trials begin, with the defense attorney objecting to all charges and requesting dismissals based on couched terms, the right to know inconsistencies of dates, and other legal jargon. Most of these objections were overruled, and the first witness was called to testify.

Lieutenant Colonel Wilbur F. Maring took the stand and testified that Byrne had in fact been an MFA&A officer from July 1, 1945, until August 12, 1946. Maring also stated that in the beginning, Byrne had accompained Colonel Howley as an unofficial bodyguard. Afterward, Herbert Stuart Leonard, MFA&A officer in Berlin, testified and redefined Maring's testimony concerning MFA&A duties as they related to Military Law 52. Leonard was only allowed to respond to questions that were asked of him. It is interesting to note that he wrote the following to Calvin Hathaway:

> Byrne tells everyone that he will get off, but I found an inventory of the Magazinbau that he made in September 1945, in which he lists the Dürer as a part of the Goudstikker collection and the Teniers as from the Weber collection and to my tired eyes that just about wraps up the case.

Both Hathaway and Leonard absolutely despised Byrne.

Emil Linden testified that his home was raided by Byrne and Mrs. Loesche and that thirteen paintings, including *The Big Horse,* were confiscated by Byrne. Kaete Berow, wife of Bero Berow, told of the raid upon her home and described her personal property, including two gold bracelets, taken by Byrne. Fritz Weber told of the raid made in his home and garage and told of the boxes of porcelain taken. The main contention in Weber's testimony was the address of the garage, and this meaningless issue caused the defense lawyer to ask for a continuance of the case until the following day. Weber also told the court that several days after the raid Byrne brought him a painting for his appraisal. At that time Byrne told him that he would return his porcelain. A day later, Helga von Corvin would tell the court that Byrne had told her when he left for the States to leave the porcelain alone and that Herta Waschow would pack it for shipment. Later, Waschow admitted that Byrne told her to ship the porcelain to the States and had given her the address, but for the most part her testimony was confusing and incoherent. At one point the prosecution stated that Waschow would be in charge of the court if she kept on with her answers. The president of the court then reprimanded Waschow and told her that she was not on trial and must answer the questions to the best of her knowledge and belief. Although much of her testimony was ambiguous, it was evident that Byrne had instructed Waschow to ship the crates to Harold Mercer, in White Plains, New York. The ambiguity of Waschow's testimony had a purpose: She was trying to prevent criminal charges from being levied against her.

On February 11, Johanna Schroeder, an employee of Kaminsky's, testified to the double dealings of Waschow and Byrne. Having been intimidated by Waschow while working at Kaminsky's, she reveled in identifying the items that had been stolen or embezzled from the Kaminsky shop. After Schroeder's testimony, Waschow, who was aware of Schroeder, was recalled to testify. This time she was most clear and concise as she identified each valuable that had been packed for shipment to Mercer's residence in New York. With clear recall she identified the items taken from Weber's garage and Kaminsky's shop. When asked if all the items stolen were present in the courtroom, she replied, "No; one box must be missing."[1]

CID agents Lester A. Kolste and Miklos A. Strauch were allowed to testify at the trial, and they identified thirty items (numbered 1–30) from the five boxes returned from the United States and six items (numbered 31–36) from the box retrieved from Byrne's office. The written confession obtained from Byrne during their trip to San Francisco was not allowed in court. The confession was ruled by the court to be an admission and not a confession. During Kolste's testimony he told the court that the investigation into the illegal art trade had begun in Berlin by a colonel who was sent to Berlin from the War Department in Washington.

Strauch also told the court that the investigation surrounding the Berlin art scene had been a top secret investigation ordered by the theater commander (General Clay) and that from three hundred to five hundred people had been investigated. He further stated that all antique and art shops had been investigated in order to determined how much was being sold to the American forces. Their investigation soon indicated that at least fifty military officers were actively involved in the unauthorized purchasing of art, but Byrne's name surfaced to the top of the list. As a tactic to discredit Strauch, the defense attorney asked Strauch for his identification card. Strauch produced his card, and the defense attorney pointed out to the court that Strauch's fingerprints were missing from his ID card and from this deduced that Strauch was a neglectful individual. Continuing along this line of questioning, the defense attorney questioned Strauch's authority to make an arrest. The exasperated Strauch replied that he even had the authority to arrest the defense attorney and explain later, but of course he would not.

After eight days the prosecution rested, and Byrne's defense began with the defense counsel moving that a "not guilty" be found on all charges for lack of sufficient evidence. This move was denied, and the defense's first witness was Norman T. Byrne.

The smooth-tongued Byrne told the court that he had taken the paintings to New York and had arranged for Calvin S. Hathaway, now working for the Cooper Union Museum, to give his expert opinion concerning their value. Once he arrived in New York, he said, he found out that Hathaway was not available and therefore did not make an attempt to have the paintings appraised. This statement was not validated by Hathaway, nor did the prosecuting attorney ask Byrne why he did not have Hathaway appraise the paintings while he was sharing the Magazinbau in Berlin with Hathaway. Hathaway, the prosecutor pointed out, had only returned to the United States two weeks prior to Byrne's furlough. Most of Byrne's testimony was mumbo-jumbo, with his talking in circles concerning various military law directives. At one point the prosecutor said, "He [Byrne] always gives me a song and dance about if, maybe, wherefore—he never answers the question." An example of this is the statement that he had given to the CID agents in San Francisco concerning the stamp collection. Byrne had ranted on about "a compound subject with a single predicate, which later can be taken to apply to both parts of the subject."

Byrne also testified that he had no prior knowledge of the boxes being shipped to Mercer by Waschow. He further stated that he had absolutely no idea how some of the valuable objects got from the Magazinbau to his apartment and then subsequently to Mercer's home in White Plains, New York. The most damaging evidence against Byrne, the signed statement taken by the CID in San Francisco, was not allowed to be entered as a confession.

One of the last witnesses for the defense was Colonel Frank L. Howley, who generally described Byrne's duties. Howley told the court that he had confidence in his officers and delegated much of his responsibility to his staff for their judgment. When asked about Byrne's decision to carry the paintings to the States, Howley replied that Byrne had used very poor judgment and had he learned of it he would have "skinned" the officer involved. Howley testified that for years he had had a four-hour meeting each Saturday morning and had given illustrations of mistakes of poor judgment. (At one of these Saturday meetings, Howley had the men vote on whether to butcher a pet pig that had been with the unit for more than a year or allow it to live. According to Lieutenant Colonel Wilbur F. Maring, the pig had become a pest, and the men hated it. Thinking differently, Howley put it to a vote by saying all those in favor of murdering and eating our mascot, raise your hand. That night the men ate barbecued pork, and Howley ate two eggs.) Although Howley was a witness for the defense, he did not seem to help Byrne's case.

The trial lasted until February 18, and at one-thirty that afternoon the members of the court submitted their secret written ballots. Judged by his peers, Byrne was found not guilty by two-thirds of the court members on sixteen charges. One charge was reduced to wrongfully accepting one pair of ladies' boots, some silk stockings, and three typewriters. He was found guilty of moral turpitude, slapped on the wrist, and dismissed from the service, effective midnight, August, 26, 1947, without a fine or any jail time.

Because of Byrne's actions, Herta Waschow, Byrne's girlfriend, first took an overdose of medication, then slashed her wrists and jumped out of a five-story window. Remarkably, she survived. After hospitalization, she was confined to an insane asylum. Helga von Corvin went to jail. Margarete Loesche, the mother of Byrne's illegitimate baby daughter, was fired from her job. Dr. Irene Kühnel-Kunze was fired from her position with the Berlin Museum. During the investigation of Byrne, Kaminsky's art shop was reestablished, to be controlled by Kaminsky by order of General Keating.

During the trial it was apparent that a large box of Meissen china was still missing from the raid on Weber's garage and that sixteen paintings and the Bronzino biblical interpretations, taken from Emil Linden, director of the Schantung Trading Company, were never returned. In addition, a worthless stamp collection that was eventually returned to Mrs. Gertrud Quiadkowski was not the same collection that had been taken from her apartment by Byrne. These incidents were dismissed and never investigated. The circumstances surrounding the Byrne case were highly complex and hard to follow, but it is a sure bet that others involved acted improperly or unwisely, to say the least.

For instance, there was Margarete Loesche's sworn statement about a Colonel Hatch of OMGUS, who had purchased a painting by Melenar and other art objects amounting to $18,700. The accusation that Lieutenant Colonel Daniel J. Horney had Weber working for him and that the porcelain taken by Byrne had belonged to the colonel was not taken seriously, but the more pressing matter of Colonel Sigmund Fisher's dealings with Kaminsky was never investigated. During testimony, Byrne tried to discuss the purchase of a $25,000 Goya painting, but the testimony was stricken under objections by the prosecuting attorney. The story that property from the Rathaus Nikolskie was given to Colonel Mercer prior to his departure from Berlin was ignored. Many more such cases escaped investigation.

Several times the defense attempted to probe into other illegal acts, and each time the prosecution objected. Each of these objections was immediately sustained by the court. Lieutenant Colonel John P. MacNeil, testifying for the prosecution, said, "I burned my notes as soon as this report was written. I didn't just throw them in the wastebasket, I burned them." Not only did MacNeil burn his notes, but the complete file concerning the looting of art objects in Europe was burned by the provost marshal's office in 1965, the year they would have been available for public scrutiny. It appears from examining all the evidence that Byrne was guilty and that his claim that he had been set up by higher authorities in the judiciary system may have been a valid point.

The Hungarian Booty

8

The General's Kingdom

I wondered back then if there was one honest person left in the whole world.

—*Captain Howard A. Mackenzie*

As Byrne was collecting valuables in Berlin, he had a counterpart who would outperform him by far: Major General Harry J. Collins, commander of the 42d (Rainbow) Division. The 42d had pushed to the Rhine near Strasbourg in December of 1944 and played an important role in stopping the last major German offensive in the west. Under Collins's command it had been a standing joke that the battle strategy for the Rainbow Division was "one man fighting, two men looting, and three men painting rainbows." During hostilities, looting was already widespread, but following the surrender of Germany, it would increase, particularly in the occupation zone of the 42d Division. This division occupied the eastern part of the Tyrol in Austria, and as other divisions were deactivated, the 42d extended its occupation duties and took over the entire U.S. Zone of Austria.

General Collins, like most conquering generals of the past, would live most comfortably. For one of his homes during the occupation, he acquired a castle in Zell am See. The small fifteenth-century residence, beautifully furnished and immaculately maintained, was the Prielau Castle. A majestic eight-by-ten-foot fifteenth-century French fireplace was built into its entrance hall. Equally imposing were the Greek marble columns and Byzantine Christ on the Cross that were the centerpieces of value for the estate. An assortment of old Austrian peasant furnishings was scattered throughout in a most agreeable manner.

The owner was Josef Thorak, a sculptor, close friend of Albert Speer, and Nazi party member. Thorak had sculpted several official busts of Hitler and other party members. He was promoted in the Nazi party by Hitler for his artistic abilities. Prior to the war, Thorak had married a British citizen from Bristol, England. Because she was of Jewish descent, Thorak soon divorced her, but Gilda Thorak remained in Germany with their small son until 1939. Realizing that the situation had become dangerous for her and her son, she and the child went to England. During the Third Reich, Thorak became a favorite artist of the National Socialist party and took on a young American woman, Erna Hoehnig, as his mistress.

Acquiring the Prielau Castle was not a difficult task for General Collins. Because of his activity with the Nazi party, Josef Thorak was in jail, but his mistress, Miss Hoehnig, was allowed by Collins to share the castle with him. While he was in jail, Thorak wrote his former wife in England and reaffirmed his love, faith, and intention to take up life with her again. Thorak also urged Gilda to make claims for alimony, which he had owed since 1939, advising her to secure claims through a mortgage on another property, the Hartmansberg Castle in Bavaria. Then, to Gilda's shock and dismay, Josef immediately married Erna Hoehnig and made her sole heir of all his property. The Prielau Castle had been seized as "Jewish property" and acquired by Thorak. Soon thereafter, General Collins was shown a document by Erna confirming that the Prielau Castle and all of its contents were her property. Thorak died in 1954, and Gilda tried to claim some of his wealth. There is no evidence that she received anything.[1]

Collins also acquired a nearby castle for his command staff. The Fischhorn Castle was at the south end of a small but deep lake in Zell am See. The castle and surrounding farmland were the property of Henrique E. Gildemeister, a citizen of Peru and former Peruvian ambassador to Germany. Soon after the bombing of Pearl Harbor, Peru severed its relations with Germany, and Gildemeister and his family returned to his native land. The medieval castle and surrounding farmland were seized by the SS in 1943, and they renovated the estate to accommodate twentieth-century conveniences, but the Germans did not take title to the land for fear of a similar action being taken by Peru against German property in that country. The SS simply evicted Hans Zillich, the farm manager, and took over the castle and farm.

The Fischhorn had been SS Headquarters for Equine Matters under the command of General Hermann Fegelein and was the last major SS headquarters in the Third Reich. In 1944, during the insurrection in Warsaw, Fegelein's troops looted Polish museums, palaces, and private homes. The loot was loaded onto a train, and sixteen railway cars of it was shipped to the Fischhorn Castle. These valuables were still there when the American army arrived in May 1945.

Hans Zillich, the manager of the Fischhorn, returned on May 23, 1945, in order to take charge of the castle. Herr Zillich, who until now had been serving in the German army, was denied entry to the estate by the U.S. Army. Gildemeister notified the American authorities that he was the owner of the Fischhorn Castle. This was done through two memoranda submitted to the War Department in Washington by the Peruvian embassy. In spite of Zillich's and Gildemeister's repeated efforts to claim the castle, it was taken over by Collins's 42d Infantry Division.

Most important, Zell am See had a rail line running through its center. This line would be used by General Collins and his immediate staff for their trips to Salzburg. The general had, in effect, acquired a private railroad for his daily trips. The 42d Division used the Fischhorn Castle for a headquarters building and had taken over the Fuschl Castle, near Salzburg, for use as an officer's R & R center.

In 1939, German foreign minister Joachim von Ribbentrop had Baron Gustav von Remitz, nephew of Fritz Thyssen, declared a state enemy and had the Gestapo seize the well-kept Fuschl Castle, the surrounding estate, and jewelry and personal possessions of Baron von Remitz. The baron was sent to the Dachau concentration camp, where he was tortured to death. The Baroness von Remitz had a nervous breakdown and was institutionalized in an asylum as a consequence of the duress. Ribbentrop reserved the castle for his personal use during the war. The large hunting preserve provided game as well as timber that was sold by Ribbentrop. In the latter stages of the war, he removed many valuable items from the castle.

Immediately after the property was requisitioned by U.S. forces, Baroness von Remitz filed a legal claim for possession. There was no question as to ownership, but the U.S. Army would not return the castle. The baroness, still affected by the nervous breakdowns suffered during the war years, filed a rebuttal through Dr. Franz Hartig, her lawyer. Dr. Hartig produced signed petitions validating the property as belonging to the von Remitz family. Nevertheless, Collins's officers would remain in the Fuschl Castle for the time being.

General Collins needed to supply himself, his private railroad car, the three castles, and his officers with the superior rewards that he felt a conquering army deserved. It did not take him very long to discover and tour the Property Control Warehouse located in Salzburg. In addition to the Hungarian Gold Train treasures, the warehouse contained the large Herzinna Library and the Rothschild Palace property of Vienna, which included marble door frames, mantelpieces, interior and exterior garden sculptures, carved wood, and wrought-iron gates.

After reviewing this large accumulation of wealth, General Collins had a letter sent by Major R. W. Cutler to Lieutenant Colonel Homer Heller, directing without delay that a large amount of household goods be sent to him for his personal use. The directive demanded that all the items be of "the very best quality and workmanship available" from the Property Control Warehouse. The general specifically told Major Cutler that he intended to hold Heller responsible for securing the requested items. The request was initially refused by Heller, and he received the following memo:

> Homer—
>
> General Collins wants you to be at the warehouse promptly at eight o'clock in the morning to give every assistance to his aides in providing furnishings, etc. for him.
> To say the least he is very displeased with the treatment accorded the aides by you today.
> I have tried to reach you by telephone this evening but couldn't.
> I suggest you do not fail to be of great help to him and the aides.
>
> Lieutenant Colonel Fredrick Gallagher
>
> *Wednesday evening, 2000 hrs*

The letter was written on August 29, 1945. The following morning, under coercion, Heller watched the general's aides take 25 Oriental rugs, 8 paintings, 60 sheets, 30 sets of table linens, 45 sets of Rosenthal chinaware, 45 place settings of silverware, and 90 highball, cocktail, wine, champagne, and liquor glasses.

The general had his railroad car stripped of all furnishings and had two rugs permanently installed by nailing them to the floor. Partitions were then reinstalled, securely fastened by wood screws into the walls and into the floor through the carpets. During early November 1945, someone removed the carpets by cutting along the sides that were nailed down. Since the railroad car was next to the Parsch Displacement

Camp, it was thought that the carpets might have been stolen by one of the persons in the camp. Accordingly, a thorough search of the camp was made, but the carpets were not found.

Pfc. Robert R. Webb had worked with rugs at a furniture store in Rockingham, North Carolina, prior to World War II. Webb was assigned to the Rainbow Division and was requested to appraise the value of the carpets. He later admitted, "I was told my help was needed to get some big officer out of trouble and to pretend that I knew how to evaluate the carpets based on the remains." With this background information Private Webb appraised the value of the priceless carpets at $69 each.

Unfortunately, this requisition of property by General Collins established a precedent for hundreds of U.S. military officers to requisition thousands of items from the Property Control Warehouse for use in households, offices, and clubs.

General Collins further let it be known that he was interested in providing proper quarters and house furnishings for families of the military and expected demands to be made upon property in the Property Control Warehouse.[2] In a wild stretch of the imagination it was interpreted by General Collins's staff that the restitution of the property in the Property Control Warehouse would "jeopardize satisfaction of the minimum requirements of the Austrian economy," and further, that the Hungarian property was required for the "essential needs" of the occupation forces.[3] Also, the release of the property was justified by a military need that could not be met elsewhere, or so the lies went.

Additionally, it was suggested that high-quality solid silverware be acquired by the chest and not be separated. Inscribed inside the tops of many of the chests of silver were the names of the owners, such as "Viktor Mayer." Generals Donald W. Brann, Willian C. McMahon, Charles Saltzmann, Henning Linden, and Edwin B. Howard were just a few who took advantage of this interpretation of the Supply Procedure for Allowances of Household Furnishings for Dependents, Bachelor Officers and Civilians, Americans and Allies. General Linden's essential needs included a camera, tripod, and printer.[4] Linden later claimed that the camera and its accessories were taken to the United States by an officer of the 42d and further stated that he would make every effort to have it returned.

Property requisitioned from the warehouse would be identified on the property sheets in the following manner: 4 pictures, 20 rugs, 1 painting—blond nude, sitting position—1 complete set of silverware. An investigation into the transfer of property from the Property Control Warehouse concluded, "The records on the property control are in confusion." Despite the confusion, heavy demands were made for securing the property due to the arrival of families of military personnel in Austria. This property represented a substantial sum of money, and most of it was taken from the Hungarian property that had been on the Hungarian Gold Train.

Captain Howard A. Mackenzie admitted that "the officers would requisition one rug, 8 × 12, light color, flower design. The rug taken and signed for would be a priceless handwoven Oriental rug. If the rug was returned, it would be a very sad looking 8 × 12, light-color, flower-design rug made in Austria. The only difference between the Germans and Americans in looting was [that] the Germans keep very accurate records and with the Americans it was free enterprise unchecked."

The Property Control Warehouse was a major source of commodities but not an exclusive supply point. The Klessheim Castle at Salzburg had formerly belonged to the Hapsburg family and was little more than a ruin at the beginning of the Nazi regime. It was completely renovated, furnished, and decorated by the Germans during World War II. These furnishings came mostly from France. The castle was used to entertain visiting celebrities. It was here that Hitler met Benito Mussolini to discuss Fascist strategy shortly after the surrender of Italy to the Allies in 1943. Early in the occupation several truckloads of antique furniture, paintings, and objects of art were taken from the Klessheim Castle to furnish General Mark Clark's residence in Vienna.[5]

As truckloads of this property headed in the direction of Clark's army headquarters in Vienna, it appears that almost everyone except Lieutenant Colonel Homer Heller was taking advantage of these guidelines for burglary. In lieu of stealing, Heller offered to purchase one of the ermine furs for $1,000, but his application for purchase of the large coat was denied. The coat was worth $10,000. Although Heller was turned down, one can only speculate upon the number of American wives who did end up with one of the hundreds of fur coats from the Hungarian Gold Train.

Had Homer known the history of the fur, he may have been reluctant to purchase it. Dr. Robert Ley, leader of the German Labor party, had purchased the coat while in Norway for his second wife, Ingar. Until 1942, Ley had been as close to Hitler as anybody in Germany. One of the main factors in this relationship was Ingar Ley. At that time it was no secret to anyone that Hitler admired the beautiful Mrs. Ley and that the admiration was mutual. Hitler was a regular weekly visitor to the Leys' home. The Führer always brought a bouquet of flowers and had tea with them. Unfortunately for Ley, one night in December 1942 she locked her bedroom door, wrapped the fur coat around her naked body, lay down on her bed, and shot herself through the head with a pistol. She had had a history of drug abuse and alcoholism and had only recently undergone treatment in a sanitarium. This tragic death ended Ley's close relationship with Hitler and started the former on a drinking binge that would last until his death. Three months after his wife's death, the grieving fifty-four-year-old Robert Ley attended the Reich Ballet in Berlin and became captivated with seventeen-year-old Madeleine Wanderer, a member of the ballet from Estonia. She soon became his mistress and had his child in September 1944. During this time she lived with him in Berlin and also became the owner of the $10,000 ermine coat.[6] After hostilities, Ley committed suicide while imprisoned at Nuremberg on October 24, 1945. Soon after, the young Miss Wanderer was killed in the course of an adventurous love affair in the Tyrol province of Austria. The jinxed coat was seized by American investigators, who assumed that it had been looted and transferred it to the Property Control Warehouse.

On November 30, 1945, Count Josef V. Markovits appeared at the Property Control Warehouse in Salzburg. Markovits had recovered from his illness and obtained the necessary travel permits that he and his family needed for the trip. Colonel Heller allowed Markovits to visit the warehouse, and the family's luggage was identified intact within clearly labeled wooden boxes. Heller explained that Markovits could not take it, however, because no policy presently existed concerning the release of the property. Markovits bemoaned the fact that he had lost his home, country, and profession and that he was now living on foreign soil with his wife, child, and governess. He further pleaded that the very basis of his existence was his private property in the warehouse, which he needed immediately to protect himself and his family from hunger during the cold winter. Although Heller was sympathetic, he had no grounds on which to release the property, so he instructed Markovits to inquire again in six months.

9

The Property Control Warehouse

DURING THE TIME THAT the 42d Infantry Division was quartered at the Fischhorn Castle in Zell am See, Polish valuables were inventoried by Bondas Urbanowicz, of the Ministry of Polish Arts and Culture. The collection contained the remainder of the collection of Count Krasinski, which had been partially destroyed by the Germans, the oldest Polish prints from the University of Warsaw, parchments and archives of Polish kings from the collection of Prince Radiwill of Nieswiez, furniture and pictures from the royal palace, and pictures from the Polish Museum. Even quite simple objects from Polish homes were found in the collection at the Fischhorn Castle. The collection filled twelve railroad cars and was shipped to the Property Control Warehouse in the early spring of 1946. The warehouse from the Fischhorn contained the following: 481 paintings, 81 tapestries or Oriental rugs, 376 art objects, 46 statuaries, 313 porcelain objects, 164 pieces of furniture, 17,000 library books, 2,584 portfolios of archives, and 2,124 engravings. About 98 percent of this loot was from Poland. Fifty-one paintings were German, and among them were a few from Hitler's private collection; there were also seven Hungarian paintings from the Count Andrassy collection.

After this shipment and as a result of other actions and demands, the Fischhorn Castle was returned to the Gildemeister family on April 18, 1946. The estate was returned to Mr. Zillich on the condition that he sign a receipt that the castle and surrounding estate were being returned in perfect condition and with a complete inventory. Zillich had not been allowed in the castle or surrounding buildings and only signed the receipt upon verbal orders. Zillich wrote above his signature that he only signed because of the order.

In truth all of the china, silver, household utensils, pillows, blankets, linen, beds, books, furniture, and pictures had disappeared from the Fischhorn. Carloads of valuables had left the estate, and a local U.S. Counterintelligence Corps agent had sold the Fischhorn's silverware to a civilian in Zell am See. Most of the furniture was used in the Zell am See Red Cross Club, but the office furniture had been taken by Lieutenant John B. Leonard, 42d Division, to be used in his office at the Strant Hotel. Two pastures were seized for the establishment of a shooting range. Military units drove across the pasture grounds, tearing down fences instead of using the roads to the range. Six heads of cattle were killed, and two horses were so badly hurt that they had to be shot. U.S. troops took two good horses and left in exchange two old, crippled mares. An additional horse was stolen, and the grounds of the farm were damaged and spoiled by troops riding through and vehicles moving willy-nilly through the pastures.

On May 30 the U.S. Army returned to the Fischhorn, seized the only truck on the estate, and loaded it with furniture from the castle, taking it to the Property Control Warehouse.

On June 3, 1946, Maria Luisa Gildemeister, daughter of the owner, obtained full power of attorney from her father, traveled to Vienna, and obtained an appointment with General Ralph H. Tate, deputy commanding general. Miss Gildemeister presented a detailed oral and written report concerning the outright seizure of property belonging to a UN national, and she demanded an end to arbitrary actions at once, asking help in obtaining restitution for damages suffered. Tate wrote General Collins a sizzling letter and demanded that he clear up the matter immediately. Upon receipt of the letter Collins wrote in the margins in his own handwriting, "Put Inspector General on this at once and expedite investigation. This is one hell of a note and it happened in our area."[1]

The complaint was investigated by Major E. H. Hilton, of the Inspector General Department, and it did not take him long to discover that the castle had been looted. Major Hilton stated that it was impossible to determine if the missing property had been removed by the German SS, displaced persons, Austrian civilians, the Polish inventory team of Bondas Urbanowicz, or U.S. military personnel. He did state that property had been requisitioned from the castle and at no time had a receipt been written for it. This requisitioned property included a complete set of silver and china that was being used in the officers' mess of the 505th Military Police Battalion. Hilton wrote that a UN national's property should not be requisitioned and recommended that the Red Cross Club and Lieutenant Leonard be instructed to return all property belonging to the castle. This property was returned during June and July.

Hilton's investigation disclosed that twenty horses were removed from the Fischhorn by the 242d Infantry Regiment of the 42d Infantry Division. The horses were entered as the property of the 242d and taken to Salzburg, where they were used as riding horses for the officers. This subject was not enclosed in Hilton's report to General Collins. Furthermore, the general was not one to forget that the Gildemeister family had gone to Vienna and discredited him and his 42d Infantry Division. He would deal with this matter in due time.

10

The Salzburg Coin Collection

COLONEL HELLER RETURNED to the United States on March 11, 1946, and Captain Howard A. Mackenzie transferred from nearby Hallein and became the property control officer for the Property Control Warehouse. The forty-three-year-old Mackenzie, like many older American men, had been inducted into a civil affairs organization and trained in a military government position.

Mackenzie arrived in England during Christmas of 1944 and trained for occupation duty in Austria. Afterward, he was sent to Italy. At the time of his arrival the Allied plans were to capture Austria through Italy from the south. But the swift advance of the Allies through France changed the strategy of the occupation forces; they would advance through southern France across Germany and into Austria from the northwest. By this route Mackenzie arrived in Hallein on July 13, 1945, where he took over as military governor of Hallein.

During the invasion of Austria, Dr. Lothar Pretzell, director of the Salzburg Museum, and his employees packed up the valuable coin collection of the museum. The collection contained examples of all the coins ever minted in Salzburg Province, dating back to the Roman invasion of Salzburg. The coins were packed in a strong wooden chest and marked "S.M." (Salzburg Museum) and secretly transported to and stored in the Wolf Dietrich salt mine of Duerrnberg near Hallein, Austria. The chest measured four by two by two feet and contained 4,086 unique and irreplaceable coins made of gold, silver, and copper. Fritz Hintze, a mine official in Hallein, was one of a handful of reliable

79

people informed about the storage of these coins. The collection was priceless.

At the time of the collapse and surrender of Germany, looting began immediately in the vast Duerrnberg salt mine. Soldiers of the U.S. Army had been looting for some time since moving into the Tyrol and Salzburg provinces. The 42d still adhered to its "one man fighting, two men looting, and three men painting rainbows" philosophy. With the surrender, looting increased, particularly among the foreign workers living in the vicinity of Hallein. There was no action taken to apprehend looters. Security procedures established by the U.S. Army to seize and secure valuables immediately after occupation were not enforced.

On May 15, 1945, Lieutenant Armand L. DeGaetano, commander of the military government detachment in Hallein, found an anonymous note on his desk. The note stated that Heinrich Himmler had stored documents of the Ministry of the Interior and other items in the nearby Wolf Dietrich mine of Duerrnberg. DeGaetano instructed his public safety officer, Lieutenant Bertrand LeVien, to investigate the matter. Lieutenant LeVien contacted Fritz Hintze, the mine engineer, and together they entered the salt mine and found some soldiers of the 3d Division looting shotguns, gold-plated Walther pistols, liquor, and many other valuable objects from a storage area about two miles from the shaft entrance. That same evening, Lieutenant DeGaetano called the provost marshal in Salzburg and requested that a military police be assigned to the mine. The following day he entered the mine and found about a dozen 3d Division soldiers looting in spite of the armed guard. He ordered them to leave the mine. The mine shaft was littered with broken toys, boxes, porcelain, pottery, and old books. Lieutenant DeGaetano reported the looting to the provost marshal's office, but no one seemed to care.

The section of the mine containing the Himmler papers and the Salzburg coin collection was over two miles from the entrance. The chamber had been blocked by huge logs. The Germans had also set off an explosion that caved in the shaft and further blocked access to the more valuable items. To discourage entrance into the chamber even more, the Germans had posted a sign stating that the chamber was radioactive.

Major John F. Back, commander of T Force, arrived at Hallein on June 4, 1945. Major Back's T Force was part of army intelligence, and his target was the Himmler documents. The major had the passage opened with the assistance of Fritz Hintze and several local mine experts. Back expected to find only the papers of Himmler, but the chamber contained the Himmler papers plus four boxes and two cases. One was marked "S.M.," three were marked "Archives," and two were cases of radium. The box marked "S.M." contained the rare Salzburg coins. Fritz Hintze was aware of the contents of the box and verified the contents as the Salzburg coin collection. The T Force team nailed the box closed and removed it from the mine. They then placed it on a U.S. truck and delivered it to the military government detachment in Hallein. The other three boxes, containing gold and silver, were taken by the T Force. They, as well as the radium cases, were turned over to the Property Control Warehouse in Salzburg. The Himmler papers were taken to Back's headquarters. According to a January 6, 1946, handwritten letter of Back's, the Salzburg coin collection was turned over to Lieutenant DeGaetano of the Hallein military detachment on June 4, 1945.

The Salzburg Museum contained thousands of coins, and only the most valuable had been removed from the large iron safe and sent to the Wolf Dietrich mine. At the museum only Dr. Pretzell and Franz Gruber were aware that the coins had been transferred from the museum. On July 14, 1945, Professor Rigobert V. Funke relieved Dr. Pretzell as director of the museum. Dr. Funke was not aware of the transfer of coins, and it was only during an inventory of the forty drawers of coins in the iron safe that he noticed that the coins were missing. Upon investigating, he was told by Dr. Pretzell of the location of the missing coins. Funke asked the Austrian police to begin an immediate investigation.

The Austrian police were told by various military personnel that the chest had been transported to Berchtesgaden, Germany. After a thorough investigation by police, and especially by the Salzburg Museum security staff, it was determined that the coins had actually been turned over to the military detachment at Hallein. This was validated by Fritz Hintze, who had accompanied the chest from the mine to the military detachment. The director of the small Hallein Museum had seen the box of coins unopened in the file room of the military government detachment. The security staff of the Salzburg Museum had actually seen some of the coins circulating among the general population at Hallein and had confiscated eleven of them from a local jeweler.

Professor Funke wrote: "My repeated efforts to locate the coins were frustrated by the harsh, declining attitude displayed by Lieutenant DeGaetano, American governor of Hallein.

On July 13, 1945, Captain Howard A. Mackenzie took over as military governor of Hallein, and Lieutenant DeGaetano became second in command. In September 1945, Professor Funke and Captain Charles R. Sattgast, MFA&A officer, came to Hallein with the permission of Captain Mackenzie and had a private conversation with Lieutenant DeGaetano. The professor and captain told him that a box of valuable coins had been deposited with him while he was commander of the military government detachment. The lieutenant stated he had never been given or seen any coins and could not understand why any officer would leave a chest of coins in such an unsuitable place as the military government detachment building. Prior to redeployment to the United States, however, DeGaetano told Mackenzie, "If anyone comes to Hallein looking for a chest of coins, tell them I sent them to Salzburg."[1]

On January 18, 1946, Sergeant Charles W. English discovered a battered wooden chest marked "S.M." on the main floor of the military detachment building in Hallein. The wooden chest was in a corner underneath other boxes, files, and papers. The box was one-third full of soiled envelopes and contained some coins. The envelopes contained the descriptions of the coins that had been removed. The chest was immediately turned over to Captain Mackenzie and placed in a safe for the night. The following morning, Sergeant English and Captain Mackenzie drove the twenty-five miles to Salzburg and turned the chest over to Captain Charles R. Sattgast.

Captain Mackenzie began an immediate investigation by interviewing the secretary of his former chief clerk, Sergeant George Kaplin. The secretary, Anna Raschek, stated that Sergeant Kaplin had once taken her to the file room and showed her some old gold and silver coins that were in envelopes in a wooden chest. The coins were found in an office formerly occupied by PFC Murray Gordon, who, like Sergeant Kaplin, had been redeployed to the United States. Maria Stendl, a close friend of Private Gordon's, said under oath that she had seen a bag of gold and silver in his possession. He showed the coins not only to her but to anyone interested in seeing them. Mr. Simon Marchetti, a local watchmaker, testified that Private Gordon came to show him approximately fifty to sixty coins from the thirteenth and fourteenth centuries and asked if they were gold. Marchetti had verified that the coins were indeed gold.

The aforementioned Bertrand LeVien, now a captain, had been the public safety officer in Hallein from May until September 1945. He had relocated to Linz, Austria, where he was assistant provost marshal. At Linz, Captain LeVien was interviewed by Miss Evelyn Tucker, of the Monuments and Fine Arts Section, and told her how he had learned about the coins quite by chance. The military government detachment at Hallein had had a Latvian woman working for them who had given him two or three large ancient Latvian coins. She left the coins for him in the office, and Lieutenant DeGaetano, thinking they had been left for him, had taken them. Lieutenant LeVien and Lieutenant De-Gaetano were arguing about the coins when Sergeant Kaplin said he saw no point in their arguing over two or three coins when there was a box full of old coins upstairs. The next day, LeVien went upstairs and asked Private Gordon where the box of coins was, and Gordon pointed out the box. LeVien looked through the box and found twelve gold and twenty-four silver coins, which he whisked away as souvenirs.[2]

A search of Lieutenant LeVien's home in Long Branch, New Jersey, by the U.S. Army, Criminal Intelligence Division, revealed forty-one silver coins and six gold coins which had been made into a bracelet for his wife. The coins were returned to the Salzburg Museum.[3]

George Kaplin was located by the military authorities in Utica, New York. Under questioning, he admitted that he had taken approximately twenty gold and silver coins. Kaplin stated that he had given part of the coins to an American soldier, whose name he had forgotten, in exchange for a German film projector. The remainder of the coins were given to people in Austria unknown to him. What was left he lost in his travels. There are no records to indicate that Private Gordon was ever located. Captain Charles R. Sattgast turned over the chest to Professor Funke, director of the Salzburg Museum. The chest still contained 1,422 coins, only 10 of which were gold; the original chest had contained 4,086 coins. Among the missing were 2,664 of the most valuable coins of the Salzburg collection.

After a thorough investigation by the Provost Marshal General Headquarters, European Command, the case of the Salzburg coin collection was closed. No censure or arrest was made due to lack of evidence.

During the six months that the Salzburg coin collection had been at the military detachment in Hallein, coins from it were definitely stolen by two officers, Lieutenants LeVien and DeGaetano, and two enlisted men, Pfc. Kaplin and Gordon. There is no hard evidence to indicate that Captain Mackenzie took any coins or property from the warehouse, but he definitely lived the good life. He, like most army captains, was paid three thousand dollars a year; but he owned a supercharged touring Mercedes, chauffeured by the former driver of General Alfred Jodl, German Chief of Operations Staff (Oberkommando der Wehrmacht, High Command of the Armed Forces).

Prior to the arrival of his wife and son, Mackenzie lived in the bachelor officers' quarters with his close military friends. He and his cohorts did considerable entertaining with young Austrian females. The women were always clothed in very elegant attire, which included numerous expensive-looking full-length fur coats. Mackenzie and his party were usually seen in the finest spas, casinos, and night spots in the Salzburg region. After the arrival of his family, Mackenzie also took advantage of the Hungarian property by furnishing his large duplex home located on Petersbrunnerstrasse in Salzburg. This duplex was shared by the family of now Captain LeVien, the officer who had participated in the looting of the Salzburg coin collection. The two husband and wives as teams spent many a night playing high-stakes games of bridge.

In April 1946, one of Mackenzie's first tasks included working with the Monuments, Fine Art and Archival officers in completing the elaborate task of cataloging and inventorying the looted Polish museum collections found in the Nazi art depot in Fischhorn Castle. This restitution, together with the Polish zoological collection recovered from Haus der Natur in Salzburg, comprised a special twelve-car freight train known as the Polish Art Train, which was sent to Warsaw on April 14, 1946, under protection of American and Polish armed guards.

The Hungarian Gold Train on a side track at Werfen, Austria, guarded by members of the 15th Infantry Regiment, 3d Division.

A grain car on the Hungarian Gold Train, converted to hold diamonds and reinforced with a locked steel bar.

China, crystal, and furniture in an American apartment taken from the Hungarian Gold Train.

Abba P. Schwartz and Colonel William G. Brey (right) reviewing some of the gold items taken from the Hungarian Gold Train.

Furniture stored in the Property Control Warehouse. The items were taken by the American occupying forces as household goods. Refrigerators were a top-priority item in Europe at that time.

General Harry J. Collins, 42d Infantry Division Commander (left), established the norm by being the first to appropriate the Hungarian valuables from the Property Control Warehouse.

These wedding bands taken from the Hungarian Gold Train are a grim reminder of what happened to the owners of the property.

The unscrupulous Captain Norman T. Byrne, Monuments, Fine Art and Archival officer, in his Berlin office.

The 17th-century Kronberg Castle was the scene of the largest robbery of World War II—the theft of the Hesse crown jewels.

Princess Margarethe, the Landgrafin of Hesse and granddaughter of Queen Victoria of England.

Princess Mafalda, the daughter of the King and Queen of Italy. Interned in Buchenwald concentration camp, she was forced into camp prostitution and died in Buchenwald.

Princess Sophia of Hanover, daughter of the King of Greece.

The jewels pictured here were stolen by Captain Kathleen Nash and her lover, Colonel Jack Durant. The diamonds, emeralds, pearls, and sapphires were removed from their settings. The gold settings were apparently sold in Switzerland. The loose gems disappeared from a parcel checkroom in the LaSalle Train Station in Chicago. The large gems and gold settings have never been recovered.

The U.S. Army placed on exhibit in the Pentagon the valuables recovered from the home of Mrs. Eileen Lonergan, Kathleen Nash's sister, in Hudson, Wisconsin.

The 44-year-old Captain Kathleen Nash (center) was responsible for the theft of the jewels of the house of Hesse.

The half million dollars' worth of jewels that were recovered from the Illinois Central Railroad Station, Chicago, were taken from this stationery box held by the author.

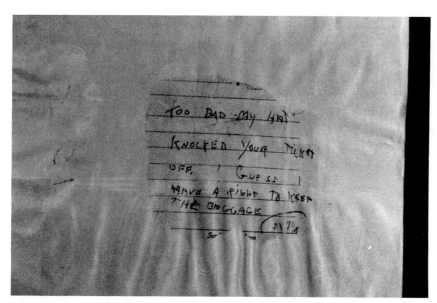

This torn piece of telegram message paper taken from behind the instruction plate of a pay telephone is the last link to the missing Hesse crown jewels. The note had been stuck to the plate with a wad of chewing gum.

After considerable inquiries, these valuables were mailed to the U.S. Army by Gladys B. Madison, the sister of Kathleen Nash.

Lieutenants Bertrand LeVien (left) and Armand L. DeGaetano were involved in the theft of the irreplaceable Salzburg coin collection. In spite of admitting his part in the theft, LeVien remained in the Army unpunished, due to a lack of evidence.

11

Robberies in the Property Control Warehouse

PROPERTY LOCATED IN THE WAREHOUSE was not guarded adequately, and large-scale looting further scattered it. Hungarian museum objects and religious relics were displayed openly in local Salzburg merchants' windows. The black market for Gold Train items was so lucrative that the Hungarian government protested the lack of security and emphasized that although Austria did not win the war with the Allies, it apparently was sharing in the war booty. More prized items were plundered in Salzburg than in any other place in occupied Europe.

The Property Control Warehouse was a large structure two stories high and approximately two city blocks square. For extra security, a fence reinforced with barbed wire had been built. It surrounded the structure, and the area was patrolled by military guards. All windows and doors were sealed except for one door, and it was secured with three locks. Captain Mackenzie had one key, Sergeant Robert J. Cloud had one, and the remaining key was kept in a safe. Procedure stipulated that the warehouse could be entered only by teams; no single individual was allowed in. Prior to entering, individuals had to remove their outer clothing and put on coveralls that had had the pockets and cuffs removed, and upon leaving, they were searched by military guards.

Guarding the Property Control Warehouse, located in the center of the military base, was the responsibility of L Company, 5th Infantry Regiment, from nearby Camp Glasenbach in Salzburg. There was a

85

small gate at the right front corner of the barbed-wire fence surrounding the warehouse. One of the sentries stood guard at this gate, where he could see the entire front and right side of the building. The second sentry station was at the opposite side of the warehouse, where the back and left side of the warehouse could be seen. The warehouse could not be entered without the knowledge of one of the guards.

Unfortunately, the guards and enlisted men were aware of the fact that high-ranking officers and civilians were raking in big profits from the warehouse, and they figured that they should get in on some of the action. Private Ira Waits had been told of the valuables by a private who had worked in the warehouse and was aware of its contents. In May 1946, Waits and Pfc. Saford R. Semones approached the guards and told them about the jewelry and antiques in the building. Waits asked the guard to let him in and said that he would share what he got with both of the guards. The young guards agreed, and Waits and Semones went to the first window on the right side of the warehouse, opened it and crawled through, and sneaked to the back of the warehouse. There the valuables were separated in another room that was not locked. Waits opened the door, and the two proceeded to stuff their pockets full of watches, rings, bracelets, gold chains, and three cameras. They then left the warehouse and went over to the guardhouse and shared the loot with the detachment of guards. Semones walked back to the barracks, removed his valuables from his pockets, and put them into his locker. Waits stored his loot in a dresser drawer in his barracks. Waits had a bit of class, however. From the drawer he removed one beautiful wedding band and another expensive gold ring and took them to one of the prisoners at Camp Marcus Orr to have them engraved with his initials.

Waits had an insatiable appetite for this kind of loot, and he and another soldier, Tech-5 Marvin Adams, entered the warehouse on June 10, 1946. They entered the same back window and immediately crept into the room containing the valuables. They collected their loot in bags and upon leaving gave the two guards a watch each. Adams took his bag, containing more than a hundred watches, and buried them in a field behind the motor pool building. He removed a ring, two women's silver lace handbags, a gold cigarette case, and a bracelet, which he gave to his girlfriend Kathe Farber, who resided in Wels, Austria.

Waits could not shake the looting habit; twice more, accompanied by Tech-5 George T. Law, he entered the warehouse. Law did not take note of what Waits filched, and the first time Law only filled up his pockets, but on the second foray, he took a small Red Cross bag with him and loaded it with rings, watches, bracelets, and cameras.

A week later Waits and Semones were themselves on guard duty at another warehouse. They left their station and walked over to guard post 418, which was the guard station for the Property Control Warehouse. Pfc. Harold Perkins, nicknamed "Blondie," and James White were the sentries at that post. Waits told them about the valuables in the warehouse. They told Perkins and White that guards had let them in before and that they would share some of the valuables. Once again the guards on duty were amenable, and once again Waits and Semones entered the warehouse the identical way. This time they had a large green laundry bag which they filled up with all the jewelry that Waits could carry. After they left they went into a small trailer and poured the jewelry onto the floor. They then scooped up several handfuls of wedding bands, watches, brooches, gold chains, and gold teeth and gave them to Perkins and White. Then Waits and his cohort Semones concealed the remainder of the stash in a small storage room nearby. Of all the loot, Perkins was most impressed with the three Swiss-made watches that he had received. White was given fifty-seven signet rings, six watches, two cameras, and two gold chains, which he took back and stored in his room.

Later that night, at about 1:00 A.M., while still on guard duty, Perkins decided to sneak into the warehouse. Guard post 418 was about thirty feet from the building, and Perkins told Pfc. Russell D. Parker to be on the lookout and let him know if anyone came into the vicinity. He entered the warehouse through the rear window with an M1 rifle in one hand and a flashlight in the other. He had been exploring the warehouse for about twenty minutes when he heard, or thought he heard, footsteps. The exterior doors were checked every thirty minutes.

Scared of getting caught, he returned empty-handed in the early-morning darkness, Perkins began to get cold, so he left the guard trailer to find some cardboard boxes to build a fire. He went to the storage room and picked up a couple of cardboard boxes. One of the boxes was unusually heavy, and upon examination Perkins found the green bag of jewelry that had been hidden by Ira Waits. He took the bag back to the trailer, removed some of the jewelry, and wrapped it up in his raincoat. He then gave some of it to Parker, who put it into his cartridge belt and also filled up his raincoat. They did not have enough room for all the valuables, so Perkins took the bag back where he had found it and left it there. At 4:00 A.M. the guard truck picked up the two men and took them back to the company area. Parker put his cartridge belt under his pillow and put the remaining diamonds in a cigar box. When he woke up thinking about the theft, Parker removed two gold bracelets, walked upstairs to Perkins's room, and gave him the remainder of the jewelry.

Later that morning, Perkins took Gerald J. Roberts to the storage room and showed him the bag in its hiding place. Roberts removed two handfuls of jewelry and put them into his field jacket. The following day, Waits returned to claim the bag and found it gone. He suspected that a "tall Mexican" (Perkins) had taken the stuff. Roberts did not store his valuables but panicked and threw them over the bridge at Camp Glasenbach into the Salzach River.

The following day, Perkins took some of his large aggregation of jewelry and gave it to Pfc. Soloman G. Cadriel, asking him to take it to his girlfriend's house. Perkins was afraid of a barracks search (quite common during that time,) that would reveal his ill-gotten gains. That afternoon, Perkins and White stopped by guard post 400 and asked Cadriel, who was on duty, where his girlfriend lived. He said her name was Maria Hoell and pointed out her house at 5 Hofkirchenstrasse, very close to his guard post. Perkins and White then walked over to the house. Maria spoke only German, which they did not understand, so they walked back to the guard post and had Cadriel accompany them. Cadriel then told Maria in German to show the valuables to Perkins and White. She took a key and opened a clothing closet and removed a box containing the cache. Both Perkins and White removed a handful of booty and put the box back in its place. Maria locked the door and gave to key to Perkins. Later, Cadriel borrowed the key from Perkins and told him that he had removed twenty rings and two gold bracelets for his own use.

Perkins now had in his possession a large quantity of watches, jewelry, gold teeth, and other items. Two weeks later he took the valuables to the home of Valerija Uzeinaite, a Lithuanian living in a displaced persons camp and known to the soldiers as Viole. She took the bag without opening it and hid it under her bed. A few nights later Perkins returned to Viole's room and found her boyfriend, Pfc. Paul Prewett, an army cook, with her. Perkins had come by to purchase some black market cognac from Viole. Perkins, known to Prewett and Viole only as Blondie, asked Viole to show Prewett the jewelry. She produced about three hundred rings, and since Perkins had decided to sell the loot, Prewett agreed to help on a commission basis. Perkins gave him approximately one hundred rings and a seventeen-jewel Swiss Girand Perregaux watch to sell. Prewett sold most of the rings the following day to cooks in his company mess for 500 schillings ($6.25) each, and he sold the watch to a Polish DP working in the mess hall for $12.50. The next night, Prewett gave Perkins his share from the sell, which was 4,300 schillings.

Viole soon let it be known that she had some valuables for sale. One of her first customers was Leo Fleischacker, who took Private Jerry Karapopolas with him and purchased a few gold rings from Viole and made a quick profit of 1,800 schillings from their sale. Leo told his cousin Ruper Fleischacker about the deal. Ruper was a slim Austrian, sporting a most uncharacteristic Hitler mustache; at the end of the war these mustaches and the name "Adolf" were dropped immediately by most Germans and Austrians. Ruper went to Viole's room and asked if she had anything to sell. She told the Austrian that her American friend had some jewelry that he might want to sell, and then she arranged a meeting with Perkins.

On June 7, 1946, a Sunday afternoon, Fleischacker, with his brother-in-law Hans Tauner, returned and met with Perkins in Viole's room. Perkins produced 175 gold wedding bands, 12 signet rings, 7 gold watches, 1 necklace, 1 collar pin, 15 gold bracelets, 81 gold teeth, and 100 scrap items of gold jewelry and asked for 25,000 schillings ($312.50) for the lot. Not expecting such a large number of items, Fleischacker and Tauner could only produce 8,000 schillings each. Tauner had borrowed the money from his two brothers, and as a dealer in antiquities and gold, he knew that they were getting a bargain, but still negotiating, Fleischacker said that he could only borrow another 8,000 schillings. After agreeing upon a price of 24,000 schillings, they caught a taxi to Ruper's cousin Leo's home. They soon returned from the house and paid Perkins in front of the building. Perkins walked away, but Tauner had to remain in the taxi due to a recent leg amputation caused by a war injury. Perkins then returned to Viole's apartment and gave her 1,800 schillings, three rings, and a watch for her help in the transaction. This was a good sum of money for Perkins, for at that time he was grossing $96 a month.

Fleischacker and Tauner, both penniless, had promised their relatives a quick return on the loans. Needing to turn the valuables over quickly, they took the taxi to Camp New Palestine, a DP camp located in Salzburg. Tauner knew a dealer there who called himself Schmul. They spread their merchandise out for his inspection. After about twenty minutes, a middle-aged man entered and gave them 30,000 shillings for the lot. In one afternoon, without any money of their own, the two entrepreneurial Austrians had turned a profit of 3,000 shillings each. Although amounting to only $37.50 each, that was a month's salary in war-torn Salzburg in 1946, and Tauner needed the money badly to provide for his wife and three children. Fleischacker used half of his profit to purchase an accordion and saved the other half. Schmul and the unnamed middle-aged man immediately dropped out of sight.

During one of his routine checks of the warehouse, Captain Mackenzie noticed that several of the boxes had been moved. Further investigation revealed that many boxes in the immediate area were empty. He had begun to notice a large number of enlisted men wearing expensive rings and that all of the cooks in the mess hall were wearing crescent rings of a similar design. Also it was noted that three young Austrian women living at 7 Glanhoferstrasse. Salzburg, were festooned in expensive jewelry. Saford Semones, known to the girls as Jimmy, had given his girlfriend Hildegard Puffal several rings and had also given her friend Maria Estl nine watches and one ring. Soloman Cadriel, known as John Hall, had given one of his girlfriends, Zilli Doblhammer, a gold bracelet and one gold ring, and to one "Estl" eight gold signet rings. Cadriel had bragged that he had so many girlfriends that he used the name John Hall so they wouldn't find out his real name.

Based on these incidents and information that enlisted men were giving away and selling a large number of rings and watches, Captain Mackenzie, on July 17, 1946, reported the incidents to the local Criminal Investigation Division.

CID agent Raymond J. Brown began the investigation by asking the cooks about their expensive rings. Their fingers immediately pointed to Pfc. Paul Prewett, who was arrested the following day. His story led to Valerija Uzeinaite (Viole) and a blond soldier known only as Blondie. The following day, July 19, a search of Viole's apartment by the CID did not yield any jewelry. Afterward, a lineup of L Company was held, and Prewett and Viole were taken through the company separately, and both identified Pfc. Perkins as the soldier known to them as Blondie. Viole then told Agent Brown about the purchase by two Austrians, Tauner and Fleischacker.

The following day, and much to his surprise, Brown was given a box containing eighty watches by Captain Marvin Jark. The box had been found by a Yugoslavian DP who had been cutting grass behind the motor pool. These were the watches hidden by Marvin Adams. Adams was positive that he had hidden more than a hundred watches. Who had siphoned off some of the loot? A few days later an Austrian working in the courtyard of the Sternbrau restaurant found a large package containing jewelry and turned it over to the proper military authorities.

It did not take the CID very long to connect Maria Hoell, one of Soloman Cadriels girlfriends, to the robbery of the Property Control Warehouse. They went to her home and searched it. The thorough search included opening a coal stove and looking into the stovepipe, where they found hidden 175 gold wedding bands, 12 signet rings, 7 gold watch chains, 1 necklace, 1 collar pin, 15 gold bracelets, 81 gold teeth, and 100 scrap items of broken jewelry. Hoell also knew Cadriel only as John Hall. It was only during the CID investigation that she learned his real name. Who was trying to steal from whom here? Was there no honor among thieves?

It did not take long for Ira Waits to receive word that the CID was investigating the robbery of the warehouse. Later, after he was picked up, Waits said:

> All the rings and watches, bracelets and etc., I threw into the [Salzach] river when I heard the CID was looking for me. I sold one camera to a boy in the Service Company named Denato for 1500 schillings. I sold another camera to Sergeant Baxter of my company for 500 to 600 schillings. I sold a pocket watch to a boy in my room for 300 schillings. I gave another boy in my room a girl's watch. I have two more rings—one a wedding band and another a gold ring being engraved for me by one of the prisoners at Camp Marcus Orr.

By August 6, 1946, both Semones and George Law had been arrested by the CID. Upon questioning, Semones claimed that he had thrown most of his jewelry into the Salzach, but Law told the CID agent that he had thrown his loot into the reservior pool in the Service Company area. Arrangements were made, and the Salzburg fire department drained the reservoir. The following list of only the recovered items gives one an idea of just how much was dumped into the reservoir: 25 ladies' wristwatches, 27 men's wristwatches, 26 pocket watches, 21 silver spoons, 3 rings, 3 gold chains, 1 bracelet, 1 brooch, 1 medal, 26 wristwatch works, 16 wristwatches without casings, 16 wristwatches without crystals, 94 fronts and 75 back casings of various type of watches, 1 Compur camera, 1 Bessa camera, 1 Balda camera, and

2 pairs of field glasses. Law had only entered the warehouse once, and Waits had made five hauls with various other soldiers. There is evidence that he had entered the warehouse three times alone. (Did Waits really throw his cache into the Salzach?)

Based upon the investigation by Raymond Brown, twelve soldiers and seven civilians were arrested. On September 25, 1946, a common trial in courtroom 69 in the Landesgerichts building was arranged for five of the accused: James White, Harold Perkins, Saford Semones, Marvin Adams, and George Law, all L Company, 5th Infantry Regiment.

Captain James H. McGuire was appointed trial judge. (More about this incredible man later.) At the beginning of the trial, all of the accused except White pleaded guilty to carrying away captured property of the United States. At that time, Captain McGuire advised the accused that they were legally and morally entitled to plead not guilty and place the burden of proof on the prosecution to prove them guilty. The best testimony for the prosecution was given by CID agent Brown. According to the prosecution, Brown's testimony, along with the recovered jewelry and nineteen other witnesses, proved the case against the five without a shadow of doubt. After three days of trial that generated 107 pages of records, the prosecution rested. Judge McGuire then advised the five accused soldiers that they had the right to do three things. First, they could be sworn in and take the stand as witnesses. If they did, they could be cross-examined and their testimony could be held against them. Second, without being sworn in they could make any statement that they desired, but it would not be given the weight of a sworn statement. Third, they could remain silent. All five chose the third option and remained silent.

On September 27, 1946, and upon written ballot, two-thirds of the members of the court-martial board present at the time the vote was taken concurred in finding the five men guilty. White, nineteen years old, was sentenced to be confined at hard labor for four years; Semones, also nineteen, was sentenced to be confined at hard labor for five years; Adams, twenty-eight, was sentenced to be confined at hard labor for five years; Perkins, eighteen, was sentenced, but for ten years; and Law, nineteen, was sentenced to five years. In addition, they were all dishonorably discharged. All were single except Adams, who was married and had three daughters. Adams had been awarded a Bronze Service Star for combat action in Germany. He had served twenty months in a reformatory training school during his youth.

General Harry J. Collins, commanding general, zone commander, Austria, reviewed the cases and reduced four of the sentences to two years' hard labor. Perkins's time was reduced to four years. Collins signed these documents at a handsome antique desk embellished with hand carvings. The desk belonged to the city of Hallein, but the general had "requisitioned" the desk for himself. He had spotted it one fall day in 1945 while visiting Captain Mackenzie, then military governor of Hallein. The next day, an army truck arrived, along with orders to ship the desk to Collins. Mackenzie protested feebly but gave up the desk. Collins's office had six rugs, eight paintings, a modernistic desk clock, and a desk set requisitioned from the Hungarian valuables to complement the antique desk.

Captain McGuire's next assignment was to preside over the trial of Lieutenant Thomas J. Correlle. This case began on October 24, 1946, and was an embezzlement charge. The twenty-nine-year-old New Yorker had served during the war as an enlisted man, but had later attended officer candidate school at Fort Knox, Kentucky, and had received his commission exactly one year prior to his trial date. Correlle was special service and post exchange officer of the 4th Constabulary Squadron and as such operated the post exchange, or PX, at Hallein. In June 1946, Correlle became acquainted with Niklos Roth, a Hallein resident, who had been hired to make small repairs around the PX buildings. During this time he approached Roth and told him that he would like to buy some jewelry if Roth could find some for sale. Roth then met with a Count Odelskalski, who offered to sell a ring and brooch for 60,000 schillings ($750). Roth showed the valuables to Correlle and stated the price. The ring contained a large diamond, 14 smaller diamonds, and 12 rubies. The brooch contained 36 diamonds and 4 rubies. Correlle then made a counteroffer of 200 cartons of Camel and Chesterfield cigarettes. The 200 cartons could have been purchased at the PX for $140. Correlle had a bargain, if one overlooked the fact that the the smokes would have fetched over $1,000 on the black market

An agreement was reached, however, so Correlle told Pfc. Frank Trinka, the PX manager, to remove forty-three cases of cigarettes and some soap and shoe polish from inventory and take them to his office. Each case contained fifty cartons of cigarettes. He told Trinka that he was going to issue the cigarettes to the troops as extra rations. Thirty-two cases of the war-issue "yellow seal of the armed forces" cigarettes were issued to the troops, but 4 cases containing the 200 cartons were taken to Roth's home, after which 120 cartons were removed by Count

Odelskalski. Roth commenced selling the remaining 80 cartons on the black market and was subsequently arrested by U.S. authorities. Roth told his story to CID agent Joseph P. Denove, who immediately, on August 20, at 5:30 P.M, closed the Hallein PX for further investigation.

Word traveled fast that the PX had been closed. The following night, during a dinner conversation in the staff officers' quarters, the subject of the CID was discussed by Correlle and Captains Martin and Lundberg. Correlle asked Martin if he had a storeroom big enough for a piano. Later that night, Correlle went to his room over the PX and lugged a wooden box over to Martin's room and hid it under a nightstand at the foot of Martin's bed. The next morning, Lundberg discovered the box and, suspecting something, took it to his room and opened it. He was flabbergasted to discover an ermorous stash of glittering diamonds. Suspecting Martin of criminal activity, he immediately notified the CID. Armed with the statement that Roth had made after his arrest, they quickly connected the box of valuables to the conniving Correlle. On September 11, 1946, he was arrested and charged with stealing 200 cartons of cigarettes.

On October 23, the first morning of Correlle's trial, the special defense counsel was involved in a case in Vienna and could not finish in time, so a continuance was granted until Wednesday, November 6. The valuables had been obtained by the CID and were signed over to Lieutenant James W. Graham, the assistant trial judge. The evidence had already been displayed on a large table in the courtroom and included cigarettes, cameras, twenty-five expensive watches, wearing apparel, pistols, ammunition, six different currencies, many pieces of expensive jewelry, including thirty diamond rings (one ring contained twenty diamonds) and one small red velvet box with a brooch that contained thirty-six diamonds and four rubies. Graham recounted the valuables, and in referencing them McGuire told Graham, "It is your baby."[1] Escorted by two MPs, Graham placed the valuables in unlocked boxes and suitcases and took them to McGuire's office. The containers were stacked against the wall, and the office was locked and guarded from the inside by a shift of men from the 505th Military Police Battalion, Company A, twenty-four hours a day, seven days a week. The guards— one MP during the day shift and two MPs during the night shift— were under the general supervision of McGuire.

On the morning of November 6, at 8:15, prior to the court's reconvening, Graham unpacked and displayed the evidence once more upon the large table. Approaching the table, Captain George Lundburg noticed that the little red velvet box with the expensive brooch was missing. The estimated value of the brooch in 1946 was $4,000. He immediately notified Graham, who started checking the valuables against the CID's inventory and discovered that also missing were two rings with one diamond each, one ring with one large diamond surrounded by six small diamonds, and 51,000 schillings. Startled, McGuire immediately instructed the MPs to search all envelopes, boxes, and drawers in the court building. The case was turned over to CID agent Arthur Miller, who investigated the missing valuables and reported that his team was unable to obtain substantial facts to accuse anyone of actually taking the brooch and rings. The CID report concluded that the loss of the evidence was due to careless handling and storage.

During his trial, Correlle chose to remain silent. He was found guilty and received a one-year sentence. Lieutenant Graham was verbally reprimanded for laxity in safeguarding the evidence. Rank has always had it privileges, but the punishments meted out by court-martial for looting by enlisted men and the punishments received for the same crimes or larger by officers were never more disproportionate than at this time in history.

In the case of the missing jewels, the prime suspect was an MP, W. Miller, who had guarded the valuables. It was merely reported that he usually had more than his share of schillings for spending money. No further action was recommended, but Salzburg CID agents began to suspect that something was blatantly wrong. During this and the Property Control Warehouse robbery trials, the more expensive of the stolen goods had vanished during or shortly after the trials.

12

Judge James H. McGuire

J AMES MCGUIRE WAS five feet eleven inches tall, forty-four years old, and overweight at 235 pounds, but his uniform gave testimony to an adventurous past. His tunic was bedecked with an impressive array of decorations that included the Legion of Merit, a Silver Star with one cluster, a Bronze Star, American Theater Camp, Croix de Guerre from World War I, Croix de Guerre from World War II, Distinguished Unit Badge with one cluster, and the Belgian Fourrage. Most impressive was the 2d Ranger Battalion patch on his left shoulder. His records showed that he had served in combat from July 1942 until May 1945 with one of the most elite units of World War II, the famed 2d Ranger Battalion. It was most celebrated for the furious assault on D day of the hundred-foot-high cliffs at Pointe du Hoc. In contrast to his battle ribbons and decorations were the two rings he wore on his pudgy fingers, one gold containing a large diamond, the other gold containing two large sapphires and a large diamond.

The captain was above suspicion; in addition to being a war hero, he boasted a Doctor of Law degree from the University of Texas (1922), a Doctor of Philosophy of Law degree from Columbia University (1928), and a Doctor of Theory of Law degree from Cambridge University (1933).

In the fall of 1946, Lieutenant Rene S. Davis, having known McGuire for several months, approached him and said that he needed some advice and assistance. At the outset, Davis thought of McGuire not as a judge per se but as a friend who happened to be trained in law. Davis confessed that he had acquired a considerable amount of jewelry and other valuables. McGuire counseled him that if the CID found the articles in Davis's possession, they would be confiscated. He advised Davis to turn the valuables over to him for safekeeping, adding that the CID could not touch McGuire in his official capacity as trial judge advocate.

At the end of hostilities, Davis had ended up in Tyrol, Austria. There he had met Hilda Rademayer and obtained a job for the twenty-one-year-old as an interpreter. Hilda had become intimate with Davis and was known by all to be his girlfriend. Davis's company had moved several times in the next two months, ending up in Vienna in August 1945. Hilda remained with Davis during the moves. In November, Davis transferred to Salzburg, leaving Hilda in Vienna. He returned two months later for a New Year's Eve party and asked Hilda to move to Salzburg to be closer to him. She declined this suggestion, and several more, during the next few months. Again in May he visited her in Vienna and pleaded with her to make the move to Salzburg. Because of her marginal living conditions and the food shortages now plaguing Vienna, Hilda assented and moved to Salzburg. There she obtained a job in Davis's company as a typist in the supply room of the 63d Signal Company A. The room was located in the former Stern Brewery buildings.[1]

On June 7, 1946, just after she accepted the job, Davis gave her a platinum ring with a large pearl and two diamonds. This was just one ring among a large number of items that he had acquired from Karl Steinhart, an Austrian citizen, in exchange for seven cases of cognac and 324 bottles of liquor. In addition to the jewelry, Steinhart had been a regular visitor to the supply room, purchasing many bottles of liquor from Davis at 150 schillings per bottle.

Davis needed the schillings because during a visit to Ernst Schubert's antique shop on Burgerspitalgasse he had seen a large twelve-place silverware set with an asking price of 8,000 schillings. The consignment of silverware was inscribed on the back with a baron's crown and had been stamped with the number 900 by a Counter Intelligence Corps (CIC) officer by the name of Strassmann who had stated that he was selling it for a Mrs. Pauline Gobiet. Davis bargained with Schubert, and they agreed on a price of 6,000 schillings. After selling 40 bottles of liquor, Davis returned and purchased the silver-ware, which, it so happened, had been taken from the Hungarian Gold

Train property. Although purchased for a value of $75, this "hot" silverware in 1945 was worth more than $500.

Two months later, at the end of July, Davis told Hilda that she must return to Vienna because his wife was expected to arrive in Salzburg during September. He told her that he wanted her out early so that nobody would be able to tell his wife about her being his girlfriend. Hilda, however, knew that Davis was seeing other Austrian girls and surmised that he simply wanted to dump her. In fact, Davis's wife was on her way to join her husband. Hilda chose not to return to Vienna and was fired from her job in Company A.

Maxine Davis arrived in Austria and in due time met Captain James McGuire. Davis had telphoned his wife prior to her arrival that he had "been in trouble" and that he had given McGuire a large amount of jewelry to get the charges against him dropped.

On December 14, Maxine Davis, John H. Bowman, a U.S. civilian, and McGuire went to the home of Anneliese Rausch, Captain McGuire's twenty-eight-year-old girlfriend. McGuire told Anneliese that he had been a lawyer for Lieutenant Davis and had gotten him out of a jam and was now going to be Mrs. Davis's lawyer in securing a divorce for her. Anneliese made a big mistake by showing Maxine Davis two diamond bracelets, a dinner ring, and several more pieces of valuable jewelry and identifying them as gifts from McGuire. Mrs. Davis asked McGuire about the jewelry that her husband had given him. Looking her straight in the eye, he told her that he had given the valuables away as gifts in order to have the charges against her husband dropped. He further stated that he had kept only the ring that he was wearing as a fee. Suspicious, Mrs. Davis began to put two and two together and, questioning her husband, was told that some of the jewelry displayed by Anneliese Rausch had been jewelry he had given McGuire. Davis told his wife to drop the issue, but she would not and told John Bowman that she would like to report the incident to someone in authority. Bowman relayed this message to CID agent Eugene F. Land.

On December 20, 1946, Eugene F. Land, one of CID agent Brown's colleagues, received a request from Mrs. Davis to come to her room in the Linzerhof Hotel in Linz. The room had been assigned to Lieutenant Davis and his wife by the U.S. housing authorities. When Land arrived, Mrs. Davis was alone in the room. After introducing herself, she said that she had arrived several weeks ago from the United States, only to learn that her husband was in some sort of difficulty. She told Land that the defense counsel for her husband in a pending general court-martial had taken a diamond ladies' dinner ring, a large diamond ring, a diamond bracelet with fifteen large stones, a set of silverware valued at $1,200, and several silver candlesticks from her husband. Furthermore, she claimed, the jewelry was intended to bribe members of the judge advocate judiciary in Salzburg. The jewelry had included the gold ring with two sapphires and a large diamond worn on the right hand of Captain McGuire. Mrs. Davis concluded by telling Land that her husband was unaware of her meeting with him. The agent told her to go ahead and tell her husband about their conversation and to arrange for a joint meeting.

The meeting then took place, but now both Davis and his wife refused to talk to the agents; Davis was perplexed as to why his wife had decided to reveal the story about the jewels. Under stern questioning, Davis would neither deny nor confirm the story his wife had told Agent Land. He further asserted that the only person to whom he would talk and give a statement was General Harry J. Collins. Mrs. Davis affirmed that her husband would not assist the investigators because the question might arise as to where he had acquired such a large amount of jewelry. The lieutenant made no friends among the CID men when he accused the lot of them of acting like "Nero detectives."

With this story from Land, Agents Raymond Brown and Philip Bernstein began to reflect upon the statement made by Mrs. Davis. Their exploration during December revealed that Lieutenant Davis had used Captain McGuire as his defense counsel after Davis had been charged with the unlawful attempt to sell 288 bottles of cognac to an Austrian civilian. He was also charged with an attempt to obstruct justice. The court found him guilty, but the reviewing authorities set aside this decision and dismissed the charges. Apparently McGuire's bribes had worked.

The agents were baffled over this series of events. On December 22, 1946, Bernstein and Brown, along with a German policeman, traveled to nearby Anger, Germany, and discussed the situation with Miss Rausch, who spoke English well and told the two agents she had met Captain McGuire in Wiesbaden in September 1945. At that time she had been employed as a secretary in the mess club and billeting office. She said McGuire had been transferred to Stuttgart and then to Salzburg in April 1946. She traveled in U.S. military vehicles with McGuire during his transfers and lived with him. The agents noticed that Rausch was wearing a white-gold bracelet containing many diamonds, a wedding band with four diamonds, an engagement ring containing three diamonds, and a yellow dinner ring with thirty-two diamonds of various sizes, with a space where one of the diamonds was missing. This missing space would turn out to be evidence linking the ring with the jewelry Lieutenant Davis had given to McGuire.

The chatty Anneliese Rausch told the agents that McGuire had bestowed many expensive gifts upon his friends in her presence. They had, for instance, visited the home of Lieutenant Colonel Clifton D. Blackford, judge advocate counsel, in November 1946, and McGuire had given Mrs. Dolores Blackford a ring with twelve diamonds and four sapphires. Mrs Blackford had shown Rausch two pairs of candlestick holders, a set of twelve silver mocha spoons, a silver Oriental cigarette case, and one silver snuff box, all gifts from the popular Captain McGuire. During this same visit and in the presence of the Blackfords, McGuire gave Anneliese a bracelet with eleven diamonds of different sizes set in eleven links of platinum. Both ends of the bracelet were attached with thin gold chains about two inches long.

She recalled that a week earlier, on Monday, December 16, that McGuire had taken the bracelet back and had told her that it was "hot." Two nights later, McGuire and an American civilian, Mr. McConnell, had paid a social visit to her apartment, and she had asked about the bracelet. McGuire had told her that he had turned it over to CID agent Arthur Miller and that he had acquired most of his valuables from a Major Snow, who was "in a hell of a lot of trouble" and was under arrest at the Osterreicher Hof hotel. McGuire then made the assertion that the major had "hundreds of diamonds" and said that Snow had called him from the maid's telephone in the hotel and that he, McGuire, had gone to the hotel and smuggled out a tie pin in his cap for Major Snow. When Rausch wondered aloud where the valuables were hidden, McGuire grew sullen and replied, "Oh no, I'm not going to tell you—but they will never find it. If Colonel Blackford knew where the stuff was hidden he would kill me."[2]

Anneliese Rausch also informed the CID agents that she and McGuire had been invited to the home of Major Cullus M. Mayes, staff judge advocate, in nearby Hallein. After dinner, Mayes and his wife Marion returned with them to Salzburg. Mayes and McGuire went to the Bristol Hotel, and when they returned, McGuire handed over to Marian Mayes an enormous bag of silverware, with one silver spoon missing. This was the silverware originally acquired by Davis from Ernst Schubert's antique shop.

Rausch then told the agents that McGuire had also given Lieutenant Colonel James Garnett, Jr., McGuire's immediate supervisor and judge advocate, a valuable set of silver. She said McGuire had told her that he had "completely furnished Garnett's apartment with silverware, rugs and china.

"McGuire told me he had been a lawyer for Lieutenant Davis and now he has to be Mrs. Davis's lawyer in securing a divorce for her." This last statement intrigued Brown and Bernstein; they began to suspect that a close relationship had developed between Mrs. Davis and McGuire. They arranged for a joint interview with Lieutenant Davis and his wife, and when they were all gathered together, Agent Brown decided to go for all the marbles and told Lieutenant Davis that if his wife had been in Europe at the time of his troubles, McGuire might not have demanded only jewelry from him—implying that he might have asked for Davis's wife instead. At this, both suspects jumped to their feet. Enraged, Davis shouted that he could charge Captain McGuire with attempted rape.[3] The agents then grasped that Mrs. Davis was after revenge, with McGuire as her target. They really didn't care what the motive was now, because they had more than enough evidence to conclude that James McGuire was a certified crook.

The agents had gone to McGuire's billet in the Bristol Hotel in Salzburg on the night of December 19, 1946, accompanied by Lieutenant Marshall S. Otsea, Military Police. They had asked McGuire for permission to search his quarters and received an emphatic no. The request was repeated, but the reply was the same. McGuire was then placed under strict bed arrest by authority of the commanding general. These unusual instructions meant that McGuire was to actually remain in bed at all times, with his hands visible above the covers, and not to venture out for any reason, without permission. Toilet and shaving privileges were to be allowed only under the strict supervision of armed guards inside the room. McGuire remained under these humiliating restrictions for twenty-four hours, after which he was placed under normal arrest and held in the brig. A search warrant was issued on December 21, and after his quarters were thoroughly inspected, McGuire had been released on a recognizance bond, and on Christmas Eve he walked into the bar of the Bristol Hotel and began drinking. Under the influence, he had told Captain Warren M. Cannefax that the CID had found over $90,000 worth of diamonds in his room.

On that same Christmas Eve agents paid a visit to Lieutenant Colonel Clifton D. Blackford, judge advocate counsel. They requested that the colonel turn over to them the valuables that had been given him by McGuire, but the colonel refused, claiming that they were gifts from McGuire that were his to keep, and declined to make a written statement.

CID agents continued to reclaim stolen valuables relentlessly. On January 3, 1947, Brown and Bernstein questioned Major Cullus M. Mayes, who told Bernstein that some silverware he had possessed had been turned over to McGuire for appraisal and that ownership was transferred to his wife. The silverware had not been returned, however.

Agent Brown then questioned Lieutenant Colonel James Garnett, who said that McGuire had delivered to him some flat silverware bearing a distinctive crest. He had told McGuire, said Garnett, that he wanted silverware with his initials on it. The crested silverware was turned over to Agent Brown on January 21. It was the same silverware that had been given to Marian Mayes. The colonel was not questioned concerning Anneliese Rausch's statement that McGuire had furnished his complete apartment.

During the CID's investigation, the normally verbose McGuire refused to talk to the CID and carried himself with an air of being untouchable; he seemed to consider himself a notch above their paltry attempts to convict him. After all, he was a well-educated war hero. Brown and Bernstein, who were paid to be suspicious, were nevertheless unprepared for what they were about to discover about their disdainful suspect.

The two men sent a routine Western Union telegram to the FBI in Washington requesting a background check on McGuire. This inquiry included requests for information concerning McGuire's educational background and legal experience. Their routine requests triggered an investigation by the provost marshal in Fort Sam Houston, Texas. The seven-page report that the agents received from Special Agent Roger A. Pendery, dated February 13, 1946, was a bombshell. The documents revealed that McGuire had never attended college in the United States or England and, in fact, had never graduated from the reformatory high school he had attended in Austin, Texas. All of the educational accomplishments that McGuire had listed on his army records were bogus, as well as information concerning his supposed former law firm. The CID agents also discovered that although McGuire claimed to be married to one Katherine McGuire, she could not be located. A first wife, however—Alcair—was located by the Texas investigators. The hapless woman reported that she had divorced James McGuire in 1935 because she had been left alone almost every night while he went out to parties and dances with other women.

The agents were also unable to trace McGuire's birth certificate or any other vital statistics about the bogus legal beagle. They did manage to locate his mother, in San Marcos, Texas. Mrs. D. A. (Cora) McGuire was working as a night nurse in an institute for retarded children. McGuire's father had died in 1931. Mrs. McGuire cleared up a bit of the mystery by declaring that James McGuire had been born on December 26, 1910, not December 26, 1902, as he had claimed.

The elderly woman also revealed that she and her Methodist minister husband had adopted him when he was three months old. Reform-school records also confirmed the 1910 birth year. This lying about when he was born was a symbol, apparently, of a life devoted to prevarication. The minister and his wife, claimed the report, had been living in virtual poverty, renting in the lowest-class neighborhoods and still not being able to pay the rent on time. The report portrayed the young James McGuire as an irresponsible braggart. Later, he was always in debt to firms and people because of his arrogant and untrustworthy attitude. McGuire had forged bad checks on his mother's account. The report contained many such revelations about McGuire's past and ended as follows: "There is serious doubt as to the integrity of subject, and his fitness to serve in a position of trust and responsibility, where absolute and total honesty is a requirement."

Even more damaging was a letter from Agent Jack Y. Canon, who stated that he knew McGuire in 1934 as a result of his passing four worthless checks for which he received thirty days in the county jail. Canon further stated that McGuire was a braggart, a notorious liar, and a man absolutely lacking in discretion and integrity.

Now the flabbergasted Brown and Bernstein contacted the War Department in Washington and requested any records concerning McGuire, which they received. These records established that McGuire had never been in combat and had, in fact, been in England until hostilities ceased in Europe! He was then transferred to Germany on May 30, 1945. All of his ribbons and medals were also faked.

During all this, McGuire, as an "officer and gentleman," was not locked up, but was confined to the immediate area of Salzburg. This restraint kept McGuire from going to nearby Anger to visit his girlfriend Anneliese Rausch. The imaginative McGuire overcame this obstacle by having her visit him at his room at the Bristol Hotel, violating yet another military rule. In order to cover himself, McGuire, accompanied by a Captain Green, went to the Oesterreichischerhof Hotel around midnight and requested a room for each of the men. McGuire introduced himself to the U.S. Army clerk as "Captain Willie Cobb" and told him that a young Austrian lady was over at the Bristol Hotel and that he, Cobb, wanted a room assigned to her. The clerk told the captain that Austrian civilians could not be billeted at military hotels. Captain "Cobb" then assured the clerk that it would be all right, that he was with the CID and that she had been questioned by them. He would take the matter up the following morning with the officer in charge of the hotel. The clerk then made out a billeting slip for Anneliese Rausch from March 20 to March 22, 1947, room 100, Hotel Bristol. As McGuire walked the authorization slip over to the hotel, he changed the dates from 22 to 25. Once housed in the hotel, McGuire renewed the authorization slip by one crooked method or the other until March 28.

At the hotel, Rausch daily had breakfast, lunch, and dinner with McGuire. James D. O'Hara, manager of the hotel, recognized Anneliese as a German and McGuire's girlfriend. The manager knew something was wrong and questioned McGuire about it. He was informed that the CID had placed her there. O'Hara insisted that Anneliese could not eat in the dining room of a military hotel, but McGuire replied that he was going to take her home anyway. O'Hara, by now wise in the ways of the military and carefully covering himself, removed the billeting slip from the file and put it in his pocket. He knew that the slip could mysteriously disappear. Surely enough, on March 31, Agent Bernstein came calling on O'Hara, who removed the slip from his pocket and gave it to the CID agent.

On this same day, March 31, McGuire was committed to the Neuropsychiatric Section, Ward D-3, of the 98th General Military Hospital in Munich, Germany, for a neuropsychiatric examination. The psychiatrists knew only that they were to evaluate the patient as to his competency to stand trial. They were not told of his background and did not know what evidence the CID had accumulated against McGuire. Their job was quite simple: They were to determine if McGuire was sane or insane. The psychiatric examinations consisted of a Wechsler-Bellevue Intelligence test that concluded that McGuire had an IQ of 104. A word association test and Minnesota Multiphasic Personality Inventory, among other examinations, indicated that McGuire had a "big-shot complex." He also was given a Bender-Gestalt and Rorschach evaluation that indicated he was a person with feelings of insecurity and inferiority.

McGuire spent the whole month of April in the neuropsychiatric section. During this time, he continued his masquerade as an educated war hero. By now this was not merely a fantasy in McGuire's mind but a solid psychological reality. His fabrications included combat in North Africa, Italy, and the European campaign. He had suffered, in his mind at least, a severe wound in the back. He had been awarded the Legion of Merit for his work in something called "the cleft chin murder trial" in England in 1945. Even in civilian life, while working in South America, he had been involved in a plane crash, sustaining a severe head injury for which he was hospitalized. McGuire lived in a Walter Mitty world of phantasms. The medical staff at the hospital knew that he was basically an emotionally unstable individual, but they never caught on that he was a psychopathic liar.

Perhaps oddly out of character, McGuire did tell the psychiatrists what seems to have been a genuine sad accounting of his unhappy childhood. His father was a strict, dominating man who enforced with severe punishments his credo of a very rigorous religious upbringing. In keeping with his dogma of no work and no fun on Sundays, McGuire's adoptive father beat the boy with a riding crop because he thought that McGuire had been swimming on the Sabbath. Worst of all, when McGuire was thirteen years old his father had told him during one of his rages that he was not his real father and called him a "little bastard." This was a real blow to James McGuire, and from that day forth he felt inferior and ashamed of being illegitimate.

McGuire also admitted a few homosexual experiences and stated that he saw nothing morally wrong in activities of this nature and that a person's sexual behavior was his own business and that anyone was privileged to seek sexual satisfaction in any way he saw fit. Naturally, these were dangerous words for an army captain to utter in 1946. Nevertheless, McGuire was pronounced sane by the medical staff and was scheduled for court-martial on July 7, 1947.

Benjamin Reich, a civilian lawyer; Captain Robert A. Baker; and Lieutenant Colonel Clifton D. Blackford, judge advocate counsel, were the appointed attorneys for McGuire. Of course, the defense was well aware of the CID investigation and psychiatric reports and asked the court to question the sanity of the accused. Reich also wanted to hide from the members of the court the statement concerning McGuire's homosexual involvements. The court dismissed his motion and asked to swear in the members of the court and the personnel of the prosecution. McGuire himself objected to the swearing in. Although McGuire had lawyers for his defense, he characteristically decided to act as his own attorney and challenged each member's competency to act as a member of the court, asking for the dismissal of each member. Well versed in military law, McGuire interrogated each member of the court after he was sworn in. During this time, McGuire managed to have Lieutenant Colonel Clarence G. Hupfer removed; he had only met the colonel that day in court. After considerable delay, the court and its members were finally sworn in.

Neither the defense nor the prosecution wanted a trial; there were too many secrets that had been swept under the rug. (In fact, the courtrooms were literally furnished with stolen rugs from the Hungarian Gold Train.) Again, Reich asked the court to question the sanity of the accused and further stated that the court must observe his client during the proceedings for signs of insanity and that should this become an issue during the trial, it must be addressed. Reich further stated that the accused should not be tried and that the court was not in the position to do so. Claimed Reich, "I firmly believe that the accused is not in his right mind. I got to know the accused in January 1947. Since that time I have met four of his former commanding officers, all of whom have stated to me that Captain McGuire is not in his right mind....I am bringing this with deep sincerity, with the fact that I would almost be conscience-stricken unless something is done."

After this statement, Captain Baker, the other defense attorney, added, "I have been here since last Thursday and I have not been able to find out a thing. I am not prepared on the issue of insanity. I care not. I have never walked out of a case in twenty years, but I will walk out of this. Thank God I am not appointed."

Reich asked for a continuance of seven days, but before the judge could consent, McGuire said, "Just a minute, may it please the court. They told me to do something and I did it. If they told me to tag a man, I tagged him. OK. They didn't say whether I was crazy or whether I was not. I am going to ask you, the convening authority, does this court believe that General Harry Collins, who is called in as a witness in this case and has personal knowledge of the actions of the accused, do you believe he is going to admit that this accused was insane while he was on his general court, representing him as the Commanding General?" After this outburst, the prosecutor began to read the specific charges against the accused. He was interrupted by the ever-demanding Reich, and after more deliberations a continuance of seven days was issued.

The trial began again on July 14, 1947, with the same challenging of each member's competency, except that this time the question of sanity was a moot point. To the embarrassment of Lieutenant Colonel Clifton Blackford, the four candlesticks and other valuables he had received from the accused that he was now defending were part of the prosecution's exhibit. The most damaging evidence presented was the testimony of Lieutenant Rene Davis. For his testimony, Davis had been given a letter of immunity to prosecution by General Harry J. Collins.

McGuire was found guilty of embezzlement by fraudulent conversion and sentenced to be dismissed from service, to forfeit all pay, and to be confined to hard labor for two years.

Captain McGuire, like many men on the run from personal problems and professional failures, had taken refuge in the army and had seen a gold mine—literally—in the confused aftermath of the war. By falsifying enlistment records, he left behind a life of passing worthless checks and the inability to hold a job. McGuire never lost his character traits of boasting, lying, and womanizing, but the scorn of Mr. Rene Davis was enough to keep him out of circulation for a couple of years.

The Looting of
the Hesse Crown Jewels

13

The Unearthing of the Treasure

Each SEPARATE LINK in a long chain of facts and circumstances, extending from the Hungarian Gold Train through Büdinger, Berlin and the Salzburg, indicated the guilt of looting by the U.S. occupying forces. As the vast treasure of the Hungarian Gold Train was being consumed, another robbery was taking place at the Kronberg Castle.

In the fall of 1944, Prince Wolfgang was the director of the House of Hesse; his older brother Philipp had been interned in a concentration camp. As director, Wolfgang was president of the board of directors of the Kurhessische Haus Foundation. This foundation owned lands, houses, jewels, and other property belonging to the House of Hesse. The jewels were known as the Landgrafin and Kurhesse jewels.

During the month of October the Allied air raids on Frankfurt increased in severity, and Prince Wolfgang's home was destroyed and his wife, Princess Maria Alexandria, was killed. Wolfgang gathered together his family, and a decision was made to place the jewels in a more secure place. On October 30, 1944, the vast collection of jewels was removed from various banks by Heinrich Lange and Marga von Bochmann and taken to the Schloss Friedrichshof, also known as the Kronberg Castle, located nine miles northwest of Frankfurt. The sixty-nine-year-old Lange was the administrator of the Kronberg Castle, and Marga von Bochmann was his secretary.

The castle was owned by the seventy-four-year-old Landgrafin (countess) Margarethe, the princess of Prussia, granddaughter of Queen Victoria, and the widow of the Landgraf (count) of Hesse. Her mother, also named Victoria, had been empress of Germany during her husband's hundred-day reign and was the mother of Germany's Kaiser William II. Victoria had built the modern Schloss Friedrichshof a few miles from the *old* Kronberg Castle, a picturesque medieval castle that had not been occupied since the seventeenth century. Friedrichshof was always referred to as the Kronberg Castle, and for simplicity's sake it will be referred to as such in this book.

The jewels of the house of Hesse—those belonging to Prince Richard, Prince Christoph, Princess Mafalda, Princess Sophia of Hanover, Prince Wolfgang, and his wife, Princess Marie Alexandra—and other property belonging to Margarethe, the Landgrafin of Hesse, were individually wrapped in secure brown paper packages that also contained lists of the contents and the names and addresses of the owners. At the castle Lange and Bochmann packed the valuables in a special wooden box with a zinc lining that had been constructed by a plumber, Peter Schellenberg, who then soldered the top onto the waterproof lining and screwed it on securely. The completed container was about the size of a wine box.

The following day, the container of jewels was taken down to the cellar of the Kronberg by Princes Wolfgang and Richard and placed into a hole that had been constructed by a stonemason. The hole was sealed up with concrete, and in this depository the millions of dollars worth of jewels were protected for the duration of the war. A month later 1,800 bottles of valuable wine, champagne, and other liquors were moved into the vicinity of the buried jewels, and a separate wall was constructed that sealed off the wine from the main wine cellar and further concealed the jewels.

Princess Mafalda's husband was Philipp von Hessen. Born in 1896, he was a descendant of Emperor Frederick III of Prussia and also of Queen Victoria of England. He became a general in the early S.A. (Sturmabteilung—storm troopers, or Brownshirts) and actively recruited agents for Nazism in Italy. In 1925 he married Princess Mafalda, second daughter of King Victor Emmanuel III of Italy. In the beginning they resided in Germany, but after three serious bouts of pneumonia during the colder months, his family thereafter wintered in Rome.

In the fall of 1940, Philipp was approached by Adolf Hitler with a request that he aid Professor Posse in acquiring paintings in Italy for the projected Führer Museum in Linz. Philipp gladly responded to Hitler's request, since it appealed to his artistic interests and further gave him reason to visit his family in Rome. Dr. Posse explained to Prince Philipp that he was of the opinion it would be scarcely possible to acquire any really great masterpieces of fourteenth-, fifteenth-, and sixteenth-century art; therefore, Philipp should concentrate on seventeenth- and eighteenth-century art. While traveling in Italy, Philipp would photograph works he had found for sale and send the photographs to Dr. Posse. Posse would then visit Italy and with Philipp would visit the dealers and private owners. They would then inspect the works, and Posse would pay cash on the spot for items destined for the future Führer Museum.

Philipp continued in this working relationship until September 8, 1943, when, for reasons unknown, he was interned in the dreadful Buchenwald concentration camp. Later, on September 20, 1943, the Gestapo took Philipp's noble wife from her home in Rome to the German embassy. Princess Mafalda was then told that she could not communicate with her husband by telephone but a special plane was available and she could fly to Germany and visit with him. Once at Buchenwald, she was imprisoned in a brothel within the concentration camp. She was kept prisoner there under a false name and was not allowed to receive any news from the outside world. During an air raid she was seriously injured and had to have an arm amputated. Due to the lack of proper medical attention, she died four days later. Also during the war, Princess Sophia's husband, Prince Christoph, was killed in Italy, in 1943, while serving in the German air force.

Prince Christoph, Princess Maria Alexandria, the Landgraf of Hesse, and two of his sons who had been killed during World War I had been interred in sarcophagi in the small chapel in the courtyard. But during massive air raids in 1944 the chapel was destroyed by incendiary bombs, and the five coffins were removed to the weapons room of the old seventeenth-century Kronberg Castle. Each day the Landgrafin Margarethe came to the room and put fresh flowers beside the tombs of her husband and sons.

On April, 19, 1945, the Kronberg Castle was seized by the U.S. Third Army. The one-hundred-room castle was occupied by the recent war widow Princess Sophia of Hanover, daughter of the king of Greece and cousin of Admiral Louis Mountbatten, and by other members of her family. Living on the castle grounds in the "cottage," a stone house with twelve bedrooms, was the Landgrafin Margarethe. Next to the cottage was a riding hall, a tremendous stable for about eighty horses. There were fifteen apartments over the stables, which no longer contained horses, but which were filled with furniture, trunks, and household goods of various kinds from the apartments of the bombed-out people of Frankfurt, who now occupied the apartments above the stables. The occupants were given the customary notice that they must leave the castle in four hours and could only take with them food and clothing. At that time the castle and its grounds were taken over by a black American tank repair unit of the Third Army.

A couple of days later, Major Joseph M. Hartley came upon the castle in his search for a suitable club for officers and enlisted men in the area of Frankfurt. Hartley talked with the repair crew and was informed that they were to move forward within a week, so he attached a headquarters command marker on the property, claiming it for head-quarters use.

Two weeks later, Hartley and Corporal Alfred B. Miller returned and explored the castle to ascertain its usefulness as a club. Hartley also met with Mrs. Lina Wolf, the housekeeper, and asked her for the keys to the various rooms. Mrs. Wolf informed them that the keys were being held by a German colonel, the manager of the estate. She told them that the troops that had first arrived at the castle had taken the keys from her in a search for wine. She was instructed to get the keys and have them made available. Hartley then requested the office of the U.S. provost marshal to have the surrounding buildings and grounds evacuated, which they did.

Hartley was then contacted by the head of the British WAACs, who asked him if Princess Sophia and the Landgrafin could remove some sheets, blankets, and other personal effects. Hartley answered that they could not take the sheets and blankets but anything that the the army did not need could be removed. Shortly, a hay wagon arrived, and as the boxes were being packed, Miller inspected the contents of each box. They contained toilet articles, women's and children's clothing, and other items. Hartley then made a spot check, and in his judgment the items were personal and of no value to the U.S. military. The horsedrawn hay wagon then departed with the royal goods.

Later, Hartley and Miller returned and found various materials useful to the army. A supply officer was called in, and his trucks hauled away several hundred desks, chairs, odd furniture, and other supplies. The army, in the process of cleaning and renovating the castle, took dresses, stockings, shoes, underwear, bolts of cloth, dolls, draperies, and sheets and pillowcases, and gave then to local Germans and displaced persons. For the 1945 Fourth of July celebration, dolls, harmonicas, stockings, and dresses were taken from the castle and distributed to various U.S. military units as prizes at parties, bingo games, and so forth. Much of the wine, bolts of cloth, silverware, linen, and draperies taken from the Kronberg Castle were used to furnish and decorate the G.I. Country Club, the local Red Cross Club, and other clubs in the Frankfurt area.

The Kronberg Castle was requisitioned as a country club for U.S. Army officers and, with the help of German servants, was redecorated in its prewar manner. The rooms contained Dresden and Meissen china and silver picture frames. The German were so meticulous that they even placed eyebrow pencils and shoehorns in what had been their original places. Afterward, Miller and a Corporal Blackwell, with the help of three German servants, made an inventory of each room except for those that were locked, namely the porcelain room, the silver room, and the wine cellar. The castle was so vast and so crammed with riches that the new occupants concluded that a proper inventory would take thirty men about six months.

Since Hartley was in charge of establishing fourteen clubs in the Frankfurt area, he put in a request to the personnel section for a hostess to be in charge of the officers' club at Kronberg. In response, Captain Kathleen B. Nash was appointed to the job on May 20, 1945. She had been born on October 22, 1902, and later attended the Immaculate Heart Academy, Saint Catherine Convent, Saint Paul, Minnesota. She had a grown son and daughter, and after nineteen years of marriage to her childhood sweetheart from Hudson, Wisconsin, she had divorced him in 1940. Prior to entering military service the forty-four-year-old Nash had been employed by the Phoenix Country Club as an assistant manager at $125 per month. In July 1942 she subtracted years from her age and joined the army as a thirty-year-old to "get away from it all." She trained at Fort Des Moines, Iowa, and remained there for one year as a mess officer; then she transferred to Aberdeen Proving Grounds, Maryland, and later to Holabird Signal Depot in Baltimore.

Hartley was impressed with Captain Nash and on June 15 turned the keys and responsibility of the castle over to her. As officer of the mess section she had full charge of the castle and was to operate it as a club and recreation center for officers. The Kronberg Castle Country Club, with its thirty bedrooms, was used for overnight guests. The stone cottage was redecorated and used as overnight accommodations for WAAC officers. From the forty servants, the thirty who had not been members of the Nazi party were retained, including the estate manager, Heinrich Lange. Nash's assistant manager at the time was German-speaking Corporal Miller, from Cleveland, Ohio. The club was furnished with the many priceless antiques found in the castle.

A few days after the club was opened, a sculpted marble hand was taken from the empress's bedroom, and a Rubens oil painting of a child, about twenty-four by eighteen inches, was removed from a wall, and both items disappeared from the castle. Highly upset, Nash reported this incident to Major Hartley. Since this was the first time something had been taken from the castle, Hartley went over that morning and inspected the faded spot on the wall where the painting had hung. He and Nash then went to the empress's bedroom and saw that the glass cover for the marble hand was there but that the valuable piece was missing. The incident was reported to the CID, which promptly investigated. It was then decided that a registration desk would be placed at the main front door so that everyone going in and out of the castle would have to register. Additionally, a German servant was to sit by the door to enforce the registration rule and also to be on the lookout for anything that looked questionable. Only a few nights later a lieutenant started out of the castle with three rugs; the German guard called out for the the military policeman at the gate, and as the MP started for the lieutenant, he threw the rugs out of his jeep and drove off. Soon after this incident, silver spoons, knives, and forks began to disappear, and almost every day someone would go down to the silver room and retrieve more silverware to replace the missing pieces. Everyone seemed intent on filching a war souvenir.

Immediately after seizure of the castle, General Eisenhower had received a letter from British general Hasting Ismay requesting that the letters of Queen Victoria to her daughter the Empress Fredericka be removed from the Kronberg Castle and turned over to Sir Owen Morshead, librarian at Windsor Castle. The empress had retired in her widowhood to Kronberg, where she had died. She had retained a considerable number of private papers, diaries, and other papers of historical importance that King George of England felt belonged in the Royal Library. Action was immediately taken to have the papers turned over to the British.

The responsibility of working with the British was assigned to Captain Julius H. Buchman, MFA&A officer, Frankfurt, Germany.

Buchman had a good sense of humor and was an architect by profession; having studied at the Bauhaus in Dessau before the war, he spoke fluent German. It was Buchman who also had responsibility for the Städel Museum, and he had just finished cleaning up the mess left by Sinclair Robinson, who had trashed the museum three weeks prior while searching for documents. On July 25, 1945, Buchman and his driver, Pfc. Lee, drove from Frankfurt to Kronberg to examine the papers requested by the British. Upon arriving at the castle, they proceeded to the library. Captain Nash, Corporal Miller, and a German cleaning lady were in the library, and as they entered, Nash told Buchman that the library was not open to him, but that the letters of Queen Victoria could be inspected in a room in the basement. Nash then stated categorically that Buchman could not work in the library with his enlisted men; she was in command and had received no prior instructions as to his mission. Buchman and Lee complied, going down to the large silver room in the basement to review the letters. Much to Buchman's surprise, the room was unlocked.

Buchman returned to Frankfurt and phoned MFA&A officer Colonel Mason Hammond, telling him that he had been unable to carry out his mission because of a lack of cooperation on the part of Captain Nash. Shortly, Buchman received a phone call that his mission had been clarified and for him to carry on as he wished. Buchman then made arrangements for the Victoria papers to be moved from the basement into the library and placed an Off Limits sign at the entrance.

On the evening of July 27, Buchman and Hammond met Sir Owen Morshead, the king's librarian, and Major A. F. Blunt, surveyor of the king's pictures, at the Rhein-Main Airport and proceeded to the Kronberg Castle. There Buchman showed the men the library where they would be working and announced that they would dine that evening at the castle. Captain Nash protested, telling the men that they had not made reservations and could not dine at the castle. Buchman, perturbed, nevertheless phoned ahead and made arrangements for a late dinner at their lodge. He noticed that Nash had removed the Off Limits sign and was using the library for her office. Irritated, Buchman told Nash that she could not use the library as her private office and further stated that if she didn't like it she could make a written request through proper channels.

During the three-day visit, the British authorities told Colonel Hammond that they had the legal consent of the owner of the papers, Landgrafin Margarethe, granddaughter of Queen Victoria, to release the papers to them. Margarethe would later testify that she had indeed given her consent for the papers to be removed for a limited time for safekeeping. On August 6, 1945, Sir Owen and Major Blunt removed the following papers from the castle by orders of General Eisenhower:

> The complete sequence of letters from Queen Victoria to the Empress Frederick, from 1858 to 1901 contained in sixty-two volumes.
>
> Letters from Queen Victoria to the Emperor Frederick from 1851 to 1888, contained in two bound volumes and one envelope.
>
> Telegrams from Queen Victoria to the Empress Frederick during the year 1858, bound in one volume.
>
> Telegrams from Queen Victoria to the Emperor Frederick during the year 1861, bound in one volume.
>
> Letters from Empress Frederick to Queen Victoria from 1863 to 1866, bound in one volume.
>
> Letters from Sir Mountstuart Grant Duff to the Empress Frederick from 1876 to 1882, contained in one envelope, relating to political affairs in England.

In keeping with the times, Colonel Mason Hammond received a letter dated August 6, 1945, from Captain Doda Conrad, serving under Hammond's command in Berlin. Conrad wrote:

> I read about your visit to Kronberg. What had attracted my personal attention was not the actual library: 32 volumes of the original Bach Gesellschaft (two of which were unbound) and 12 volumes of the *Urtext* Schutz Ausgabe, both from Breitkopf & Haerte plus the entire (much less interesting) Beethoven and Mendelssohn output in the *Urtext* (also the B. & H.) are stored on the organ balcony over the entrance of what they call "das Boudoir." You get to the place by climbing a little staircase at the right of the door to the boudoir. If these books could be handed over to some institute like the Warsaw Conservatory of music, for instance, where everything has been looted or destroyed or systematically confiscated, I would applaud enthusiastically. But to leave it for the use, or neglect, of some sort of 100% Nazi-Junker-Snob type of Hohenzollern-Hessen-Hanover heiress, when so many people could derive from it seems to me to be contrary of "what we are fighting for." ... All this leads

to the idée fixe that Doda would like to have the Bach and the Schutz for his personal use, for the greatest glory of (Music) God.

As we shall see, there were many more military personnel who would agree with Doda Conrad and his "idée fixe" concerning the valuable troves within the Kronberg Castle.

In August 1945, shortly after Captain Nash had been placed in charge of the Kronberg Castle, Colonel Jack Wybrant Durant ("J.W." to his close friends), born September 25, 1909, arrived in Europe and was assigned as executive officer to Major General James M. Bevans; the assistant executive officer and assistant to Durant was Major David Fassett Watson, Quartermaster Corps. General Bevans, Colonel Durant, Major Watson, and General Bevans's aide, Captain L. M. Knowlton, shared a hotel known to the Americans as "Spin Inn," but the official name of the four men's thirty-room home was the Parkhotel, Bad Homburg. The four officers had four enlisted men living there as aides and an additional twenty-one German servants. Bevans's butler, a former German prisoner of war, had been a sergeant in German intelligence. He was also a former hotel operator and spoke English and French fluently. Their home consisted of fifteen bedrooms, seven living rooms, seven dining areas, a kitchen, a washroom, a storage room, and a swimming pool. There were two entertainment rooms where movies were shown twice a week. The house also contained a bar and wine cellar.

Situated ten miles north of Frankfurt and untouched by war damage, Bad Homburg was one of Germany's most attractive spas. Basking in the grandeur of turn-of-the-century Europe, the village consisted mostly of hotels and had been a popular resort since Roman times. Located in the middle of the spa's park, with its well-maintained gardens near the thermal springs, was the Spin Inn, the luxurious home of Knowlton, Bevans, Durant, and Watson. Watson mused that he was invited to live there because Bevans and Durant were embarrassed about occupying a house that large by themselves. Considering the number of homeless DPs in the immediate area of Frankfurt, they should have been more than embarrassed.

Durant was thirty-eight years old, six feet tall, slim and dark complexioned, with brown hair and eyes. He had spent the entire war at a desk job in Washington, where he had been rated superior in all of his efficiency ratings. Prior to military service he had graduated from the

University of Illinois in 1931. In 1939 he had obtained a job as a law clerk in the U.S. Department of Labor, earning $200 a month.

Watson, the son of Albert Watson, a wealthy San Francisco accountant, was thirty-five years old and married. Watson had graduated from Pomona College in 1934 and had been employed by Safeway Stores as a manager, earning a large salary at that time of $375 a month. He had entered the service in 1942 and was a native of Burlingame, California. For the first year, he was stationed in San Francisco as a statistical officer. From July 1943 to August 1944, he was stationed as a PX officer in Belfast, Ireland, where he met and developed an intimate liaison with Mrs. Peggy Harvey and her baby daughter. Afterwards, he transferred to France, where he was in charge of all supplies necessary for the care and evacuation of all prisoners of war who had been captured by Germany. Under his direction, American, British, French, and Russian POWs were quickly located, reported, supplied, and given priority in being sent home. He arrived in Frankfurt at about the same time as Durant and was immediately promoted to the rank of major. Watson was grateful to Colonel Durant because, as he claimed, his father had been a major in the last war and had told him, Watson, not to come back until he achieved the same rank.

Once stationed in Germany, Durant quickly became acquainted with Captain Nash and was a frequent visitor to the Kronberg Castle. During the fall and winter of 1945 and 1946, Durant would drive his car to the castle and park in the backyard behind the kitchen, then enter by a back door not used by ordinary visitors. He stayed overnight two or three times a week in the second bedroom of Nash's apartment, located on a mezzanine between the first and second floors of the castle. During Durant's visits a German maid by the name of Annie was specially assigned to serve him his meals and drinks. She did not serve anyone else when Durant was present. Also, the bartender, Walter Weidmann, delivered drinks, as he later testified, "during various hours of the night, around midnight, sometimes between six and seven in the morning, sometimes in the evening between nine and ten o'clock, almost anytime during the night or day." Although the delivering of drinks to private rooms was not permitted, they were brought to Captain Nash's bedroom whenever requested.

Major Watson generally accompanied Durant to the castle, and they and Captain Nash became close friends. Major Watson also stayed overnight at the castle, as did some of his lady friends. On one occasion he and a Colonel MacDuff, along with some British officers, went through the bookshelves in the room they were sharing, looking for souvenirs. After the British officers left, MacDuff and Watson opened a desk drawer and found three letters written by Florence Nightingale, the famous English nurse and philanthropist. The next morning, Watson told Mrs. Lina Wolf about the letters and recommended that she get them out before they were taken.

Other than that, nothing out of the ordinary happened at the castle until November 5, 1945. On that day, thirty-one-year-old Corporal Roy C. Carlton from Kilgore, Texas, was rummaging around in the basement and found two electrical wires leading into a wall which they had never thought of as being a wall to a room. He then took a large sledgehammer and knocked out a few bricks; smashing through, he discovered a cache of sixteen hundred bottles of wine in the secret room. The following day, Carlton asked Ludwig Weiss, a driver and electrician for twenty-one years at the castle, if there were more valuables hidden in the cellar. Weiss said that he did not know, but they both agreed to meet that evening in the cellar at six. Corporal Carlton was in charge of social activities at the castle. Several officers had complained that during Nash's absences, Corporal Carlton exceeded his authority and was disrespectful at times. It was the consensus of the officers involved that Carlton was not fit for the job, either by personality or education.[1]

When Weiss and Carlton met in the cellar, Carlton had a flashlight, and as they stepped into the formerly concealed wine room, Carlton spotted the concrete patch on the floor. Weiss chiseled away at the concrete as Carlton went to fetch Captain Nash and the bartender, Walter Weidmann, to come down and help with the hard digging. Finally the group chiseled the concrete open and dug down another inch or so through the dirt and found the container, but were unable to remove the wooden box from the hole, and continuing to use hammer and chisel, they tore the wooden top off and ripped through the waterproof soldered zinc lining. Inside were several individually wrapped packages that had been placed in the container in the fall of 1944. Carlton, Nash, and the two Germans removed the wrapped packages, which weighed from a pound to six pounds each, and carried them to Captain Nash's room.

As Weiss later recalled, he did not get as much as a thank-you for his help, but Weidmann received a bottle of wine. On his way back downstairs to the bar Weidmann stopped by Lina Wolf's office and told her about the discovery. In a matter of a few hours the local German population knew that the vast collection of jewels had been uncovered.

The following morning, Nash and Carlton locked Nash's door, opened the individual packages, and spread out the millions of dollars' worth of valuables on the floor of her room. There lay nine diamond-studded tiaras containing hundreds of diamonds and a long line of bracelets aglitter with diamonds and rubies. One platinum bracelet contained 125 diamonds and three rubies; another bracelet contained 365 large diamonds. There were four folding fans made of mother-of-pearl and gold and embossed diamonds. One diamond wristwatch glittered with so many gems that it was difficult to see the time-telling hands. There were miniatures of porcelain, assorted trinkets, and a twelve-carat diamond ring and hundreds of other gold and platinum pieces studded with emeralds, diamonds, rubies, and turquoise. The two spent the whole morning gawking at the amazing loot. Afterward, Nash put the valuables into a box and stored them in her clothes closet and locked the door. Later, Carlton would deny ever seeing them.

On the morning following the discovery of the zinc-lined wooden box in the subcellar of the Kronberg Castle, Ludwig Weiss, who had helped dig up the box and remove its contents, reported the incident to Herr Lange. Shortly thereafter, on November 8, 1945, Lange called upon Captain Nash and told her that Margarethe, the Landgrafin, wanted a statement concerning the discovery of jewels and that the Landgrafin wanted to know if the jewels would be delivered to the Military Government or if the family would get them back. Lange particularly requested a written certificate referring to the objects taken from the basement. Although Nash refused to give him a receipt, she told him to "tell the Landgrafin that when the family comes back to the castle, they will find the jewels as they left them." Nash then told Lange that in light of the discovery of the wine and jewels, she had called in the CIC and had been instructed by them to issue orders that anything else which was hidden in the castle should be delivered to the officer in charge. Lange then told her of the presence in his safe of the property of Prince August Wilhelm, the fourth son of the Kaiser and SS major general. Lange then surrendered the sealed envelope containing Wilhelm's valuables to her. Lange had received the property on April 7, 1945, after the arrest of the Prussian prince. The valuables had been transferred to Princess Sophia, and she subsequently gave them to Lange for safekeeping.

Not being satisfied with this answer, Lange wrote Dr. Bleibaum, who was responsible for the protection of all historical objects in Greater Hessen. Bleibaum told Lange that he had taken up the matter with the American authorities in Heidelberg and that the necessary steps had been taken to protect the jewelry.

After this discovery, Captain Nash revoked the passes of all of the German employees in the castle, and it was understood by them that they were being punished for their failure to reveal the presence of the wine in the castle and that they were to reveal the hiding places of any other valuables. Shortly thereafter, Nash rescinded her order revoking the passes.

Sometime on the afternoon of November 6, 1945, Durant received a telephone call in his office in Frankfurt. He asked Major Watson to leave the room and, when the telephone conversation was completed, asked General Bevans for permission to be absent for the remainder of the afternoon. Later the same day, Major Watson received a call from Durant in which Durant directed him to investigate and report to him whatever he could find regarding the disposition of abandoned and found property. During this conversation, Watson could hear Captain Nash's voice in the background. On the way to their quarters that evening, General Bevans asked Watson what he thought Durant was "up to," and Watson replied that he thought something else must have been found in the wine cellar.

On the following morning, Watson reported to Durant that he had consulted the Legal and Fiscal Branch, G1 Division, relative to abandoned and found property, and that he had been told by Lieutenant Colonel James R. Boyd that he had walked past some ruins a few nights before and found a copper kettle, which he had mailed home. Durant huffily replied that he was not interested in copper kettles but in something much bigger. Watson then returned to the Legal and Fiscal Branch and asked what should be done if Kaiser Wilhelm's crown jewels were found. He was informed by Lieutenant Colonel Boyd that he knew of no hard-and-fast rules with respect to the disposition of war trophies, that it was common practice for officers to appropriate some trophies as souvenirs.

The two officers then discussed the Hitler and Göring silverware and Göring's crystal goblets from the palace of Napoleon that had been looted from Berchtesgaden by Colonel Willard White. He had mailed them to his home at 1900 Townes Lane, Austin, Texas. As noted in the July 30, 1945, edition of the *Austin Statesman*, "The stuff he has sent home and is continuing to send home makes Colonel White a strong candidate for Souvenir Hunter No. 1 of this war."

(White's wife was the sister of then congressman Lyndon B.

Johnson. After the war, White and later his widow sold many of the items for more than $25,000 each.)

Boyd and Watson also discussed the fact that many of Eva Braun's jewels and other valuables had disappeared before the entire collection was to be placed on exhibit in Frankfurt and also that many of them had disappeared afterward. Watson was further told that all items having military or intelligence value should be turned over to the proper authorities but that they knew of no similar requirement in the case of personally or individually owned property.

The following day, Durant asked Watson if he would like to see "a sight for sore eyes." They drove to the Kronberg Castle. Once there, Durant told Nash that he thought that Watson "has smelled a rat; we better cut him in." They then told Watson about the valuables as they spread them on the floor. Based on the information Watson had obtained from the Legal and Fiscal Branch, it was ill-advisedly decided by the three that the jewels were loot, but as Nash pointed out, there was no inventory on the property in the officers' club which listed or hinted that any such jewelry was in the castle. They discussed the background of the possible owners and determined that they were either dead, SS members, or ardent Nazi party members and as such the property would never be returned to them. In the beginning they discussed keeping only a few of the valuables; then greed took over, and they decided to keep the entire cache. Greed begot more greed, as they now reasoned that anything in the castle was theirs for the taking.

Over a period of time, the three of them removed the diamonds and other gems by pushing them from the settings or cutting them loose from the various tiaras, necklaces, and bracelets. The jewelry was packed into Nash's footlocker and taken to Durant's and Watson's apartment at the Spin Inn. During drinking bouts they would discuss that with the proceeds from these possessions they could form a joint venture after leaving the service. They had plenty to drink, as several cases of Saint Julien Bordeaux, 1923, had been delivered free to the Spin Inn's wine cellar as well as to several other high-ranking officers' cellars.

A few days later, Ludwig Weiss was asked to make three wooden shipping boxes. After completing them, he discovered that Captain Nash had mailed two of the boxes back to the United States, while Roy C. Carlton had filled one of the boxes and mailed it back home. Each box was about eighteen by ten inches. Nash's packages were actually mailed by Tech/5 Richard Gawlowski, who later claimed that the packages were mailed to Arizona. Gawlowski also remembered that

Nash was "grouchy, mostly drunk, and always had something to holler about."

Meanwhile, at the Spin Inn, Durant, Watson, Nash, and a young lady from England whom Watson was dating, Angela Justice Harding, spent quite a few weekends together. Harding was employed by the United Nations Relief and Rehabilitation Administration (UNRRA) and was stationed in Frankfurt. Watson enjoyed showing off the looted diamonds and told Miss Harding that he was collecting them. Harding advised Watson to lock the stones up, but he replied that if he left them lying around no one would think that they had any value. He also showed her a picture of Peggy Harvey and her baby daughter. During her weekend visits the only present she received was a Ronson lighter that Watson purchased for her from the PX.

Quite often the four occupants of the Spin Inn would have private dinner parties that included Nash, Harding, and WAAC captain Leola F. Birmingham. Birmingham had transferred from Paris to Frankfurt during August 1945 and reported to Major Watson. Shortly thereafter, while preparing a chart, she met Durant for the first time. Several weeks later Durant extended an invitation to Birmingham to attend a dinner party General Bevans was giving at their home. Because of a previous commitment, she was unable to attend, but a week later she was again invited to attend a surprise birthday party for General Bevans. She went to the party with Major Day Weems, a WAAC friend. Among the guests was Kathleen Nash. Birmingham had previously met Nash briefly at the Kronberg Castle one evening when she had approached her in the ladies' room and introduced herself as the club officer.

Birmingham did not make the connection between Nash and Durant until the following Sunday. She had been invited by Captain Ken Boots to attend a football game. Boots drove up, and in the car was Durant and twenty-eight-year-old Vada R. Ward, an army civilian employee, whom Birmingham did not recognize. As they watched the game, she gathered from the conversation that Nash was in the hospital and that was why Durant had invited Miss Ward.

It was the young, attractive Birmingham who was most active in planning surprise birthday parties and Thanksgiving meals and who decorated their quarters with a Christmas tree and other trappings. As Birmingham would later tell it:

Captain Boots redeployed during the later part of October, and shortly thereafter Captain Larry M. Knowlton replaced him as a member of the general's household. Captain Knowlton and I were very congenial, so with the general's consent we planned to decorate the house and put up a Christmas tree for the holidays. I was at the place once or twice a week while we were making plans and doing that time. Colonel Durant and Major Watson would have dinner with us but would immediately depart for the castle. On very rare occasions Captain Nash would be there for dinner, but she never remained long because of her responsibility to the club. The general gave a small dinner party on Christmas Eve, and Christmas Eve was celebrated in the usual manner, but as soon as they could reasonably do so, Durant, Nash, Watson, and Hardy departed to go to the castle.

On New Year's Eve, General Bevans gave a party for all the officers in his command and their guests. Once again Captain Knowlton and I made all the plans and arrangements for the party. Although Durant and Watson were members of the general's household, they never took any interest in the house and never offered their services in making plans or arrangements for social events, and as far as I know, they rarely ever entertained themselves or guest at any place other than the Kronberg Castle.[2]

As Birmingham described it, she became a frequent visitor because the general and she shared a common interest in photography and he had equipped a small room in the house as a darkroom. Birmingham shared most evening meals with the group, which normally included Ann Hardie, or "Hardie," as she was called. She noticed that after most meals, Durant, Watson, and Hardie would leave immediately for the Kronberg Castle. Also, during her visits she noticed a pair of silver candelabra and some demitasse cups which Bevans said were from the Kronberg Castle.

One evening in early January, General Bevans and Leola Birmingham went to Kronberg for dinner. After dinner they were joined by Nash and Durant in the lounge, and Nash suggested that they might like to visit the wine cellar and silver room and called Corporal Carlton, who escorted them to the cellar. After they looked over the impressive wines, Carlton unlocked a heavy door with two locks on it and showed them the silver room.

This room was equipped very much as a jewelry store or department store would be, properly displaying very valuable silverware. The room had fourteen-foot-wide, twelve-foot-high, glass-paned bookcases with silver plates displayed behind the glass. The wide cases contained felt-lined drawers, which Carlton pulled out, to reveal about five hundred forks; another drawer contained five hundred knives, and yet another held five hundred spoons. There were more than four or five thousand pieces of silverware in these cabinets. There were innumerable silver beer steins, china, glass, tea service sets, coffee sets, candlesticks, vases, miniatures, decorative pieces of bric-a-brac and the Tornow collection of antique clocks and watches. Birmingham noticed many large cartons on the floor that were packed with assortments of things; the boxes were not sealed, but she did not notice the contents, giving them only a brief glance. The party remained in the room for about fifteen minutes, pausing long enough, though, for General Bevans to pick up a perfume bottle and a small heart-shaped silver picture frame and carry them upstairs with him.

He showed the valuables to Nash and laughingly asked, "Would I be shot if I took these?" Nash replied no, so Bevans gave them to Leola Birmingham. She later removed the picture of the small child from the frame and inserted a picture of herself into it.[3] Bevans thanked Nash for letting them visit the basement and remarked upon the beautiful silver service, idly commenting on the immense wealth of a family with so much silver. Nash admitted that she "borrowed" some of the silver when an important dinner demanded it. During an earlier conversation, Birmingham had mentioned that she was a collector of demitasse cups. A few days later Nash sent her a cardboard box containing three cups and saucers that she had removed from the silver room. Bevans also gave Birmingham an eight-inch silver plate with an engraved title and name in a foreign language.

Major Watson was one of the first to dispose of some of the Hesse jewels. During the latter part of November he returned to Belfast, where he had been stationed. There he had met Mrs. Peggy Harvey and had been smitten by her. During this particular trip he surprised her with a large baroque pearl surrounded by diamonds and valued in 1946 at $2,500 and also presented her with a small mirror for her daughter. As Mrs. Harvey was to state later:

When Major Watson visited Belfast in November, 1945, he brought me a present of a pearl set in diamonds and a little mirror for my daughter. He seemed pleased that he had been able to bring these nice little gifts and suggested that I take the pearl to a jeweler and have it made into a brooch. He also thought I should have the jeweler change the name on the mirror to that of my daughter.[4]

Later, on another trip to Belfast, the major entered a pawn shop called the Belfast Gold Exchange and sold proprietor William Corran a quantity of scrap gold, including old-fashioned Victorian ladies' gold mesh handbags, broken jewelry, bangles, chains, and other miscellaneous items, which he professed to have obtained in Italy. Corran paid him 80 pounds ($430) for the lot and put it in his window for resale. The items included a wide bracelet of braided gilt, a piece of gold chain, a gold Easter egg with enamel and forget-me-nots, a red Easter egg set with diamonds, a German gold ten-mark coin, an old coin of Savoy with a representation of the Annunciation, a gold coin with the head of King Victor Amadeus of Savoy, and a gold medal with the head of King Umberto I of Italy. All of these items were the rightful property of Princess Mafalda, daughter of the king and queen of Italy. The gold chain was a piece of the watch chain of her grandfather, King Umberto I of Italy. The ten-mark coin bore the head of Emperor Frederick III, grandfather of Princess Mafalda's husband, and had been given to her by Queen Margaret of Italy. The red Easter egg had been made by the well-known jeweler Fabergé, in St. Petersburg. The scrap gold apparently came from the settings that had contained the jewels from the tiaras and various other large valuable objects.

Also in November of 1945, a German gardener employed at the Spin Inn saw Durant and Major Watson in the basement one evening sawing a plywood top for a wooden box. He offered to help, but they curtly dimissed his offer. The box was lined with an unusual type of heavy waxed paper used by the German navy, a roll of which had been left at Spin Inn by some German marines during the war. The strong waterproof paper had been used at times to replace windows destroyed by Allied bombing. Durant and Watson intended to place most of the valuables in the box and mail them to Durant's brother in Virginia.

In November, Durant wrote his former secretary, Mrs. Martha Lucille Orwig (she had reverted to her maiden name), an intriguing letter. In this missive Durant also enclosed a note addressed to his brother James E. Durant of Falls Church, Virginia, which Durant asked Orwig to deliver for him. Durant stated that he was sending her a package for delivery to his brother and that he wanted her to acknowledge receipt by cable, using specific coded words. Orwig complied with his request. Later, however, she received the following cablegram: "PLANS CHANGED NO PACKAGE DESTROY NOTE KEEP ME ADVISED YOUR STATUS PERIODICALLY EVERYTHING FINE HERE."

Upon receiving this message, Orwig destroyed the note addressed to Durant's brother, but before doing so, she read it. The note instructed the brother to put the package which he was to receive from Mrs. Orwig in a bank deposit box; Durant added that he was "never more serious in my life."

After deciding not to mail the bulk of the jewelry in one package, over a period of a few months Charles M. Marino, the mail clerk in Durant's office, mailed about thirty packages to the United States for him. These packages were addressed to a "Mr. Durant" in Falls Church, Virginia, and to a city called "Hudson." The same clerk also mailed a package for Major Watson to Burlingame, California, and he later remembered that at least one of the packages had Captain Nash's return address on it and had been mailed to Gladys B. Madison, Nash's sister in Los Angeles.

In January 1946, Durant and Nash decided to sell some of the scrap gold that had been cut and separated from the Hesse jewelry. On January 18, Durant dropped by his office and told Leola Birmingham that he was going to Switzerland on leave but had left his money at his quarters and needed to borrow fifty dollars so he could buy a money order. She loaned him the money, and the next day Watson repaid her. That same day, Durant and Nash left Frankfurt in a green 1942 Ford, U.S. Army sedan, and drove to the U.S.-Swiss Leave Center, located at Mulhouse, France. They were traveling on military orders calling for a seven-day temporary duty assignment in Switzerland. Prior to their arriving at the leave center, the car had a flat tire, and Durant walked to the center, Nash remaining in the car, and had someone return with him and fix the flat. The following day, they drove through St. Louis, France, and on to Bern, Switzerland. Because of their official assignment, the car was not inspected at the Swiss border. After arriving in Bern, Durant cashed three U.S. postal money orders for three hundred dollars at the Finance Office of the U.S. Military Attaché, which was standard procedure for U.S. military personnel visiting Switzerland.

At around eleven that night, Durant and Nash checked into extravagant adjoining rooms at the Bellevue Palace Hotel, the most luxurious hotel in Bern. As they were checking in, they appeared to the reception clerk, Robert Ammann, to be very tired and dirty, and both expressed a desire for a bath. Ammann noticed that Nash was very plain and unprepossessing and further thought to himself that they must have had a flat tire and fixed it themselves. The maid would later describe Nash as being a "dumpy blonde," and as she laid out Nash's clothing, she noticed that Nash's underthings and negligees were of excellent quality. They were traveling light, wearing mostly dull colors, but what they had was most expensive. When they checked out of the hotel, Durant left his white bathrobe behind.

While in Bern, Durant went to several jewelry stores with two small, dirty linen bags. One contained gold in the form of cut and mutilated rings, bracelets, and other items from which precious stones obviously had been removed, and the other bag contained diamonds. The more legitimate jewelry stores turned down his offer to sell the items because it was obvious that the items had been acquired illegitimately. The smaller shops and the black market quickly acquired the loot.

Durant and Nash remained at the hotel for three days, until January 22, when they departed for Basel, Switzerland. From there they went to Zurich and registered first in the Dolder Grand Hotel in rooms 271 and 272. The maid who took care of their rooms commented that it appeared as if they were on their honeymoon, as they remained in their rooms most of the time, and that they really liked to drink whiskey. While there they purchased a new suitcase and gave the old one to the maid. They stayed in the Dolder Grand for two days, then checked out and moved into the most expensive hotel in Zurich, the exclusive Hotel Baur au Lac. Again they obtained the finest adjoining rooms. They were living well beyond the means of the three hundred originally received from the Finance Office of the U.S. Military Attaché.

In Zurich, Durant sold more of the gold, seemingly oblivious to the fact that he appeared surreptitious and shady and was selling and spending in a freewheeling manner. The unconscionable amount of gold and precious stones he offered soon aroused suspicion in the minds of the tradespeople. Nevertheless, the Swiss, notorious for their secretive attitude toward finances, purchased the valuables, and to this day no information has been divulged concerning Nash's and Durant's financial transactions in Switzerland. The gold from the bracelets and the gold connecting the necklaces and trimming were not recovered and apparently disappeared on this trip into Switzerland.

The pair returned to Frankfurt from Zurich on January 28, by way of Transadingen, a Swiss village that leads directly into the Black Forest area of Germany. Upon their return to Frankfurt, they presented Watson with one of three watches they had bought in Switzerland.

Shortly before Durant's trip to Switzerland the deputy chief of military personnel, air forces in Europe, had received a telephone call from Durant in the course of which Durant asked "if it would be possible to send a present to a lady friend at headquarters in Washington by official mail" and was informed that it would not be feasible. Durant was still trying to determine how he could send the bulk of the valuables to the United States without a customs check. He got lucky when, shortly, he learned that his former secretary, Martha Orwig, had been transferred to England.

Like many young women during World War II, after graduating from high school, Orwig had proceeded to Washington for the lucrative job market. Prior to arriving in Washington, she had married a serviceman. On March 28, 1944, the nineteen-year-old Orwig, after a week of orientation, was assigned as a secretary to Jack Durant. She and Durant became very friendly, both in and out of the office, calling each other by their first names and going out together several times a week. Orwig knew that Durant was married with children, but as she stated later, "I think it is fair to say I was in love with him—certainly I was infatuated. I knew Jack was married and had two children, but I knew his wife was divorcing him—in fact, I typed copies of his decree, which was issued in December 1944. We never contemplated getting married—never even discussed it." Their affair and her job continued until Durant went overseas.

After Durant went overseas, they kept in touch by writing five or six letters a month. It was in November that she had received his enigmatic letter with the enclosed note to his brother. After receiving it, Orwig ceased writing Durant and took December off to return to Illinois and obtain a divorce. Referring to her marriage, Orwig would say, "We were unable to get along, even for the short time we were together before he went overseas—within a matter of weeks I saw that sooner or later we would be separated, and in May 1945 I started divorce action in Illinois, based upon desertion."

Upon returning to work, Orwig wrote, "I came back after my divorce was granted and heard that people were wanted for United Nations work in England. I felt free now to do anything I wanted and I liked the idea of getting away, so I applied and was accepted." She obtained a ninety-day temporary assignment in England. She did this in hopes of meeting Durant. After confirmation that she had been assigned to the stenographic pool for the American delegation in England, she wrote Durant and said she would drop him a short note when she got there, telling him where she was.

Orwig arrived in England on January 12, 1946, and wrote Durant that she had arrived. Not hearing from him, she later wrote that she would be leaving London for the United States in two days. Immediately upon receiving the letter, Durant called from Frankfurt to say that he was coming by air on Wednesday, February 13. She drove to Bovingdon Air Base, more than one hour away, to meet her lover. It was a foggy night, and Durant's flight did not arrive. Orwig, working the night shift, returned to work, where she became ill and nauseated. From there she returned to her room in the Berners Hotel near Oxford Circus. She remained in bed, taking only aspirin and drinking tea and eating toast for two days. On Friday, Durant called to say that he had just arrived. He came to her room shortly and was not carrying any luggage or briefcase. Orwig was in bed, still very ill[5] After they had talked for a few minutes, Durant reached inside his large jacket and brought out a handful of jewelry, saying, "Here, Marty, will you take these back for me? I hate to have them in my pocket, and they are funny things for a man to have." Too ill to care much, Orwig got out of bed and put the following jewelry in a drawer in a cardboard box where she kept her costume jewelry:

DESCRIPTION	OWNER	1946 VALUE
Bracelet, platinum, 3 rubies, 125 diamonds	Mafalda	$3,000
Earrings, platinum, 2 sapphires, 76 diamonds	Mafalda	800
Necklace, coral	Maria Alexandra	150
Pendant, gold, heart-shape, 4 diamonds	Maria Alexandra	110
Brooch, gold, enamel, pheasant-shape, 4 diamonds	Maria Alexandra	50
Brooch, ruby, 70 diamonds	Mafalda	700
Brooch, gold, platinum, 4 sapphires, 128 diamonds	Mafalda	600

Orwig's roommate, Mrs. Emerson, came in, and Orwig introduced Durant. The two of them went downstairs and had dinner without Orwig. Since she could not join them, Orwig insisted that they put the meal on her bill. When they returned, Orwig told Durant that she had not cashed her paycheck because of her illness and was worried that she might need some cash. He immediately reached into his pocket and plucked out 50 pounds ($200) as a loan until she could get back on her feet.

The next morning, Lieutenant William Galloway came by to see Orwig and insisted that she have something to eat and see a doctor. Galloway was an aide to General Balmer, and as such he drove Orwig to the general's house, since Orwig also knew the general. Balmer insisted that she lie down and then called a British doctor, who attributed her illness to liver and gallbladder trouble. The doctor gave her some medicine and recommended that she stay in bed. The general and Galloway insisted that she stay in the general's home, and she did for the remainder of that day and night.

The following morning, Orwig received a phone call from her roommate, who said that the hotel maid had let Durant into her room and that she was most worried about him. During the phone call it was obvious that the two of them had been drinking together. Orwig told Emerson that she did not want to see anyone.

Feeling a little bit better and fairly doped up from the medicine, Orwing let Galloway take her back to her hotel. Durant had a gold mesh ladies' purse with him and asked Orwig if she could sell the purse for him. Not feeling well enough to go out, she said no. He called several more times while she was in bed, but Durant did not bring up the subject concerning the jewels. The next day, Monday, February 18, he returned to Frankfurt.

On Tuesday, Orwig managed to get up, and Galloway took her to dinner and a movie. Afterward they went by General Balmer's house to see him and demonstrate that she was back on her feet and on the road to recovery. At the general's home, however, she collapsed. The next day, she was admitted to the infirmary and was hospitalized for one month with hepatitis. She took two bags and an overnight case with her to the hospital. Her remaining items were shipped back to the United States, but the jewelry remained in one of the bags that she had brought. She remained there until April 21 and, in the meantime, received a note from Durant saying that he was going back to America.

Prior to her sailing back to the United States on the *Queen Mary*, Orwig opened the cardboard box and looked at the jewelry. She remembered later a pheasant-shaped brooch, a pin with a frog on it, a string of irregular pearls, a string of orange beads, a silver bracelet colored with red and white stones, a brooch with matching pierced earrings with a blue pear-shaped stone. Going through customs in New York, she carried the cardboard box in her overnight case. Customs officials opened the overnight bag but not the cardboard box. Thus, the valuables entered the United States undeclared. Orwig's girlfriends from Washington met with her for a weekend in New York. Afterward Orwig returned to Washington and began a new job assignment in the Pentagon on April 7, 1946.

In early February 1946, Kathleen Nash was put in charge of the Cogen House, which was a new club being opened for colonels and general officers, but she still lived in her apartment in the Kronberg Castle. Cogen House had been the home of General Robert Q. Brown, who had by now transferred back to the States. It was wildly rumored at the time that Nash was transferred to the Cogen House because Krongberg Castle was not as pleasant a place to visit as it once had been because of the rampant drinking that was going on and most people felt that Nash had failed to handle the club management as she should have.

Within a few weeks after Nash's new assignment, Leola Birmingham dropped by one afternoon to look the place over. She had been given the assignment of preparing posters and invitations for the opening-night party. Nash told her that she expected to be leaving soon for the States. She planned to move to New Mexico or Arizona and resume her civilian occupation as a manager or hostess in a resort hotel. Nash told Birmingham that she would write, but never did.

The day before her departure from Germany, Captain Nash had dinner at the Spin Inn, at which time she presented Captain Knowlton, Captain Birmingham, General Bevans, and Colonel Durant each with a silver tankard and Watson with a silver pitcher, as "souvenirs of Kronberg Castle." Durant mailed his silver tankard to his brother in Falls Church. Major Watson mailed his pitcher to his family in Burlingame, California. The silver tankards were the property of the Landgrafin and had a value of $75 each. The silver pitcher, which had a value of $250, was also the property of the Landgrafin, having been presented to her by the king and queen of Italy.

Nash left Frankfurt and reported to Camp Home Run at the port of Le Havre, France. After waiting five days, she sailed from there on February 20, 1946, and the *Mormacsea* arrived in New York on March 2. Her destination was Camp Beale, California, where she was to be processed for separation from the army.

Nash returned to the United States in such a hurry that she did not pack her personal belongings. Major Watson, a few days later, went to the Kronberg Castle and with the help of Lina Wolf packed a footlocker with Nash's clothing, writing utensils, a sewing kit, and toilet articles. The footlocker had been partially packed, with a blanket over the items in the bottom, among them two valuable Victorian books taken from the Kronberg Library. The footlocker with Nash's items remained in the castle until June 8, 1946.

On March 6, 1946, orders were issued by Headquarters, U.S. Forces, European Theater, directing Durant to return to the United States by air for seven days' temporary duty with the War Department and granted him leave for thirty days in the States upon the completion of the temporary duty. The order designated him an official courier and exempted from censorship packages he might carry in that capacity. Under the terms of the order, he was directed to return to the European Theater at the expiration of the leave granted. Prior to leaving, Durant asked Birmingham if she knew "the customs procedure when you return to the United States." Birmingham did not, and Durant told her that he was taking back a watch he had bought in Switzerland, a handbag, and some perfume for General Bevans's wife. Birmingham assured Durant that if that was all he had to declare he had nothing to worry about. But Durant had much more and apparently had found a safe way to get valuables into the United States and convert them into U.S. currency.

At the same time, Watson took fifteen days' leave and went to Ireland. After his return, Birmingham saw him around the office and at the snack bar frequently. She couldn't help noticing that he had not been able to find any friends to while away the time with after Nash and Durant had left.

In January 1946, Princess Sophia, through Lange, had requested an interview with Captain Nash relative to the return of her jewels, as she was contemplating marriage in the near future and would like to have the jewels for the occasion. At the same time, the princess asked for the return of her silver, books, linen, and some furniture. Captain Nash declined to see her at the time of the request, and shortly thereafter Princess Sophia repeated the request by letter. Nash finally told Lange that she could not see Princess Sophia just then but that she would see her in the near future.

Meanwhile, Lange again contacted Dr. Bleibaum, who was responsible for the protection and care of historical and artistic valuables. Bleibaum promised to search for the jewels in accordance with the American policies that had been established by U.S. Army Headquarters. In spite of several more requests, Lange never heard from Dr. Bleibaum.

Suddenly, Nash had left the Kronberg Castle, supposedly for the United States, without saying good-bye to Lange and the staff of Kronberg and leaving behind her a partly packed footlocker. Later, Lieutenant Philip Seymour caught wind of the story and told Major Watson that a news story was about to break concerning Captain Nash and some missing jewels. Watson immediately went out to the castle and removed the footlocker. Lieutenant Seymour later would say that Lieutenant Virginia Sue Speidel told him about the missing jewels, but Speidel would deny this charge.

At this point, Princess Sophia decided to take up the matter with Lieutenant Clyde K. Harris of the Monuments, Fine Art and Archival branch in Frankfurt. She had met Lieutenant Harris previously. On April 9, 1946, Harris checked with the local property control offices and could not establish that any items had been seized from Kronberg. He was told by Colonel Owen Summers that many unorthodox developments had come to his attention. Among other things it had been established that clothing was being doled out to German civilians and that children's toys and other belongings were being distributed freely to the local populace. The following day, Harris visited the castle, without any success, although he did go down into the cellar and view the hole that had once contained the valuables. Harris spoke to secretary Marga von Bochmann, who told him that she had no idea what had happened to the jewels and that she had no further information about Captain Nash except that she drank to excess and had several male visitors. By now the management of the castle had been taken over by Lieutenant Speidel.

Meanwhile, Princess Sophia went to the CID in Frankfurt and filed a report concerning the missing jewels. During the CID investigation they questioned Walter Weidmann, who was located in a German veterans' hospital where he was recuperating from injuries sustained in an automobile accident. He told the investigators that he had helped Nash and Carlton take the jewels from the subcellar to Nash's room. He went on to say that while in the room Nash opened some of the packages and he saw some of the jewelry. Weidmann continued by saying that the only time he saw any of the jewels again was during a trip to Frankfurt, which he made with Carlton. At that time, Carlton showed him a watch with a small gold chain which was described by

Carlton as being part of the jewelry found in the subcellar. During the investigation, Sophia wrote, "I wish to add that on the same day in which Captain Nash made the discovery, she called a general, whose name is Brown, I believe, who viewed the jewels in a room in the castle."

Heinrich Lange would also sign a statement stating that General Brown had viewed the jewels. The CID investigators concluded that Nash and Carlton had committed an act of grand larceny by taking and carrying away the jewels of the Hesse family.

During the end of April 1946, the CID began making inquiries concerning the missing valuables. On April 20, 1946, Mr. Tibor J. Papp, an American civilian employee, appeared at the CID office in Frankfurt and stated that Lieutenant Hartley S. Shea had been a frequent visitor to the Kronberg Castle and had had the reputation of being an "operator" and said that he had personal knowledge that sometime prior to his departure, Shea had mailed home a large package containing a jewelry box. It was confirmed by the servants at the castle that the twenty-six-year-old Shea had acquired a large quantity of silver from Kronberg and that much of the silverware had been looted from the castle. Shea had been assigned to the Transportation Section of Headquarters Command and was assigned to the Bosch Garage and made responsible for the assignment of German sedans to military personnel. Lieutenant Shea found it necessary to keep in contact with Nash because he was responsible for the maintenance of her vehicle, and, further, it was necessary that he supervise the operation of a bus line to and from the castle in the evenings and on holidays. Additionally, Shea was dating Nash's secretary, Marie Seidler.

The first time Nash used a vehicle from the motor pool, she provided Shea with a bottle of whiskey. Nash managed to have a permanent car assigned to her; on one occasion in October 1945, she was in Shea's office waiting for some repairs to be completed on her car. Shea later confirmed that he had never seen any small valuables around the sections of the castle that the officers were allowed to visit. Nash told Shea that all the small articles had to be locked up, as the officers visiting there would carry everything off as souvenirs. Shea told Nash that he himself would like to have a souvenir from the castle, and Nash told him to come by the castle some afternoon and she would give him one.

A couple of days later, he went out to the castle, and Nash told Carlton to take him downstairs and let him pick out a souvenir. Carlton took him to the silver room in the basement and told him to take his pick, so Shea walked around the room, laying out things that he liked. He took so long that Carlton finally told him to hurry up because he had to make a trip to Frankfurt. Shea then picked up a plush-lined stone-studded jewel chest, a large handmade pewter stein with a gold-plated top with the inscription "ZUM, 23 November 1894," a small silver cup, and a solid gold brooch bearing the emblem of the crown. Carlton told him to cover up the valuables so that the German employees working there would not see them. He put the articles in his car and then went back to Nash's office. Shea then mailed the articles home in two separate parcels addressed to Mrs. Hartley S. Shea, Rutland, Vermont.

During the CID investigation, Speidel admitted that she had taken a satin-lined box that held a lace fan with a mother-of-pearl framework, a gold crown with the initial "V," and a "brownish knicknack" hand-carved in the shape of a snail. She also said that she had given a WAAC friend of hers a letter opener.

Now that the story was out concerning the systematic disappearance of valuables, Colonel Owen Summers, headquarters commander in June of 1946, ascertained that there were many valuables, including silverware, art objects, historical items, and books, that should not be lying about, but should be stored in a secure place. He requested that the valuables be evaluated by an MFA&A officer and that they be removed to the Wiesbaden Collection Center. After some delay, MFA&A officer Mr. Edward S. Peck visited the castle from September 9 through 11.

Under his direction the historical furniture was removed from the two dining rooms and the ballroom and placed in a locked room upstairs. The finer Oriental rugs were removed from the hallways to avoid further excessive wear. Valuable books were removed from the library and stored in cardboard boxes. Unframed paintings were removed and stored. The large tapestries and paintings remained on the walls, since they were too large to be considered easy prey for looters. The silver royal miniatures and fine porcelain were locked in the basement in two secure rooms. Peck also recommended that the solid silver and gold table service in use at the club should at the earliest possible time be replaced by less valuable pieces and that the castle items be locked away. More than a year after the castle was seized, precautions were finally made to protect its valuables from looting by U.S. officers, a classic case of closing the barn door after the horse had escaped.

14

Washington D.C.—1946

DURING THE SIX MONTHS preceding March 1946, five packages bearing the return address of Jack Durant were received at the home of his brother James in Falls Church, Virginia. One of these contained a silver tankard that had belonged to the Landgrafin of Hesse and which had been given to Durant on the eve of his departure for the States by his lover, Nash. Other items were a shell-shaped silver dish taken from the cottage; two boxes of knightly orders belonging to Prince Wolfgang; a large watch and two handsomely bound books; a silver cigarette box bearing the monogram of the late Prince Christoph of Hesse, which belonged to his widow, Princess Sophia; a barometer which matched the large watch; a dagger; a porcelain statue; three large silver star-shaped designs encircled in gold; and a nutcracker.

On March 13, following his return to the States, Durant went to his brother's home. James at the time worked for the U.S. Government Printing Office. Durant showed James numerous loose diamonds and other stones that he had brought back from overseas. James Durant helped his brother remove a large number of diamonds from two tubes of shaving cream, and as they were removed, Jack placed them into two plastic tubes. These diamonds and more valuables were stored in the attic.

When Durant returned, he, like thousands of other former servicemen, wanted a new car. Cars had not been manufactured for more than four years, and the demand was excessive. It was impossible to simply go to a car dealer and purchase outright. James Durant told his brother that he knew Miguel Carrasco, who operated a service station in Falls Church and who was reported to have connections which enabled him to secure the delivery of a limited number of automobiles. James contacted Carrasco and told him that his brother wanted to barter with precious stones for a new car. At the gas station, Durant produced from his pocket a small packet containing more than fifteen diamonds of various sizes. Carrasco agreed to try to get a car for Durant. A few days later, Durant and his brother called upon Carrasco and were told that the purchase price of the car was too much, and they called off the deal. Carrasco told the brothers that he was interested in purchasing some of the diamonds for himself, however.

Colonel Durant then gave his brother two diamonds and told him to make the best deal possible with Michael Carrasco. A few days later, James Durant returned to the gas station and showed the diamonds to Carrasco, claiming that they had been in his family for many years. He also stated that he had had them appraised in Washington for $400 and advised Carrasco to also have them appraised. Carrasco said that he was not interested in the diamonds but that his wife was and that it was up to Maria Carrasco to purchase them.

She had them appraised at several places. Some jewelers quoted her a price, but several stated that they would not buy the diamonds because they were so old and the carbon marks were so numerous. She finally managed to settle on a price of $400, of which $200 was to be paid upon delivery and the remainder at a later date. After turning the diamonds over to Maria Carrasco, James Durant did not see them again. Maria later took the diamonds to El Paso, Texas, to the home of her parents, with instructions to have the best diamond mounted and to sell the other one. The remaining gem was sold just across the Mexican border for $400 to a family friend.

On March 14, 1946, Colonel Durant entered the jewelry store of Shah and Shah in Washington, D.C., and offered to sell certain diamonds. Although no sale was effected on that day, Durant returned on March 16 and sold three old cut diamonds, weighing 3.38 carats, for $357. Durant gave his name as "Colonel J. W. Gable" and accepted a check made out in that name. This check was endorsed "Col. J. W. Gable." Durant gave the check to his brother and asked him to cash it for him and told him that it was from the sale of three small diamonds. It was cashed on March 19, 1946, by James at a Washington bank.

Still determined to procure an automobile, on March 15, Durant entered the salesroom of the Burrows Motor Company, 900 M Street in

Washington, D.C., and was informed that there was a long waiting list. Durant then tried to bribe his way into the purchase of a new car by offering to give the owner, John S. Burrows, three small diamonds if he would sell him an automobile without waiting. Mr. Burrows declined, stating that he could not accept a gift, but expressed interest in buying a larger diamond. Durant then promised to bring in a larger diamond which he claimed he had bought for his wife.

The following day, Durant brought in the larger diamond, and the two of them took it to Max Zweig, a pawnbroker on D Street, who appraised it for them at a value of $600. Durant then sold the diamond to Burrows for $500. The diamond weighed 2.29 carats and had a value of $2,600. Burrows then sold him a new two-door, light blue, six-cylinder Hudson Brougham at the list price of $1,375.29, which Durant paid for by a personal check drawn on First and Merchants National Bank in Richmond, Virginia. Later, Burrows had Florence Ryan Inc., 1021 Connecticut Avenue, mount the diamond in a platinum setting containing fourteen small diamonds and two marquises. The mounting was picked out by his wife.

The first thing Durant did was to drive the new car over to his brother's house and show it off. While there he telephoned his two young sons and told them that he would pick them up in twenty minutes.

In the last week in March 1946, Durant told his brother that he was going on vacation, but prior to his leaving, Durant received a phone call from Kathleen Nash, who was living in Hollywood, California. Durant left Washington in his new Hudson and drove seven hundred miles to Chicago.

In 1946, with Berlin destroyed and Tokyo firebombed, only New York, London, and Paris had populations larger than Chicago's. Among the earth's large cities, none was younger than Chicago, and certainly no city was more closely associated with raw energy, success, and violence, American style. All over the world, Chicago was notorious for its gang wars and rackets. Seemingly, Jack Durant was seeking this shady side of Chicago.

Once in Chicago, Durant would meet with Dr. Reuben Mark, a physician he had known for a number of years. They had met about three years earlier while Durant's two young sons, ages ten and eleven, were left in the care of Mrs. Emma Block, the sister of Durant's former wife. At that time, the Durants were having domestic difficulties, and the boys were living in Oak Park, a surburb of Chicago, with their aunt

Emma, a widow. Whenever the boys were sick, Dr. Mark would either see them at his office or would drop by Mrs. Block's home. Emma Block would tell Mark to send the bill to Durant in Washington, but Mark considered the Block family good friends and never billed them.

In 1943, Durant had made a trip to Chicago to inspect an aircraft installation and had stopped by to see his two boys in Oak Park. During the visit, Mrs. Block telephoned Dr. Mark and told him that Jack was in town and would like to meet him. Mark then drove over and spent the evening with them. Durant was staying in downtown Chicago at the Knickerbocker Hotel, so Mark drove him back. Mark could later remember clearly his first meeting with Durant because it was just after a famous incident in which President Roosevelt had put his dog Fala on a plane, and to allow extra space for the animal, several G.I.s had been bumped from the flight. Durant had been very closemouthed, and Mark had not known how to converse with him. This incident had been the icebreaker they discussed as they struck up a friendship. Durant told Mark that if he was ever in Washington to please look him up. After that they met perhaps a dozen times in Washington, where Durant and Martha Orwig introduced Mark to Durant's current girlfriend, Rose Griffith, a WAAC stationed at Walter Reed Hospital. Griffith and Orwig became close friends and remained close until Durant went to Germany.

After arriving in Chicago, Durant telephoned Dr. Mark and asked him to join him at the extravagant Palmer House Hotel, a magnificent edifice that had been built in 1927 at a cost of $20 million and which was now the flagship of the Hilton Hotel fleet. Mark agreed to meet with Durant later that night. It was a Saturday, and Mark had already agreed to a party with his family, so he did not arrive at the Palmer House until just after midnight. They met in the Empire Room, which was decorated in brilliant green and gold and reflected the elegance of the French Empire period. Its mirrored walls were decorated with gold reliefs of Napoleon and Josephine. In this room, Veloz and Yolande and the Merriel Abbott Dancers opened for a long cavalcade of international entertainers, including Pearl Bailey, Tony Bennett, Jimmy Durante, Nat King Cole, Louis Armstrong, Maurice Chevalier, Jack Benny, and a host of others.

Against this splendid backdrop, Durant told Mark that he was on thirty days' leave and that he had a girlfriend coming to Chicago to meet with him and that she was from Hollywood. He described her as a divorcée who had been overseas with him and had been married to a wealthy man in Arizona. Then Durant changed the subject, discussing old times; there was no mention of diamonds.

Two days later they met again, this time at Isbell's Restaurant on Diversay Boulevard. Kathleen Nash was with Durant, and he introduced her as "Katie." Mark noticed that she appeared to be a nice girl, nothing unusual about her. After dinner, Durant took a tissue out of his pocket, unfolded it, and showed Mark fifteen or twenty diamonds, which, Durant explained, he had obtained cheaply in Europe, and asked Mark if he knew of a jeweler who might be willing to buy. Mark wanted to know exactly where Durant had gotten them, and Durant responded that he had picked them up in Frankfurt. Given the climate of the times, it never occurred to Mark that any impropriety was involved; he knew that many soldiers were returning from Europe with valuables.

The following afternoon, Durant telephoned his former sister-in-law, Emma Block, in nearby Oak Park. She was most surprised to hear from Durant; she hadn't heard from him in three years. She had always considered the man cold and unemotional and as a result was never close to him. Block remembered the first time she had met him. Her sister, Folly, had been attending the University of Illinois, where she had met the young Durant. One day she came home with him on her arm and told her sister that they had been married for some time. Folly also told her that they were expecting a baby and that it was up to her, Emma, to tell their parents that they were married.

During the Depression both Durant and his wife dropped out of school. Durant worked off and on for Emma's first husband. Several years later he took a civil service examination and landed a job in Washington. The Durants bought a car and loaded it with all their belongings and drove to the nation's capital. Emma did not see her sister or brother-in-law for nine years, but was told that both of them were working and getting along very comfortably. Shortly before Pearl Harbor, the Durants returned to Illinois and visited Folly's parents at Lake Geneva. Emma remembered that Durant was wearing an army air corps uniform. In 1943, Folly returned to the Chicago area with her two children and later returned to Washington, while the two boys remained in Oak Park and spent the balance of the summer with Emma.

Now, three years later, Durant was calling her on the phone. When Durant began by saying that he would like to see her, Block replied that she had guests, Dr. Mark and his girlfriend, but added, "Fine, come out if you will take potluck supper with us."[1] Durant told her that he had a lady friend with him whose name was Katie. Durant drove to his former sister-in-law's house and upon entering gave Emma a bottle of perfume and a bottle of whiskey. They then had dinner with her and the guests, including Emma's son Bill, who had recently been discharged from the air corps after serving in the South Pacific.

Later, as the women were doing the dishes, Kathleen Nash came into the kitchen and said that she was in a very uncomfortable position coming to the home of Durant's former sister-in-law. Block's response was, "Katie, why don't you let water over the bridge be? We are all trying to forget it. I know Jack—he is the father of the two children." Block then noticed a very large stone on Nash's hand and asked what type of stone it was. Nash responded, "It's a goose diamond." She then handed it to Emma, who looked at it and asked if it was a yellow diamond. Nash answered, "Yes, it is. My former husband was a playboy, and whenever he went out and did something he shouldn't, he came home with a gift like this." Block then asked if she and Durant would get married, but Nash responded, "No, I think he's a playboy like my first husband." As Durant and Nash left, they mentioned that they planned to take a trip out west. Nash also mentioned that she would love to have a private lunch with Emma, but the lunch never materialized.

In response to Durant's previous question at Isbell's Restaurant concerning the selling of some diamonds, Dr. Mark took Durant to a patient of his, a jeweler, Hyman Horwitz, to whom Dr. Mark introduced Durant as "Colonel Jack." On the way over, Durant told Mark that he wanted to take care of him for his time and for the favors that he had done for him in the past. Mark responded, "Skip it. I don't need it, and anyway, you talk about getting out of the service and going back to law practice and you need it, but in due time, if you and Mr. Horwitz come to an agreement, stipulate that I shall have the right to, or he will sell me, a few stones at the price he pays you." Durant agreed that this sounded like a fair deal and explained to Mark that he wanted his name concealed because army officers were not supposed to engage in business while they were in service.

In Horwitz's office, Durant produced a large quantity of diamonds, and Horwitz agreed to buy seventy of them at a price of $130 a carat. Durant asked for cash, but Horwitz insisted on paying by check and further emphasized that every deal he made was by check. Horwitz then said that he had to call the police to see if everything was okay. Durant's retort was, "Go ahead and call."

At that, Horwitz called the Chicago police and told them the story. The police told him that it was okay to buy the diamonds provided they had been declared at customs and that a duty had been paid on them. Durant declared that he had mailed the stones from Europe and that he was in Chicago for pleasure and was headed to Mexico. As he started to gather up the stones, he told Horwitz that he would take care of the duty tax at some later date. Horwitz stopped him at this point, wanting to make a deal. "If it's a matter of duty tax," he said, "we'll figure something out."

At that point, Horwitz's son asked his father to step out into the hall with him. When they came back in, Horwitz suggested that they make out the check to Dr. Mark and for him to cash it and give the money to Durant. Mark objected, but over his objection, Horwitz left the room to make out the check. Alone in the room, Durant said, "Now Ruby, you do anything you want; you can either do it or not." Horwitz entered the room and gave Mark a check made out to Dr. Mark, dated April 1, 1946, in the amount of $6,379.10. This check indicated the purchase of seventy old mine-cut diamonds. "Mine-cut" referred to the manner in which diamonds were fashioned prior to 1840 and an indicator that the diamonds were over one hundred years old.

That night they went out to dinner and returned to Durant's room in the Palmer House and continued a long-running series of gin rummy games. During one game, Durant said, "Ruby, you don't have to go back to Horwitz to buy any of those stones." He pulled out a tissue and there were four stones. Durant said, "Take these—they didn't cost me much anyway." Mark thought, All right. I'll take these few as a gift.

Meanwhile, after writing the check, Horwitz called the Internal Revenue Service and asked them whether it was permissible to buy jewelry from one who was a member of the armed forces. The IRS promised to check into the matter and call back. Waiting for their response, Horwitz called his lawyer and asked the same question. His lawyer told him that there was nothing wrong with purchasing items from members of the armed forces, but advised him to check with the customs office to make sure that the merchandise had been declared and the duty paid. If it had not been declared, the lawyer advised, Horwitz should not go through with the deal and should put a stop payment on the check, which he did immediately. The following morning, Horwitz notified Mark that he had stopped payment on the check and would not go through with the deal unless his "Colonel Jack" produced the customs receipt showing that the diamonds were declared and duty-free.

Following Horwitz's phone call, Mark contacted Durant, worried about the the size of the transaction, not the legality of it, and insisted that Durant return with him to Horwitz and rescind the transaction until arrangements could be made to take care of the customs duty on the diamonds. They entered Horwitz's office around noon, and the check was returned to Horwitz, and the diamonds were returned to Durant. Horwitz gave Durant the name and address of the Chicago customs officer and told Durant that he would pay half the customs fee and purchase the diamonds should Durant acquire a customs document. Durant said he was returning to Washington to request a ten-day extension to his leave and would attend to the matter when he returned. After they left, Horwitz wrote the Bureau of Criminal Information, Chicago Police, advising them of the purchase from Durant. Apparently the bureau contacted the customs authorities.

From Chicago, Durant and Nash drove south and visited his mother, Annie Evelyn Durant, in St. Petersburg, Florida. From there they drove to Texas and arrived on April 5 in Kilgore to pay a surprise visit to Roy C. Carlton, the corporal who had found the buried Hesse jewels. When they arrived, Carlton was not at home, so they decided to leave, and Nash wrote a note. As she was placing it in the mailbox just before dark, Carlton and his wife, Billie, drove up. Nash hastily retrieved the note and tore it up. Durant then collected a bottle of gin from his new Hudson, and they entered the house and had several drinks. The visit lasted about two hours, and in addition to talking about their trips from Germany and other general subjects, it was mentioned that Durant and Nash were on their way to New Mexico to see about placing his children in a school. Afterward, Durant and Nash climbed into the Hudson and drove away, he in his uniform and she in civilian clothes. Where they traveled for the week after that remains a mystery. Why they decided to visit Carlton in the first place is unknown. Since the pair never seemed to do anything without an ulterior motive in mind, it is hard to believe that it was merely a social visit, but there is no evidence of any business dealings taking place.

Durant returned to Washington on April 14, 1946, accompanied by Kathleen Nash, and visited his brother James. James told Durant about the Carrasco diamond sale, and Durant told his brother to keep the proceeds for himself.

James also told his brother that Dr. Mark had made two phone calls that seemed extremely important. Mark had insisted that Durant was in Mexico City, and he had given James the name of two hotels where his brother might be staying. Mark insisted that James phone the hotels and notify Jack that he should immediately phone Mark. James placed a person-to-person call to Colonel Durant in Mexico City and suggested to the operator that she might be able to reach him at either of the two hotels Mark had mentioned. While he waited on the line, he heard the two hotel operators tell the long-distance operator that there was no Colonel Durant registered there. One can only wonder why Mark himself did not make the phone calls to Mexico City from Chicago. What was Dr. Mark concealing and from whom?

Mark had stressed to James Durant that his brother must be in Chicago before a certain time, a matter of hours. Mark reemphasized the importance of timing, and James received the distinct impression that it was highly imperative that Durant be in Chicago at that time.

Durant, however, told his brother that Mark was an extremely excitable person to whom he should pay no particular attention. He then placed a long-distance call to Mark and talked in hushed tones so that his brother could not overhear the conversation. Afterward, Durant asked James if he would meet him at National Airport on the following day, Monday, April 15, and bring Nash back to Washington so that he could leave his car at National Airport in order to have transportation available upon his return from Chicago. James Durant agreed to the request and dropped Nash off in downtown Washington at the corner of Fourteenth Street and Pennsylvania Avenue.

The following day, James Durant received another phone call from an anxious Dr. Mark; although James was certain that his brother was in Chicago, Mark gave James the impression that his brother had already departed Chicago and returned home. Mark firmly stated that the person whom Colonel Durant had seen wanted to see him again. The elusive Durant returned to his brother's house two days after he had left Washington for Chicago and was informed of Mark's frantic phone call.

On April 23, Durant telephoned his former girlfriend Martha Orwig at her office and suggested dinner. She declined his invitation but suggested that they have lunch on the twenty-fifth. On that morning she took the jewels she had received in London from her cardboard box and put them into a cigarette box and wrote a check for two hundred dollars, the amount of the loan from Durant. She put both items in her purse and went to work.

At lunchtime, Durant picked her up in the Hudson, and they drove to an eatery in nearby Virginia. With no questions asked, Orwig took out the cigarette box and gave it and the check to Durant. He took the check and box without opening it and said, "Don't ask any questions in connection with this jewelry. If you are asked any questions, you don't know a thing." They resumed dating during this period, and on May 1 he went by her apartment and stayed for dinner. Afterward, he dictated a letter to be sent to Chicago customs officials and had her type it for him. He showed her a vial of diamonds but refused to tell her where he got them and admonished her not to say anything to anyone.

In the meantime, however, a customs agent had called upon Dr. Mark. The frantic doctor made repeated attempts to reach Durant by telephone, and after about ten days he succeeded. On April 17 the customs agent received a telegram from Durant in Washington, D.C., which stated that Durant would come to Chicago by air. Durant called the agent on April 19 and explained to him that he had obtained diamonds in Germany in exchange for an Elgin wristwatch and three thousand marks and had mailed them in a cigar box to his brother without a declaration, which was a lie. Durant then surrendered 102 diamonds to the customs agent, which, Durant stated, included those he had sold to Horwitz. The customs agent accepted the 102 diamonds, gave Durant a receipt, and informed him of his right to file a petition for a remission of forfeiture. Shortly thereafter, on April 22, the four diamonds Durant had given to Dr. Mark were delivered by Mark to the Chicago customs officials.

Several days later Durant returned to Washington and told his brother that he had trouble with the customs authorities in Chicago over 106 diamonds which had been impounded and that he had seen the Chicago agent concerning them. Durant also told him there would possibly be a customs agent from the Baltimore office calling for him because the Chicago agent required more information than he had given him in the first interview. The two brothers then concocted a story that Durant had mailed a package the approximate size of a cigar box, wrapped in brown paper and tied with heavy string. The mythical package had been mailed to Colonel Jack Durant at his brother's address. The made-up story included the assertion that Colonel Durant picked up considerable mail at his brother's house and opened it all and read it, except for the package, which Durant took unopened with him when he left the house.

Later, Durant dropped by the Pentagon and told Colonel Charles Maylon, general staff corps, that he would like his help in getting released from his assignment in Germany and obtaining an assignment in the States. Maylon agreed to speak to one or two officers and see what he could arrange, but the following day, Maylon was hospitalized with a heart attack. Visiting Maylon in the hospital at Bolling Field, Durant asked if he could send a personal wire in Maylon's name at his expense to General Bevans in Germany. Maylon read the draft, which asked Bevans to release Durant from the German theater in order to give him an assignment in the United States. The reason given for the transfer was that Durant was now divorced and had custody of and responsibility to his two sons. Maylon agreed to the request, but unknown to him, Durant used this request to ask for separation from the army. Durant forged Maylon's name to legitimize his own separation papers.

Durant and Nash later visited his brother's house on Easter Sunday, April 21. Durant turned over to James an envelope containing fifty small diamonds averaging between three-quarters and one carat, plus two large diamonds about the size of the nail of an index finger, emerald cut, approximately three-eighths of an inch long, one-quarter inch wide, with an extreme depth of three-eighths of an inch. He also gave his brother some pure gold in the form of wire, weighing approximately one-half pound. Durant boasted that it had been given an acid test and was determined to be pure gold. He didn't want the gold wire and asked James to hold it until a future date. There is some confusion about what happened next, but it appears that Durant and his brother buried two containers on a county road off the Lee Highway. One was an ink bottle containing about fifty small diamonds; the contents of the other is unknown. A little later, Durant or his brother or both dug up the containers.

The next time Durant and Nash came by James Durant's home was on Saturday, May 4. A citizens' association was holding a dance, and James and his wife attended, leaving Durant and Nash in their home. Durant told his brother that he might be placed on "terminal leave" and wanted to go through his effects in the attic, where they had been stored since he left for overseas duty.

Durant and Nash did not visit again until May 18. On this date, Durant told his cohort, "We can't stay here long. We want to be in Chicago tomorrow night." Then he suggested that he and his brother "take a ride." When they were outside the house, he told James to bring a trowel. They drove westward on Lee Highway, looking for a good spot to bury a small package. James suggested that they drive three or four miles to a large stand of trees into which several roads led. When they reached the trees, Durant turned left off the highway and drove approximately one hundred yards into the woods. Durant took the trowel and a glass jar out of his small leather handbag and circled behind the car.

They buried the jar, which contained both loose amethysts and white envelopes containing loose diamonds, and then returned to the car. Colonel Durant attempted to turn the car around and became stuck in the mud. After trying several minutes to get the car back on the road, James suggested that he travel into Falls Church and bring back a tow truck. He walked to the Lee Highway, boarded a bus, and rode into Falls Church to Frazier's Garage, where he got a tow truck.

Arriving at the scene, tow truck driver John W. Ayers determined that a winch was needed to pull the car out and that his truck was not adequately equipped to do the job. Ayers tried to turn around in the woods and also became stuck. After freeing his truck, Ayers said that he would return to Falls Church and have another truck return. In Falls Church, Ayers called Harry N. Nalls and told him that a car was stuck in the mud about three miles south of Falls Church on Highway 211 on a section of land known as the Old Stafmead Estate. Nalls drove out to the place and found two men sitting in a new Hudson. It was 5:00 P.M. and it had just stopped raining after a bad storm. While pulling the car out of the mud, Durant remarked to Ayers that they had been looking for a spot to build a tourist camp.

Driving back home, Durant told his brother to remember where the jar was because there was enough there to set him up for life and if anything happened to him, he wanted him to have the jar's contents. Durant never mentioned how or where he had acquired the jewels other than that he had picked them up in Germany. Upon arriving at his home, Durant picked up Nash and left for Chicago. Several days later, James Durant received a letter from Nash saying that they had arrived in Chicago the following night, Sunday, May 19, after a fast trip through the rain from Washington.

Jack Durant and Kathleen Nash checked into the elegant Hotel Sherman and dined most nights with Dr. Mark and his girlfriend, Rose Griffith, in one of the hotel's several fine restaurants. Griffith had been discharged from the army in March and moved from Washington to Chicago, where Mark had put her up at the Drake Hotel. One of their favorite places to eat while at the Sherman was the Pump Room. The food in the Pump Room, aside from being exquisitely delicious and served by an expert team of waiters in brilliant uniforms, was distinguished by being highly mobile and usually in flames. There were wagons of all kinds—hors d'oeuvre wagons, roast wagons, pastry wagons, cheese wagons and fruit wagons. But the pièce de résistance of the Pump Room was the flaming swords on which were served an endless variety of dishes. On these occasions Nash would wear a platinum wristwatch and bracelet set with 606 diamonds, which had belonged to Princess Mafalda and which was valued at $7,500.

Dr. Mark especially remembered the watch; as he said later, "The only reason that I paid any attention was because we were out one evening and one of the other women had just gotten a little watch from her husband for an anniversary gift and it was very scrimpy in comparison with the one Katie was wearing, which was very beautiful. However, I figured she was divorced from a wealthy man—so what."

They also frequented the Hotel Sherman's College Inn, the oldest nightclub in the country. The room was decorated in the then popular South Seas style, with bamboo, animal skins, and murals of black leopards that graced the entrance to the ladies' room. The College Inn was a temple to frenetic swing music, cigarette smoke, and jitterbugging. The bands performing there included those of Benny Goodman, Gene Krupa, Vaughn Monroe, and Woody Herman. It was said that the formula for entertaining returning war veterans at the Pump Room was: "Surround them with lots of pretty girls, put whiskey on the table, and then retire to a safe distance." On one of these occasions, Nash wore a ring set with an eleven-carat diamond that also had belonged to Princess Mafalda and which was valued at $14,000. The sometimes naive Dr. Mark, observing the jewels, remarked, "Katie, gee, that thing looks like a real diamond," to which Durant replied, "Well, that's the lighting effect." Durant, however, later told Mark that Nash had received the jewelry from a divorce settlement with her wealthy Arizona husband.

A few nights later, while dining out at the Chez Paree, Dr. Mark introduced Durant and Nash to entertainer Danny Thomas, who was also a patient of Dr. Mark's. Mark noticed that Durant and Nash were heavy drinkers and that it was sort of a barrier between them. Mark and Rose were more the active types, enjoying golf and playing religiously every Saturday, Sunday, Wednesday, and holidays. Mark had enviable office hours: 2:30 P.M. to 7:30 P.M. four days a week.

During this trip, Durant and Nash decided to pay a surprise visit to the Block family and drove out one afternoon. The Blocks were not at home, so they decided to sit in the yard on the nice afternoon and wait for the Blocks to return. After a half hour or so, the Blocks, Rose Griffith, and Dr. Mark returned, all dressed in golf clothes. They had just finished playing a foursome. Emma Block noticed that both Nash and Durant had been drinking considerably. As they entered the house, Block noticed that Durant was carrying a bottle of whiskey with him. As they sat down, Durant asked for a glass of water, which Nash got for him. At that point Emma Block thought to herself, I am not against drinking, but I am to the extent that you can't be without liquor.[2]

They began to talk about their trip and how they had traveled together, at which time Emma Block asked if they weren't afraid of the Mann Act, a federal law that prohibited taking a person over a state line for immoral purposes. The tipsy Durant only responded that "they won't hurt a man like me." During the conversation, Durant mentioned that he might marry Nash. In privacy, Block asked her husband, "What does he want with someone that much older?" They agreed that Durant was only marrying her for her money. From there the drunken couple drove out to the Town Inn on Ogden Avenue for dinner. They arrived at 9:57, and the waiter told them that they had only three minutes to order, as they closed at 10:00. After dinner they drove back to the Blocks'. Later, in a drunken stupor, the two staggered into the Hudson and drove off in the early-morning light. The Blocks did not see them again.

One May evening, while the four of them, Durant, Nash, Rose Griffith, and Dr. Mark, were dining out, Durant said, "Ruby, I've decided to get married. Where can we do it?" Mark told him that he could take their blood test but he would need a couple of days. On May 28, 1946, Durant and Nash were given a premarital blood test in Chicago by Mark, and in the afternoon of the same day, they were married in the county building in Chicago by Judge William P. Boynton. That night the Durants, Rose Griffith, and Dr. Mark had dinner at the Rio Cabana and reveled well beyond midnight. They then drove the four hundred miles to Nash's sister's home in Hudson, Wisconsin, a small town of 2,900 residents.

The following night, May 29, 1946, at nine o'clock, the noose began to tighten, woven by the CID investigation in Germany. Captain Nash* received official orders to report to Fort Sheridan, Illinois, immediately.

---

* In order to avoid confusion in names, Captain Kathleen Durant will continue to be referred to as Captain Nash, the name by which she was known throughout her army career.

Apparently unaware of Nash's recall to active service, Durant returned to Chicago and told his brother to bring the jar they had buried on May 18. James made an attempt to locate the jar, but after failing to do so, on Thursday evening, May 30, he called Durant and informed him that he could not find it. James then canceled his reservation to Chicago for Pennsylvania Central Airlines (PCA) Flight 401 on Friday, May 31. He next heard from Durant early the following evening when he called and asked James to meet him at National Airport in Washington at 12:30 A.M. on Saturday, June 1. Several hours later he called again, saying he couldn't make connections and for his brother James to go to bed.

The mysterious goings-on and high jinks continued. It is remarkable that Durant could charm people into doing almost anything, at almost any hour of the day or night. At approximately 4:00 A.M. on Saturday, June 1, James's bedroom door was opened, and a voice called. It was Durant saying, "Get dressed and let's go." As daylight was breaking, James dressed and returned with his brother to where they had buried the diamonds. Durant took a shovel and began digging. He soon located the jar, but broke it during digging, necessitating their scrabbling around in the dirt by hand for the white envelopes and the loose amethysts. Durant tossed the broken jar into the underbrush. They then returned to the car, carrying the shovel and the jewels, which Durant placed in his small leather handbag.

Colonel Durant then asked his brother to drive him to National Airport for the 8:00 A.M. flight to Chicago. They arrived at the airport before the restaurant opened, so they went into the coffee shop and had coffee and doughnuts. After they finished these, they noticed that the restaurant was now open and went in for more coffee and a sweet roll. Later, they sat on the balcony in the waiting room, where they talked for a short while before Durant handed his brother two small packages containing twenty-eight thousand dollars in bills. He asked him to bury this money in a jar at a site near the Leesburg Pike, approximately one-quarter mile south of the intersection of U.S. 50. After passing these packages to him, Colonel Durant said it would not be necessary for his brother to stay to see him off.

The same afternoon, June 1, James Durant put the two packages containing the cash in a quart mason jar, screwed on a zinc cap, and sealed the jar with red sealing wax, after which he buried it at the agreed-upon location near the Leesburg Pike.

15

The Tightening Noose

AFTER FURTHER INVESTIGATIONS by the CID in Germany, the magnitude of Durant's and Nash's thefts was more clearly understood. The adjutant general, M.M. Bentill, had agreed to issue telegraphic orders on Nash directly from Washington without going through the separation centers. This was followed by mailed orders to Nash. The investigators decided to interrogate Nash on a polygraph, and for this purpose the offices of Mr. Leonard Keeler, the inventor of the polygraph, were selected. Telegraphic orders were accordingly sent to Captain Nash at her sister's address, in Hudson, Wisconsin, informing her that she was recalled to active duty effective May 29, 1946, and instructing her to report to Fort Sheridan, Illinois, immediately.

The CID considered it extremely important that Captain Nash be questioned as soon as she reported for duty, before she could communicate with others who might be involved in the case. Her terminal leave was about to expire on May 30, and as she had been ordered to report to Fort Sheridan on May 29, Colonel A. C. Miller, director, Provost Division, Lieutenant Colonel Ralph W. Pierce, chief, Criminal Investigations and Apprehensions Branch, and Major John D. Salb, chief, Criminal Investigations Section, left Washington, D.C., on May 29 for Chicago. Upon arrival, they contacted the provost marshal of the Sixth Service Command and immediately requested to ascertain from Fort Sheridan whether or not Captain Nash had reported for duty in compliance with her orders.

Fort Sheridan replied that Nash had not reported. Arrangements were then made to send military police and an investigator from Camp McCoy, Wisconsin, to Hudson to attempt to locate Nash at her sister's home. It was early on the morning of June 2, and the family was not up, so as the military authorities left, Nash dressed and left by the back door and caught a taxi, driven by twenty-year-old Thomas O'Connell, to nearby St. Paul, Minnesota.

As the search continued, the provost marshal of the Ninth Service Command was requested by telephone to check at the Coronado Hotel or the Old Pueblo Club, Tucson, Arizona, and at 7570 De Longpre Avenue, Hollywood, California, in an effort to locate Nash. Fort Sheridan was also requested to call Nash's sister in Hudson and ask whether Mrs. Lonergan knew where Nash could be located. This met with negative results; Lonergan claimed to know nothing of the whereabouts of her sister.

On May 31, Nash had sent a telegram to Fort Sheridan in which she stated that she could not understand her being recalled to active duty, that she had recently married and was going on her honeymoon, and that she would go to Washington and appeal for discharge. She then called the base and repeated some of the information she had previously furnished by telegram, again offering to go to Washington if necessary.

On Saturday, June 1, Nash placed a long-distance, person-to-person call from St. Paul to Durant at his brother's home. When James Durant informed the operator that Colonel Durant had taken PCA Flight 401 that morning and that he should be in Chicago, Nash requested to speak to James. She told him she had just left Hudson, one step ahead of the military police, and that she had wanted Durant to know.

On June 1 investigators in Hudson learned that Captain Nash was now married to Colonel Durant. Nash was now considered AWOL, and the investigators were instructed to take her into custody when she was located. Subsequently a telephone call was received from the military police in Hudson, who furnished the information that Captain Nash had made reservations on PCA to fly from Minneapolis to Chicago. The MPs in Hudson agreed that as long as Nash was flying to Chicago she would not be taken into custody now but would be allowed to fly to Chicago, where she could be taken into custody by Chicago military police.

Nash, in the meantime, was to be placed under surveillance and, in the event she did not take the plane, would be taken into custody at Minneapolis. Major Salb, with Lieutenant Hergert, assistant provost marshal of the Sixth Service Command, and Sergeant Elizabeth

DeYoung, WAAC, immediately proceeded to the Chicago Municipal Airport but did not arrive until after the plane had landed. Passengers from the flight still remained in the building, but Nash could not be identified from the meager description they had been supplied with. The flight stewardess was located and checked her passenger list, which showed that Nash was included as a passenger on her plane. She then checked her ticket stubs for the flight and could not find one for Nash or Durant, which, she said, would indicate that Nash did not make the flight.

Upon returning from the airport, the investigators received news from the MPs in Hudson that they had talked with the cabdriver who had picked Nash up and that he had driven her to the railroad depot in Minneapolis, where she was to have taken the "400," a fast passenger train, due in Chicago at about 9:20 P.M. Major Salb, in a military police car, drove to Evanston, Illinois, to board the train before its arrival in Chicago. Arriving in Evanston ten minutes before train time, he made arrangements with Western Union to prepare a telegram for Nash, aboard the 400.

Major Salb boarded the train at Evanston and had the porter go through the train with the telegram, paging Captain Nash. Although Nash heard the page, she ignored it, reasoning that if her husband was paging her he would use their married name of Durant. In the meantime, Colonel Miller, Lieutenant Colonel Pierce, Sergeant Elizabeth DeYoung, and Mr. Keeler, having been apprised of the facts of the case, had gone to the Northwestern Station to meet the train upon its arrival in Chicago. Arrangements were made to have Nash paged over the public address system in the station. These efforts to locate Nash aboard the 400 and in the Northwestern Station proved ineffective. She was now dressed in civilian clothing and sported newly bleached blond hair. She boldly walked right past the investigating team without being identified and continued on her way.

On Sunday, June 2, the War Department issued orders canceling the unexecuted portion of Colonel Durant's terminal leave and ordered him back to active duty at Fort Sheridan, Illinois, immediately.

Later that same evening, investigators determined that both Durant and Nash were holed up in room 301 at the posh LaSalle Hotel and had registered at approximately 5:00 P.M., Sunday, June 2. They were not, however, in their room now. A detail consisting of Lieutenant Chester Weinstock, two MPs, and Sergeant DeYoung was placed in room 300, next to the Durants' room, with instructions to take Mrs. Durant into custody when she returned.

At two in the morning they heard the Durants enter their room and waited a few minutes to listen for any conversation. They could not hear anyone talking, so Lieutenant Weinstock knocked on the door. Durant, in uniform, answered the door, while his wife ran and hid in the bathroom. Durant grew pale and agitated. The police then asked to see Nash, and Durant called her out of the bathroom. Weinstock informed her that she was under arrest. Nash asked why she was wanted, and she was told that she was AWOL. The arresting team then insisted on searching their luggage, over Durant's objections. They found nothing of any importance. Durant asked if he could drive Nash to Fort Sheridan, but was told that Nash had to go with them. Weinstock told Durant that he had been ordered back to active duty and was to report to Fort Sheridan that day, Monday, June 3. Durant agreed without further argument. Weinstock asked Durant if he wished to accompany them to Fort Sheridan, as it was quite a long trip. Durant turned down the offer, saying, "No, I'll get there before midnight."

The two enlisted men and DeYoung drove Nash in an army sedan to Fort Sheridan, where, at four in the morning, she was turned over to the provost marshal and booked and fingerprinted. During the ride, Nash told DeYoung that she had seen her at the train station but just walked right by, adding that she had heard them page her but did not answer because it was for "Captain Nash" and if her husband had been calling for her he would have paged for "Mrs. Durant." After fingerprinting Nash, the clerk procured some clean sheets and gave them to her; by now it was five in the morning. Nash was told that she must be ready for the six o'clock mess hall, so she showered and ate breakfast, and at seven-thirty, with no sleep, she was headed back to Chicago, for what would be the most portentous day of her life.

She was taken to Dr. Leonard Keeler's office at 134 South LaSalle Street for questioning. Lieutenant Colonel Pierce asked her if she knew why she was there, and Nash replied that she did not know, unless it was for being AWOL. He informed her of her rights under the twenty-fourth Article of War. She was then asked if she was willing to take a polygraph test. Nash had never heard of the test, so it was explained that it was a so-called lie detector examination. Without being told what she was going to be questioned about, Nash further swore that she had nothing to conceal and agreed to submit to the test, which was conducted by the forty-one-year-old Keeler and witnessed through a one-way mirror by Lieutenant Colonel Pierce and Major Salb. Dr. Keeler, a civilian criminal investigator and the inventor of the machine, had been employed to assist army investigators.

A blood pressure cuff was fastened about Nash's upper arm and inflated so that a continual tracing of blood pressure pulse variations was recorded by a stylus on a moving strip of paper. A tube was fastened about her chest for transmitting respiratory changes to the instrument. A pair of electrodes was fastened on the palm and back of her hand for recording galvanic skin response. A normal question was first asked, then two irrelevant questions, and finally questions pertaining to the theft of the Hesse crown jewels. Captain Nash showed definite reactions to questions pertaining to jewelry. She was asked if she had ever taken any jewelry, or other items, from Kronberg Castle. During the initial stages of the questioning, she maintained that she had not. The polygraph, however, indicated that she was not telling the truth. When this was pointed out to her, she admitted that she had taken "a few things" from the castle and specifically mentioned a couple of silver mugs and a few bracelets. The polygraph again indicated that this was not the whole truth.

After approximately two hours of intensive questioning by Dr. Keeler, Nash admitted her complicity in the thefts and implicated Colonel Durant, Major David F. Watson, and former Corporal Roy C. Carlton. Nash then voluntarily gave a written statement to Lieutenant Colonel Pierce and Major John D. Salb. This statement was taken down in shorthand and transcribed by Captain Mary Cowie, WAAC. In it, Nash admitted having the box of jewels taken to her room in the castle after they had been discovered in the basement; showing the jewels to Colonel Durant, Corporal Carlton, and Major Watson; deciding to take a few pieces; deciding to keep all of it; bringing a portion of the jewels with her to the United States, with the rest remaining with Colonel Durant; and hiding that part of the loot in her sister's home.

In this sworn statement, Kathleen Nash was asked what portion of the jewels was mailed to her sister's house. Nash responded, "Why, I think I probably have about one-half of it. I mean the small stuff." She said the rest had remained with Colonel Durant and that he had buried most of his share someplace in northern Virginia.

She further stated that it was their intent to sell the bulk of the valuables in the States and divide the money up four ways, between Nash, Durant, Watson, and Carlton. Nash went on to say that Carlton was the least involved of the three and that Major Watson seemed to have the most courage to go ahead with the heist of the jewels. She further stated that "practically the whole blame should be placed on the three officers involved."

Captain Mary Cowie observed the polygraph test from the next room through a specially constructed one-way mirror and listened to the conversation being recorded on a machine in the room.

Afterward, Nash said that she wanted to address a letter to her sister authorizing her to turn over the jewels and other items to Major John D. Salb. She handwrote the following note:

To Kileen, Jack or David—

I have confessed to having the box of jewels, Bibles and fans that I hid in the attic. Will you please give same to officer presenting you this note. Major John D. Salb, our code— "cemetery"—goes. Sorry to have caused you so much grief and I don't deserve you to worry over me anymore.

Love, Vonie
(Kathleen B. Durant)

When questioned concerning the meaning of the code word "cemetery," Nash explained that this was the word agreed upon by her and her sister whereby if Nash wanted the jewels she would mention the word and her sister would send the jewels.

A special army plane was acquired, and Major Salb, accompanied by Lieutenant Hergert and a photographer, flew from Chicago to Hudson, Wisconsin. They proceeded to 1409 Third Street and, after talking to a guard who had been dispatched to the house about an hour earlier from Camp McCoy, Wisconsin, were told by the Lonergans' grown son, David, that his parents were not at home. After the guards from Camp McCoy had arrived, the Lonergans and their landlord had driven downtown to see their district attorney.

The landlord living downstairs in the two-story house had become quite agitated with an armed guard stationed six feet from his front door, and he wanted them removed. The district attorney advised the Lonergans, meanwhile, that he did not know the federal law and did not know their rights as civilians. As they left, John Lonergan considered that there was nothing else to do, so he suggested that the landlord drop him and his wife off at a movie. They had gone with the landlord because the guards had told Lonergan that he could not move anything from the house, and that included his car. As soon as the movie started, at seven o'clock, their son had them paged and said that "someone from the army" was outside and wanted to talk to them. They left the movie, and waiting for them at the corner of Main Street in downtown Hudson were Major Salb and his party.

After a short conversation they got into an army station wagon and rode back to the Lonergans' home. When they arrived, the house was surrounded by four armed guards. Major Salb dismissed the guards and entered the Lonergans' upstairs apartment by the back door. The note from Nash was not shown to her sister because investigators were suspicious of Nash's explanation of the word "cemetery." Salb informed Mrs. Lonergan that he did not have a right to search her house, but that he had come for the valuables that had been placed there by her sister.

Voluntarily, Mrs. Lonergan and her husband began bringing articles of jewelry, silverware, goldware, gold-plated ware, silver mugs, boxes, and Bibles from various rooms in the house. Some items were even in the bedroom under the bed. They turned many items over to the investigators, but not the main cache of diamonds, which had been concealed in a blue box. Salb then stated that Nash had supposedly stored the bulk of the valuables in a cubbyhole off the attic. The Lonergans professed complete ignorance of anything hidden in the attic but gave their permission for Salb to search it. It was located just off the kitchen. The Lonergans supplied Salb with a flashlight, and after about twenty minutes of fruitless searching, Mrs. Lonergan reappeared after having left the house for a few minutes and said that she had the jewels. She thereupon turned over to Major Salb a quart mason jar which she was carrying and which contained jewels of every description. Salb and his investigators set up a table in the living room and started to itemize, inventory, and photograph the valuables. As they proceeded with this, Mrs. Lonergan made ice water and coffee. At three o'clock in the morning the army investigator and Mrs. Lonergan signed the following receipt which accounted for about half of the missing valuables:

DESCRIPTION	OWNER	1946 VALUE
Bracelet, pearl, 114 diamonds	Maria Alexandra	$2,875
Brooch, moss rose, 77 diamonds	Landgrafin	700
Bracelet, 11 turquoise, 68 diamonds	Landgrafin	1,400
Bracelet, platinum, 405 diamonds	Mafalda	3,300
Pin, platinum, 209 diamonds	Mafalda	3,500
Bracelet, 142 diamonds, 74 rubies	Mafalda	3,000
Wristwatch, platinum, 606 diamonds	Mafalda	7,500

DESCRIPTION	OWNER	1946 VALUE
Bracelet, gold, 27 diamonds, emerald	Maria Alexandra	550
Ring, gold, pearl, 9 rubies	Landgrafin	50
Ring, chalcedony, 34 diamonds	Mafalda	$75
Ring, gold, 9 diamonds—one 11-carat	Mafalda	14,000
Ring, platinum, 336 diamonds	Mafalda	4,000
Ring, oval turquoise, 14 diamonds	Maria Alexandra	350
Ring, emerald, 20 diamonds	Mafalda	2,700
Ring, 5 rubies, 24 diamonds	Landgrafin	300
Ring, gold, 24 sapphires clips, 6 rubies	Mafalda	5,400
Clips, 2 pearls, 148 diamonds	Mafalda	1,900
Clip, sapphire, 62 diamonds	Mafalda	4,000
Brooch, gold, 21 rubies, 19 diamonds	Mafalda	600
Brooch, gold, 22 rubies, 8 diamonds	Landgrafin	75
Clip, platinum, 122 diamonds	Mafalda	4,800
Clip, platinum, 105 diamonds	Mafalda	2,350
Earring, turquoise, 82 diamonds	Maria Alexandra	550
Earrings, 2 sapphires, 76 diamonds	Mafalda	800
Cuff links, gold, red enamel, 4 diamonds	Richard	135
Cuff links, gold & platinum	Mafalda	50
Cuff links, gold, 4 rubies	August Wilhem	200
Cuff links, 4 emeralds, 63 diamonds	August Wilhem	500
Buttons, 4 turquoise, 16 diamonds	Mafalda	65
Cuff links, gold, 4 sapphires	Landgrafin	250
Cuff links, gold & platinum	Mafalda	100
Shirt studs, pearl	Wolfgang	250
Cuff links, 24 diamonds, 8 sapphires	Richard	225
Shirt stud, 2 moonstones, 45 rubies	Richard	175
Shirt stud, sapphire, 20 diamonds	Wolfgang	260
Shirt studs, gold, pair	Richard	40
Bracelet, 42 rubies, 168 diamonds	Mafalda	10,000
Bracelet, 5 aquamarines, 240 diamonds	Mafalda	1,250
Bracelet, 54 rubies, 321 diamonds	Mafalda	1,727
Bracelet, 3 rubies, 125 diamonds	Mafalda	3,000
Bracelet, 88 sapphires, 112 diamonds	Mafalda	3,500
Necklace, 52 pearls	Mafalda	30,000
Necklace, 49 pearls	Maria Alexandra	3,000
Necklace, 51 pearls	Mafalda	10,000

Description	Owner	1946 Value
Necklace, platinum, 18 pearls	Maria Alexandra	1,100
Necklace, gold, stones	Maria Alexandra	75
Necklace, gold	Landgrafin	$200
Necklace, gold, lapis lazuli	Maria Alexandra	75
Necklace, coral, large stones	Maria Alexandra	200
Necklace, coral	Maria Alexandra	150
Necklace, gold	Maria Alexandra	45
Necklace, gold, 7 pearls	Maria Alexandra	50
Necklace, gold	Maria Alexandra	15
Pendant, gold, 4 diamonds	Maria Alexandra	110
Brooch, gold, 4 diamonds	Maria Alexandra	50
Brooch, ruby, 70 diamonds	Mafalda	700
Brooch, 2 pearls, 1 diamond	Maria Alexandra	325
Scarf pin, 12 rubies, 26 diamonds	August Wilhem	150
Brooch, 3 sapphires, 2 diamonds	Maria Alexandra	425
Scarf pin, 26 diamonds	August Wilhem	115
Brooch, sapphire, pearl, 2 diamonds	Maria Alexandra	200
Cuff links, 14 amethysts, 62 diamonds	August Wilhem	625
Brooch, crown, 37 diamonds	Maria Alexandra	650
Locket, moonstone, 21 diamonds	Elizabeth	330
Locket, gold, 39 diamonds	ELizabeth	650
Cuff links, 56 diamonds, 17 sapphires	August Wilhem	210
Brooch, 4 sapphires, 128 diamonds	Mafalda	600
Pendant, 16 pearls, head of Queen Victoria	Landgrafin	750
Necklace, 29 pearls, 30 diamonds	House Jewels	3,000
Bracelet, gold, pearl, 12 diamonds	Maria Alexandra	175
Vase, silver & enamel	Mafalda	15
Watch, buried in crystal	Landgrafin	150
Watch, gold antique	Landgrafin	500
Watch, gold, monogram	Landgrafin	75
Watch, gold, enamel	Landgrafin	150
Napkin rings, silver, 2	Sophia	6
Snuff box, miniature of Marie Amelie	Philipp	200
Bracelet, gold, 8 charms	Landgrafin	450
Bracelet, gold, 6 garnet hearts	Landgrafin	330
Miniature, Princess Louise of Prussia	Landgrafin	200
Miniature, George V, King of Hanover	Landgrafin	150

Description	Owner	1946 Value
Brooch, 6 rubies, 56 pearls	Landgrafin	200
Miniature, 76 diamonds	Landgrafin	1,000
Miniature, Fred. Wm. IV, King of Prussia	Landgrafin	$75
Miniature	Landgrafin	5
Miniature	Landgrafin	10
Miniature	Landgrafin	25
Miniature	Landgrafin	75
Miniature	Landgrafin	50
Charm, chalcedony, ruby	Landgrafin	25
Brooch, gold, head of Queen Victoria	Landgrafin	25
Piece of uniform	Wolfgang	None
Ivory box	Landgrafin	25
Brooch, gold, 2 pictures	Landgrafin	100
Pin, 1 sapphire	Landgrafin	50
Pin, 6 rubies	Landgrafin	75
Pin, 31 diamonds	Landgrafin	50
Ring, gold, picture Frederick the Great	Landgrafin	100
Jade Buddha	Sophia	10
Easter egg, gold, iron cross	Landgrafin	45
Mecca stone	Landgrafin	1.50
Souvenir insignia, gold	Maria Alexandra	25
Letter opener, agate, ruby diamond	Landgrafin	10
Cross, silver gilt	Sophia	10
Easter egg, gold, enamel crystal	Landgrafin	25
Hat pin, amethyst, 4 diamonds	Landgrafin	50
Pen holder, silver	Landgrafin	1.50
Necklace, gold	Maria Alexandra	40
Necklace, platinum, 4 diamonds	Maria Alexandra	75
Necklace, platinum	Mafalda	100
Tankard, silver gilt, monogram Fred III	Landgrafin	100
Cream pitcher, monogram Fred III	Landgrafin	25
Coasters, silver 12	Landgrafin	48
Bell, silver, tortoise shape	Sophia	40
Box, cigarette, silver	Landgrafin	50
Candlesticks, pair	Sophia	25
Cups, egg, silver, 2	Landgrafin	40
Box, silver	Landgrafin	25
Box, match, silver	Landgrafin	20

DESCRIPTION	OWNER	1946 VALUE
Pot, mustard, silver	Landgrafin	25
Tray, silver-plated, small	Landgrafin	20
Saucer support, silver	Landgrafin	$75
Bowl, silver, embossed, antique	Landgrafin	50
Plate, silver	Landgrafin	75
Ash tray, silver	Landgrafin	25
Plate, silver, small	Landgrafin	10
Cup, collapsible, silver, w/case	Rainer	10
Pencil, silver	Wolfgang	15
Penholder, silver	Landgrafin	25
Fan, gold, 95 diamonds, 4 rubies, 3 sapphires, hand-painted arms & pictures	Landgrafin	5,000
Fan, tortoiseshell, gold inlay	Sophia	50
Fan, mother of pearl, gold inlay	Sophia	500
Crucifix, silver	Sophia	10
Smelling bottle, silver	Landgrafin	25
Chess man, metal	Landgrafin	10
Chess man, metal	Landgrafin	25
Chess man, metal, gold trim	Landgrafin	50
Fruit set, 12 each knives, forks, spoons	Landgrafin	900
Fork, salad	Landgrafin	20
Spoon, salad	Landgrafin	20
24 spoons, 12 knives, 11 forks	Landgrafin	380
Coffee spoons, silver gilt, 12	Sophia	180
Butter knives, 3	Landgrafin	9
Spoon, silver, monogram Empress Friedrich	Landgrafin	40
Spoon, silver, antique	Landgrafin	40
Spoon, jam, silver	Landgrafin	15
Spoons, egg and salt, 5	Landgrafin	15
Spoons, mustard, 2	Landgrafin	6
Pusher, child's, silver	Rainer	5
Spoon, monogram Empress Friedrich	Landgrafin	2
Spoon, porridge, silver	Sophia	5
Spoon, silver, monogram Empress Friedrich	Landgrafin	30
Spoon, silver	Landgrafin	4
Scissors, grape, monogram, silver	Landgrafin	20
Frame, silver	Landgrafin	40
Field glasses, zeiss, w/case	Christoph	100

DESCRIPTION	OWNER	1946 VALUE
Bible, gilt binding, writing Queen Victoria	Landgrafin	300
English Book of Common Prayer, gilt binding, pictures Queen Victoria, Prince Albert, markers w/turquoise, pearls	Landgrafin	$150
Book, imitation of Christ, velvet	Landgrafin	
Catalog to 187, red velvet	Landgrafin	
Album, paintings, autographs, velvet	Landgrafin	
Bible, German, leather	Landgrafin	
Catalog to 187, silk	Landgrafin	
Bible, German, leather	Landgrafin	
9 volumes correspondence between Empress Friedrich & dau. Pr. Fredrich	Landgrafin	
Box, wooden, St. Michael	Philipp	
Diamonds, 2	Landgrafin	

During the search, Salb also found a wooden box addressed to Captain Nash, Hudson, Wisconsin, and bearing Major Watson's return address. The box was lined with an unusual type of heavy waxed paper used by the German navy and in fact was the box constructed by Durant and Watson in Germany.

During the investigation, neighbors of Mrs. Lonergan and Mrs. Betty Nash Wilcox (Captain Nash's daughter, now married to Donald Wilcox, an automotive mechanic) said both women had displayed precious stones, bracelets, and other articles which they reported had been sent to them by Captain Nash from Germany.

What they did not know was that prior to mailing the valuables to Nash, Major David Watson had removed several of the most expensive items and mailed them to Peggy Harvey in Northern Ireland. Mrs. Harvey thought that she was receiving a box of mints, but when she opened the box it contained the following, shown with their 1946 dollar value in parentheses: Bracelet, platinum, 365 diamonds ($18,000); bracelet, platinum, 162 diamonds ($5,000); necklace, pearl, double strand ($500); hand mirror, silver ($35); pin, gold, pearl, 2 diamonds ($150); ring, gold, 2 diamonds, 1 ruby ($150); ring, gold, 2 diamonds, 1 ruby ($150); pin gold, 2 pearls, "Baby" Maria Alexandra ($20); brooch, platinum, 5 diamonds ($75); safety pin, gold, pearl ($20); sapphire, 116.20 carats ($5,800); amethyst, drop-shaped, 103.73

carats ($150); amethyst, 80.85 carats ($40); 1 pearl, 19 diamonds, 20 rose-cut diamonds, part of a diadem ($3,000); ring, sapphire ($800); ring, sapphire, 74 diamonds ($200); ring, garnet, 10 diamonds ($250); ring, 2 diamonds, 1 ruby ($50); chain, platinum, with pearls ($150); pendant, platinum, 18 diamonds ($100); chain, platinum, with gold lock ($65); 589 diamonds, 20 rubies, 4 emeralds, and 1 miniature heart-shaped ruby ($20,000).

Accompanying the jewels was a note for her to keep them until Watson reclaimed them. Mrs. Harvey hid them in a baby powder tin.

In the meantime, after Captain Nash had signed her statement, Lieutenant Colonel Pierce called the LaSalle Hotel in an effort to contact Durant. Told that Durant was not in, Pierce left a message that Durant was to call Pierce at Dr. Keeler's office. It was most desirable to locate Durant before he had an opportunity to dispose of any jewels that he might have in his possession or before he seized an opportunity to warn others involved.

That same afternoon, on June 3, Special Agent John F. Swartz was ordered to go to the LaSalle and wait for Durant to return. Swartz waited in the hall on the third floor, and at 3:20 P.M. Durant returned to his room. As he was inserting his key into the door, Swartz approached him and presented his credentials as a criminal investigator for the army and told him that he had been requested to escort him to see Lieutenant Colonel Pierce. Durant asked for permission to enter his room and freshen up, which was granted. Durant asked what the problem was, and Swartz replied that he had no knowledge whatsoever pertaining to the matter. Durant told Swartz that he was on leave until midnight and did not see any reason to deviate from his leave orders. Durant then asked bluntly whether he was under arrest, and Swartz replied, "Not unless you refuse to come of your own free will." Durant agreed that he would go peaceably and was escorted to Dr. Keeler's office.

Upon arrival, Durant was spotted by Nash as she sat in the waiting room. Durant was read his rights under the twenty-fourth Article of War and was warned that anything he said could be used against him. He was then questioned for several hours by Dr. Keeler and Lieutenant Colonel Pierce. After some conversation, Durant was asked to submit to a polygraph test. At first he refused, and Keeler told him that he did not have to take the test. Durant then replied, "I know that. I know my law. I know what I have to do and what I don't have to do; I am a lawyer." A few minutes later, however, he consented to submit to the test, but after less than one hour of questioning, he refused to submit to any further testing on the machine. The results of this test are unknown, but from ancillary material it was learned that Durant, testing the machine's accuracy, had stated that half the cache had been buried in a cemetery, and the test had verified the statement, scaring Durant.

Later, Durant was told that his bride had confessed to the theft of the Hesse jewels, and he was shown her signed confession. He expressed doubt, saying, "You might frame that on me." Durant then requested permission to be alone with his wife for a short time, asserting that he would tell her something that would be of benefit to the case and then she could tell them if she wanted to. He was then permitted to talk with Captain Nash in solitude. She was brought into the interrogation room and left alone. As she entered the room, Durant put his finger to his mouth as a signal for Nash not to speak. They kissed and she sat on his lap while they conversed in whispers for about fifteen minutes, and although the lovers were observed through a one-way mirror, their comments could not be picked up by the obligatory bugging device. When they left the room, Nash told the investigators that the larger pieces of jewelry had been broken up and the stones removed. Durant made no denial of the truth of the statement but would add nothing to it.

After the conversation with his wife, Durant was asked to submit to another polygraph test. By then the investigators had obtained a list of cemeteries in northern Virginia and the Chicago area, and they wanted to read the list to him and watch the reaction of the polygraph machine. Durant refused to be further tested by the machine. He then asked Dr. Keeler to take a walk with him. Durant was wise in the ways of the military and had asked to take the walk in order to avoid the bugging devices that were placed in Keeler's office. During this walk, Durant said to Dr. Keeler, "I know what you have said to me, what you have said about the case, is true; but I am in one hell of a jam. I don't know how to get out of it. I don't think I can get you back the jewels; I wish I could. You fellows have been decent to me, and I wish I could get them back, but it's impossible."

At 9:00 P.M., as they prepared to leave Keeler's office, Pierce and Salb took Sergeant Robert A. Nichols into the corridor and told him that Durant was "an unqualified son of a bitch of a crook" and was entitled to no consideration and to see to it that he was shaken down before he was taken to Fort Sheridan. Shortly afterward, Pierce and the military guards took Durant back to the LaSalle Hotel to pick up his belongings. As they were leaving the hotel in the darkness, Durant said to Pierce, "Don't you think I need some consideration?" to which Pierce replied, "If you want consideration, you just tell us what you do know." Durant replied, "The car that I have in the lot is of some value," implying that the car should not just be left there. The three men then walked to the parking lot, where Durant's Hudson was searched, and Pierce said they would move it to the army storage garage at Garvey Court and Lake Street. In the glove compartment was a camera on which was pasted a note that read: "Please mail to Mr. Robert A. Elliott, Santa Barbara, California."

Durant was then searched by the sergeant, and they proceeded to Fort Sheridan. On the way, Durant claimed that he had a headache and asked permission to go to a drugstore for an aspirin. The request was refused.

At Fort Sheridan, as they were getting out of the car, Durant dropped down and tried to conceal a piece of paper under the seat of the car. Nichols retrieved the paper and noticed that it contained the names of First State Pawners and Fidelity Home Loan Bank, two pawnshops on South Clark Street in Chicago. Nichols gave the paper to Pierce. Durant was placed in general officers' quarters, but Nash was confined to ward 2, cell 7, behind bars in a psychotic ward. All her clothing and valuables were removed, and she was issued hospital pajamas and a robe. A screen was placed in front of the bars to obstruct the view into the cell by the other patients. Nash was only allowed out to use the toilet. She refused to eat any meals while confined in the cell. After protest from Durant, Nash was confined under twenty-four-hour guard in ward 713, an open ward usually used for WAACs and the wives of military personnel, in the Regional Station Hospital at Fort Sheridan.

On the following morning, June 4, Durant was again interrogated in Keeler's office in Chicago. The investigators talked incessantly as Durant sat quietly for long periods of time with his head hung down. He refused to make any oral or written statements. Lieutenant Colonel Pierce couldn't help noticing that Durant seemed very mysterious and that there were certain things about him that were "just screwy." The investigators played along with Durant, though they knew that he was stringing them along; when they tried getting tough with him, he would just shut up, so they played along in a cat-and-mouse game.

At around 1:00 P.M. Durant again asked to talk with Dr. Keeler in the corridor. In this second conversation, as they walked to and fro in the hall, he reiterated, "You fellows have been swell to me. I wish I could get the jewelry back but I am in a hot spot and I'm afraid I can't. We might make a slip and these were tough men to get along with, and somebody might get hurt." By this statement it was apparent to the investigators that Durant was implying that to reveal the names of his accomplices would place Durant's immediate family in danger. After pacing the hall for some fifteen minutes, Durant asked if he could be released and left on his own for two hours so that he could recover the jewels. This absurd request was denied, and then Durant suggested that Keeler go along with him because he didn't want a man with a uniform along. Lieutenant Colonel Pierce absolutely refused.

It was finally agreed to permit Durant, Keeler, and Major Salb to leave the building so Durant could make some telephone calls in private. As they walked down Adams Street, Durant saw a drugstore and asked to make a call from a public booth without anyone listening. After consulting with Major Salb for a minute, they consented to allow him to make the call. Major Salb and Keeler agreed that at this stage of the investigation the chance should be taken. Durant led them to the LaSalle Hotel, where he scanned a telephone directory and then entered a booth. Keeler attempted to have the hotel operator trace the call but failed. Apparently Durant had observed Keeler approaching an assistant manager and the manager in turn going to the telephone operator, who was outside his booth. As they left, he took Keeler off to one side and said, "What are you trying to do, double-cross me?" Then he led Major Salb and Keeler to another drugstore, where he again apparently attempted to make a phone call. Every few moments, he would lean over to look out of the booth and then suddenly pull his head back as if talking on the telephone. The call lasted fully ten to twelve minutes. Upon completion of the call, he declared, "I've contacted one of the men and it is agreeable with him that the jewels be returned to me and now it is only a matter of contacting another. I am confident now that I can get the jewels back."

A little while later, Pierce, Salb, and Keeler accompanied Durant to Keeler's apartment at 1507 North Dearborn Street, where dinner was served. Pierce and Salb were house guests of Keeler during the investigation. Durant requested the privilege of taking a shower. He was treated as a guest throughout the evening. The investigators were being most friendly with Durant in hopes that he would recover the valuables. During the evening's conversation, Durant asked to make another telephone contact. Durant refused to talk on Keeler's home phone, so once again Salb and Keeler accompanied him to an army car, and they drove off.

Keeler suggested that they go to a drugstore at a given corner, but Durant adamantly refused. He said he would pick his own telephone. After being driven around several blocks, he finally said, "We'll stop here and use the phone in that drugstore." Salb and Durant left the car, and it was later reported by Salb that Durant apparently attempted to make a telephone call. They returned to the car, and Durant claimed that he was unable to contact the right person. However, he told the exasperated investigators, whose patience was wearing thin, he was sure that at 11:00 A.M. the following morning he could make the contact.

The next morning, June 5, as Durant was being taken from confinement at Fort Sheridan back to Dr. Keeler's office, the *Chicago Daily Tribune* reported that thousands had watched as the LaSalle Hotel was completely consumed by fire. The article reported that the 1,048-room hotel had been erected in 1909 as the biggest, safest, and most modern hotel west of New York City. At least sixteen persons were reported killed in the blaze. Durant requested a follow-up call from the previous evening and was accompanied by Salb and Pierce again as they walked to a drugstore selected by Durant. Following the call, Durant said that he was to receive a call someplace in town, which he refused to identify, at 4:00 P.M., but had nothing to do in the meantime. Pierce, Salb, Durant, and Keeler decided then to make a tour of the lower floors of the LaSalle Hotel, to inspect the fire damage. Durant was particularly interested in the condition of room 300, where he had stayed the night of June 20.

Following lunch, Major Salb and Durant walked about the neighborhood streets and were finally joined by Pierce and Keeler a little before 4:00 P.M. They were then led by Durant to a bar on Monroe Street. Here they waited, and promptly at four o'clock a pay station telephone call was received by Durant. While he was being returned to the front of the bar where the investigators were waiting, Salb noticed that Durant's face was "long and hanging clear down to his heels." Durant commented that "it was too bad but he had discovered it was impossible for him to recover the jewels." After rejoining the group of investigators, he said, "It looks bad. I'm afraid it's all off."

Growing tired and angry at Durant's attempts to stall the inevitable, the investigators returned with him to Keeler's offices and questioned him more intensively. Durant still professed that he had nothing further to say, but after hours of interrogation finally admitted, "Well, when I tell the story, I'll tell it all, but now I can't tell you anything. When the right time comes, I'll tell the whole story about the jewels." He claimed furthermore that he knew that they were aware that he had the jewels but that it was impossible for him to recover them and that his interrogators should do with him whatever they desired. As Pierce would later repeat in his written report:

> It is the damndest thing I ever saw. Now we have given him every possible courtesy, we have given him every leeway we could and we are about at the end of the rope as far as giving him any consideration. I'd like to take those eagles off and take that Bronze Star and Legion of Merit off. We're getting thoroughly disgusted with him frankly.

During the conversation, Pierce and Miller agreed that Durant had lost control of the deal and would probably never get his share of the valuables because of his and Nash's current circumstances.

At 8:15 P.M. the military police arrived for Durant and drove him to Fort Sheridan as Nash was being driven in the opposite direction. At 9:30 P.M. Nash arrived in Keeler's office, accompanied by MPs. During the interim, Pierce and Salb left the office and went to search Durant's car for additional clues. Upon arrival, Nash seemed in good humor, appeared friendly, and stated that she wished her husband would make a clean breast of the whole thing, that she was tired and wanted it over with. Finally, during the interview, it was suggested that she call her husband at Fort Sheridan. She stated, in substance, "I'll be glad to but I am afraid he won't talk. I wish he would tell me everything. I wish since he is afraid to tell himself, that he would tell me and then I could tell you everything."

She then telephoned Durant as Salb went into the next room and listened in on the long conversation. Pierce and Keeler stayed in the room with Nash and listened to her end of the conversation. She told Durant that she "wished we could tell all the truth and get this thing over with" and went further to urge him to tell the whole story in both their interests. Salb reported that little of importance was said by Durant. She left the office at 11:10 P.M. in the company of the MPs. Around midnight, Durant called Pierce at Keeler's apartment and requested to talk to his wife. Pierce denied the request, but said that they could get together in the morning.

The following day, Thursday, June 6, at 9:00 A.M., in Keeler's office, Durant and his wife were allowed to converse alone. Their conversation was not overheard. Durant, following the interview, still refused to make any statements regarding the whereabouts of the jewels. During the conversation which followed, Durant said, in essence, "Yes, we did break them up in Germany. The larger jewels were broken up and the stones removed in Germany and the loose stones brought back." Nash insisted she did not know the whereabouts of the jewels but asserted, "We broke the jewels up in my room at the castle and broke some of them up in Major Watson's room. I do not know what happened to the loose stones after the jewels were broken up."

Apparently the investigation team was at a dead end, but as luck would have it, a noted criminal psychologist happened upon the scene by pure chance.

As inconceivable as it sounds, the jewels that had been recovered in Hudson were then taken that evening to Keeler's apartment, where Salb and Pierce made a second inventory and both initialed the cards on each item previously attached by Major Salb in Wisconsin.* During the inventory, Dr. Lemoyne Snyder, medical-legal director of the Michigan State Police, with his wife and Mrs. Mulbar, wife of Captain Harold Mulbar, arrived from Lansing, Michigan, to take Keeler on a vacation trip. Captain Mulbar was in Japan reorganizing the Japanese police force for the U.S. military occupation authority.

After their arrival, Pierce invited them to inspect the gems and give some estimate as to their value. The entire story concerning the jewels and other valuables was told to forty-eight-year-old Dr. Snyder. Dr. Keeler asked Snyder, as an impartial individual, if he would talk to Durant in an effort to get him to cooperate in the return of the jewels. Snyder, a Harvard Medical School graduate, and not one to turn down an interesting challenge, agreed to the request.

At noon the following day, June 7, Durant and Nash returned to Dr. Keeler's office, where Lieutenant Colonel Pierce introduced Durant to Dr. Snyder. He was presented to Durant as a physician and lawyer and member of the Michigan State Police, and not officially connected with the case. Snyder began the conversation by stating that he was a disinterested person in the matter and had had no connection with the

---

* With the secure facilities available at Fort Sheridan, why did these professionals use Keeler's apartment to verify the original inventory? This incident was never reported by Pierce, Salb, or any official army documents. The valuables taken to Keeler's apartment were reported in notes of Dr. Lemoyne Snyder.

army since he was a soldier in 1918. He then went on to say that for many years in the practice of medicine he had made his living by giving advice to people in trouble and that he thought that he in a friendly way could give Durant some advice which would be of benefit to him and all parties concerned. Although Durant was highly skeptical, he responded to Snyder's approach and seemed willing and agreeable to discuss the matter.

Durant began the conversation by saying he was entirely familiar with his rights under military law and that he thought the best thing to do was to demand counsel on his arrival in Washington and let the matter run its course without making any further statements or admissions or further attempts to return the jewels. Snyder replied to the effect that while he knew nothing of military court procedure, he could not conceive of any good lawyer undertaking his defense as long as it was still under his power to return the stolen property. They then discussed this concept at length in a friendly sort of way.

Dr. Snyder explained to Durant that in the practice of medicine, doctors are called upon to give advice to people suffering all manner of complaints, some purely mental, many physical, some curable and others hopeless, but that in all cases pain and suffering can be lessened. Continuing to apply this to Durant's case, Snyder said, "I have no doubt that during the last few days you have been undergoing mental torture more severe than almost any physical pain that can be imagined." Durant emphatically agreed. Snyder stressed that in this case there were things he could do that would greatly lessen the mental punishment he was enduring. The first was to restore the jewels insofar as it was in his power to do so, so that the wrong which had been done would be mitigated to the greatest possible extent. Snyder further stated that there were, no doubt, some things that could not be undone, such as the breaking up of the jewelry and that possibly some articles of jewelry were beyond his power to get back.

"I think I have a good idea why you haven't made a greater effort to return those jewels," Snyder then interjected, surprising Durant, who was now all ears. "I think," said Snyder," that probably you have placed them in the hands of a fence or some third party here and that you are afraid to reveal his name or whereabouts or try to contact him." Durant's nervous reply was, "You're goddamn right I'm afraid of him." Snyder felt that progress had been made and hoped that before the afternoon was over, Durant would return the stolen property.

Following their conversation, Durant paced the floor and then asked to be permitted to talk with Nash. He was allowed to do so, and Keeler observed their interview through the one-way mirror. Nash urged Durant to tell the entire truth and assist in the recovery of the jewels. She put her arm around him and kissed him, patted him on the back, and implored him to tell the whole story. After considerable conversation between them, Durant agreed with his wife: "Yes, I think I better get the jewels back in your interest and in our interest." Pierce entered the room as if on cue, and immediately Durant said, in substance, "Okay, I've decided this is the best thing to do for everyone's sake, particularly for my wife. We'll get the jewels back. I need your promise, though, that the man who has them will not be implicated." No definite promise was made by the army investigators, however.

Lieutenant Colonel Pierce then asked Durant if he had really been trying to recover the jewels during the past week, and Durant replied, "Well, I have contacted the individuals who have the jewels, but I really didn't make an effort to get them back; but now I have changed my mind, and I will make every effort possible to recover them."

Pierce also asked Durant if there were others involved in the Kronberg jewelry theft, and he replied that Major Watson, Captain Nash, Corporal Carlton, and himself were the only ones involved.

At that time, Durant, Nash, Salb, Pierce, Snyder, and WAAC Sergeant DeYoung went down half a block to the elegant Martin's Restaurant at 120 South LaSalle Street. Durant asked Keeler, "How can we get it without the man who has them being identified?" They discussed several procedures, and finally Durant offered to call him, have him take the jewels, which were in a small stationery box, to one of the railroad stations, and deposit them in a baggage locker. Keeler suggested then that the key be placed in an envelope and left under a fictitious name, with a cigar counter cashier at a newsstand.

They then went to an open public telephone. Durant claimed to have forgotten the number of the man he had to contact and said he would obtain it from another friend. Keeler stood near him while he placed the call; Durant apparently obtained the number and placed the second call. Durant gave instructions to the second party to leave the entire box of loose stones in a locker at some railroad station and to leave the keys as suggested. When he finished the call, he said, "It's all arranged; he's going to follow instructions and we'll get another call back at eight-thirty P.M. regarding the location of the locker." From there the party drove over to Keeler's apartment and lounged away the afternoon.

At approximately 8:00 P.M. the same group that had been in Martin's Restaurant earlier left Keeler's apartment in army cars for the restaurant to receive the expected call. At eight-thirty, the call was received. "Everything is all right. We can get them anytime we want to," claimed Durant. Then he and Lieutenant Colonel Pierce and Major Salb went to the Illinois Central Railroad Station. There Durant walked to a telephone stand, reached up over the light above the stand, and removed a key, then proceeded to one of the dime-in-the-slot steel baggage check-in lockers, opened it, and took out a small light parcel wrapped in brown paper. He handed the package to Major Salb and asked that it be opened only in his presence. To this request, Pierce and Salb consented. The four officers then returned to Martin's Restaurant and rejoined the other members of their party, with Salb tightly clutching the box.

They then returned to Dr. Keeler's office, where Durant indicated to Dr. Snyder that he would like a private conversation with him. They entered a private office, and Durant said, "I don't know how much our conversation this afternoon had to do with my getting these jewels back, but at any rate I want to thank you for the way you talked to me and the friendly attitude which you have toward me. Well, what I want to talk to you about now is, I don't know what to do from this point on. They will want me to sign statements and tell everything I know, and I don't know whether I ought to do that, or just let them carry the ball from this point."

Dr. Snyder replied that he "couldn't conceive of how such an attitude or procedure would improve his condition, that the best way out of it would be for him to do everything that he could possibly do to undo that which had been done." Snyder then said that it was a pity that the jewels had been broken up, to which Durant replied, "Yes, that's too bad. I am sorry we did it." Later in the conversation Snyder asked, "How in the world did you get involved in this mess anyway?" Durant replied that it was simply looting and made the remark to the effect that at the time this happened, everyone was carrying everything they could out of Germany and nothing was being done about it.

When their conversation ended, Durant expressed a desire to see the jewels. The box, which had previously been used for stationery, was opened in Keeler's office by Major Salb in the presence of Colonel Durant, Lieutenant Colonel Pierce Dr. Keeler, and Dr. Snyder. After slitting open the box, they found several small packets, each sealed with gum paper; there was also something wrapped in a sock. Several stones of different kinds and sizes were loose in the box. Its contents and their estimated value were as follows:

Diamonds, 566.33 carats	$127,000
Amethysts, 65 stones	5,674
Emeralds, 67 stones	138,794
Sapphires, 3	11,344
Turquoise pearls and other valuables	36,461
Total 1946 value	$319,273

Suddenly Durant exclaimed angrily, "I've been double-crossed; the bigger stones are missing!" Durant looked up as if in dismay and inferred that Salb and Keeler had opened the box previous to his coming upstairs and had taken some of the jewels to double-cross him. They assured him that nothing had been removed from the box and that it would be ridiculous for them to put themselves in such a position. He then asked to talk to Dr. Snyder again, who in turn assured him that nothing had been removed.

He then left the office and from a public phone booth made another telephone call, after which he said, "They admitted that they didn't put all of the stones in there." Durant then stated that he thought he would be able to get the other stones but that their recovery would be difficult and that he would be unable to get the others until Monday, June 10. It was now one-thirty in the morning of Saturday, June 8.

The paper packets in the package secured by Durant bore longhand notation as follows: "miniatures," "V.L.," "seed pearls," "very small colored," "Large colors semi-prec," "pearls," "E.R.S." and "M." The contents were then replaced in the box and retied. The box of jewelry, along with Durant and Nash, was taken to a waiting army car.

In anticipation of their departure for Washington, Durant and Major Salb then went to check on Durant's Hudson, which was in the army garage in Chicago, to secure the clothing and personal equipment belonging to Durant. Durant reached into the glove compartment of the car and took out an automatic pistol and holster, which he handed to Major Salb, saying, "I guess you'll want this, too." Durant said that the pistol had not been signed for and that it was not on receipt to him.

Also on that same Friday night, Leonard Keeler gave to the press U.S. Army Signal Corps photographs showing a portion of the loot acquired from the home of Eileen Lonergan in Hudson, Wisconsin. Keeler would not discuss the case, but apparently wanted the publicity connected with the case because of the polygraph tie-in. Concurrently, the *Chicago Daily Tribune* published the story in its Saturday edition, and the story was immediately picked up by papers throughout the world.

While Keeler was displaying his photographs, the U.S. Army had placed on exhibit in the Pentagon the valuables recovered so far. Under heavy guard in a secluded office, the valuables were heaped on a black cloth–covered table some fifteen feet long and four feet wide. Eye blinding in brilliance, the display included four handfuls of cut diamonds lying on as many sheets of ordinary typewriter paper. A pile of rough-cut emeralds was surrounded by a double handful of pearls. A line of diamonds and ruby bracelets valued at at least twenty-five thousand dollars each bisected the table. There were miniatures of porcelain, trinkets, and a diamond ring with a reported twelve carats. One of the miniatures contained the portrait of Queen Victoria in her youth. On close examination, one could see that the gold casing containing a glass cover had been ripped from the tiny minature. On one side of the table was a thirty-six-piece solid-gold table service with handles of precious stones.

Among the Hesse family heirlooms were nine bound volumes of letters written to Queen Victoria of England by her daughter. Also lying on the table was a Bible which Queen Victoria had received from an aunt and had in turn presented to her daughter with the following inscription in Queen Victoria's own hand:

> This Bible given me by our dear late aunt when I was a child I give to you, my beloved child, Victoria, in recollection of the last Sunday we went to church together before you leave your parental roof and your beloved native land. May He who gives us such words of comfort and hope help and protect you and your dear, excellent husband and may you both ever be a blessing to one another and to your country and to your parents and relations. This is the fervent prayer of your devoted mother, Victoria, January 31, 1858.

An autographed book in the collection contained the signature "Elizabeth, Princess of Great Britany, 1613."

The following day, Saturday, June 8, when the investigators along with Durant and Nash returned to Washington, Durant called his brother and requested that he visit him at Fort Myer, where he was being detained. When James arrived, Durant gave him $600 in cash, two $100 money orders issued overseas and made payable to himself, his May 1946 paycheck in the amount of $422.87, a refund check of $6.83 from the Burrows Motor Company, a personal check in the amount of $1,350 drawn on the First and Merchants National Bank of Virginia, and the title to the 1946 Hudson.

While this was going on, Pierce and Salb were consulting with their superior officers, and it was decided that they should return to Chicago, since Durant had assured them that he would try to get back more of the missing stones. On Sunday, June 9, Durant, Pierce, and Salb left for Chicago by B & O Railroad, arriving the next morning at 8:15. To avoid recognition, Colonel Durant was dressed in the uniform of a Corps of Military Police major.

Durant had avowed that he could not make telephone contact before 1:00 P.M., so the men spent the morning at the movies. At one o'clock Durant made the telephone call and soon received one back at the same booth, after which he remarked, "It looks good," but averred that he would have to make another call at 4:15. After making that call and receiving one in return, he stated, "We will get them back." Then, at Durant's direction, the group went to the Northwestern Railroad Station, and Durant searched about for some time. After considerable time spent in searching, Durant told Pierce and Salb that the jewels had been placed in a parcel checkroom and that the claim check was supposed to have been placed behind the instruction plate in the sixth telephone booth across from the parcel checkroom. Then Pierce and Salb joined in a fruitless search for a sixth phone booth. A little later Durant said that he had the number in case anything went wrong; it was 110, he claimed. They then went to the parcel checkroom and found out that the storage bin numbers did not go as high as 110. Out of desperation they located a coin locker numbered 110 and had the train security force open the locker. It contained only a suitcase and not the package for which they were searching.

At Pierce's request, Durant made another telephone call and then said that they were in the wrong train station and that they would have to go to the LaSalle Street Station. He explained that he had received his previous instructions from a third person, but that now he had received them directly from the source.

They proceeded immediately to the LaSalle Street Station, and Durant led them directly to the parcel checkroom and located a bank of six phone booths adjacent to the checkroom. He entered the sixth booth and emerged with a note printed on a torn piece of blank telegram message paper that he had retrieved from behind the instruction plate. It was printed in ink as follows: "Too bad my hat knocked your ticket off. Guess I have the right to keep the baggage." The note had been stuck to the plate with a wad of chewing gum.

They immediately went to the parcel checkroom and inquired about a package stored under claim check number 110. They were told that the number 110 only referred to the bin in which the parcel was checked. Durant told Malcolm C. Smith, the attendant, that the package they were seeking was as long as a shoe box, but not so deep, and wrapped in brown paper. Smith seemed to recall such a package and that it had been left overnight and placed in storage. He remembered it because the package felt light and had been left for longer than usual without being picked up. He searched for it and returned saying that it had been called for and the claim check surrendered at about ten o'clock that morning, June 10. At Pierce's request, Smith searched through the claim checks that had been returned and produced a stub which bore the number 110 written in black pencil across the face. It bore a time stamp indicating that it had been presented for pickup at ten o'clock that morning. The back of the check also contained a bit of reddish sticky substance and appeared as if a layer of the light cardboard from which it had been made had been stripped from it. This indicated that the ticket had been stuck to the back of the telephone instruction plate.

Pierce made further inquiries, and the thirty-three-year-old Smith claimed that the man who had picked up the package was of medium height, with brown curly hair, and was wearing a light blue suit which had stripes and dots woven into it. Smith said that at that time, he had checked the bin but had not been able to locate the parcel, and he had asked the man to describe it. The man had been very nervous and said, "I am picking up the package for a friend." Smith had finally located the parcel and presented it to the man, charging him the thirty cents due for storage.

Lieutenant Colonel Pierce asked Durant to make another call and tell his contact what had happened, that the remaining jewels had not been recovered and to ask him if he could help in the recovery. Durant told Pierce that he had the utmost confidence in these people and he knew for a moral certainty that they had no connection with what had happened. He refused to tell Pierce or Salb the name or phone number of the contact. Durant further refused to make any effort to help locate the remainder of the loot, and from that point on he refused to give any details about his part in the robbery of the Hesse jewels.

This large box of jewels has never been recovered.

That night the men returned by army plane to Bolling Field, near Washington, D.C.

What was it in the message "Too bad my hat knocked your ticket off. Guess I have the right to keep the baggage" that scared Durant and kept him from making further efforts to retrieve the lion's share of the valuables? Whatever it was, Durant made good on his word, as he continued to refuse to make a written or oral statement concerning one of the greatest robberies of all time.

On June 12, Durant called the office of the CID and said that he would like to discuss the case involving his brother. The following day at 9:00 A.M., both James and his wife, Helen, arrived at the branch and were interviewed by Lieutenant Colonel Pierce and Major Salb. They stated that they knew nothing about the jewels but signed a certified statement swearing that Durant had mailed to them a package the approximate size of a cigar box, wrapped in brown paper and tied with heavy string. They further admitted that the package was addressed to Colonel Jack Durant. The statement included the fact that Colonel Durant picked up considerable mail at his brother's house and read it all except for the package, which Durant took unopened with him when he left his brother's.

That same day, Major Salb drove out to their house, looked it over, and recovered several small miscellaneous items that had been sent to them by Durant.

On June 14, Durant told Pierce and Salb that his brother James had more information about the case which he could give them. The two investigators drove out to Fort Myer to discuss the case with the two brothers. They asked Durant if he wanted them to discuss the case in his presence, and he said no. The two investigators then took James out to their car, where they discussed the theft of the jewels once more. Based on information from James, Pierce and Salb left immediately for Chicago for the purpose of interviewing Dr. Reuben Mark and also to recover the jewels from Chicago customs. As it turned out, they had no luck, but they did order Captain John W. Nichols to follow up on the case.

On or about June 17, James Durant began to panic at the publicity given the theft of the Hesse crown jewels and his brother's implication in the crime. He did not want to be caught red-handed with the gold wire that his brother had given him, so he drove along the 200 block of George Mason Road in Falls Church and tossed the gold wire into the underbrush.

On June 19, James Durant and Captain Thomas R. Smith, an agent of the Provost Marshal General, drove to the 200 block on George Mason Road and searched the underbrush, where they recovered the gold wire. From this site they drove to Leesburg Pike southward from the intersection of U.S. 50 and entered the thick undergrowth. At the base of a tree thirty feet from the road, Captain Smith dug up the jar which James had sealed and into which he had placed the twenty-eight thousand dollars in cash Colonel Durant had given him on June 1. This money of assorted denominations was wrapped in twenty-eight packages bound with bill straps. Some of the information on the straps had been altered in ink, and the bills had been issued from two to six years before. Most had been issued from the Federal Reserve bank in Chicago, which indicated that the bills were most likely obtained in that area.

On June 20, Captain Thomas R. Smith and James Durant drove to James's home, where Smith examined Colonel Durant's personal effects in the attic where they had been stored, and attempted to determine whether any article could be identified as belonging to the Hesse family. No article examined could be identified as such. On completing the search, Smith and James Durant drove to the location where on May 18 Colonel Durant and his brother had buried the jar containing the white envelopes and loose amethysts and recovered the cap, bottom, and various other pieces of the broken jar. They further sifted the dirt in the immediate area in an effort to recover any small jewels that might have been lost when Durant broke the jar, but to no avail.

While U.S. investigators were busy hammering away at the case, the CID in Germany was questioning Major David Watson about his participation in the Hesse affair. Watson was arrested on Friday night, June 7, 1946.

On June 9, Watson told the CID about his involvement and about his trips to Northern Ireland. He gave a CID agent the following pathetic letter to hand-carry to Peggy Harvey:

9 June 1946

Peggy beloved

The papers have probably told you what has happened and

now I want you to return all of the things I gave you and left with you to keep.

I honestly didn't believe that taking the things was wrong, darling—but the Army thinks so and I'll have to pay for it

Please don't hold back anything as I haven't lied in this case and shall continue to tell the truth. I am giving to Benzell who is delivering this an itemized list of the things that I can recollect. I may not remember everything.

They have promised me to keep your name and all references to you out of this.

I can never forgive myself for having let you in for worry and unhappiness, darling. I will write you a long letter right away.

Mommie, I am so scared and I love you so much.

David*

The army investigator hastened to Belfast and retrieved the mirror, the pearl surrounded by diamonds, and the contents of the package that Watson had given Peggy Harvey. The pearl surrounded by diamonds was identified as a part of the pearl-and-diamond diadem that was one of the principal Hesse family jewels. This diadem was the first item on the inventory of the house jewels which were placed in the zinc-lined box. Following his interrogation, Watson was confined in the Post Guardhouse in Frankfurt, Germany. He was incarcerated with several enlisted men who were either awaiting trial or had been sentenced to serve up to six months only. Being the only officer in the brig was a torment to himself and to his father, who was visiting and who had once told his son not to return home unless he became a major. Now the son was dishonored.

During this time the Chicago police received an anonymous handwritten letter from Ireland that read: "This Major Watson spent many of his leaves at Peggy Harvey, Antrim Road Belfast, N.I. Gave presents of valuable jewels valued at jeweller in Belfast for hundreds of pounds also valuable ornaments and wine."

Meanwhile, Captain John Nichols flew from Washington to Chicago as the interviews with Dr. Mark continued. Mark told Nichols off the record that Rose Griffith was well acquainted with Durant and that she had dated him quite a bit, but once Nash appeared she had become an offensive object. It is unknown why Mark would make this

---

* Several letters written to the Department of Army from Mrs. Harvey have been removed from the Archives. One can only guess what they contained.

statement, since the four of them had double-dated on many occasions. Of these interviews, Nichols wrote, "Dr. Mark is an extremely nervous individual and gives the impression that he might be hiding something, but a very thorough questioning and attempts to find discrepancies in his story were to no avail. The best description that I can give of Dr. Mark is that he is slick or oily."[1]

Nichols also traced the phone calls Durant had made from the hotels he had stayed in while in Chicago. The calls were to Dr. Reuben Mark; Jim Archambault, 6728 Lemoi Lincolnwood Towers; Atena Sheet Metal Works, 412 North State Street; Joseph Dullar—Durant's former father-in-law—and Mr. and Mrs. Arthur Rocque, 1322 Euclid Street, Berwyn, Illinois. Jim Archambault was a friend of Dr. Mark's and also a partner of Dr. Mark's in the ownership of Atena Sheet Metal Works. The CID continued to tail Mark and followed him to Lake Louise, Canada, where he registered as none other than "Jim Archambault." The CID continued to follow the Mark/Archambault angle but could not develop any further leads. Nichols suspected that Mark might be a fence and wrote, "The Dr. Mark referred to in the preceding paragraphs would be a likely suspect."

Nichols then teamed up with Phil G. Fraser, a customs agent, and they drove south in search of Roy C. Carlton. His military records indicated that Carlton lived in Texarkana. They arrived in Texarkana the morning of June 10, and after a thorough search of local draft board records for both the Texas and the Arkansas sides of the border, as well as for the Red River ordnance plant, they failed to find a record of residence for Carlton. Finally, at the post office, they found a change of address from 605 Olive Street, Texarkana, to Box 1615, Kilgore, Texas. They then drove to Kilgore.

With the assistance of the postmaster in Kilgore, they learned that Carlton was living with his wife at 1009 Broadway. From the postmaster they learned that Carlton had the reputation of being a hard worker and had never been in trouble to anyone's knowledge.

When they arrived at Carlton's home in the early afternoon on June 12, he met them at the door and stated that he had been expecting a visit from someone investigating the case of the jewel theft, which had been filling the papers for the last few days. He stated that he had read about the theft in the newspaper and that because of the description and the fact that it had taken place at the castle in which he had been stationed, he knew that he was the one that they were referring to as having discovered the cache. He said that immediately upon reading the newspaper article, he had gone to the local police and tried to turn himself in as the army corporal who had discovered the gems. The city police would not take his report, but advised him to go to Tyler, Texas, and report to FBI agent Glen White. Carlton was unable to locate White at his home or office on June 8, so he returned home and waited for someone to call on him.

Agent Phil Fraser then asked Carlton if he would agree to make a sworn statement. Carlton agreed, and Fraser administered the duly sworn oath and asked Carlton several questions relating to the valuables taken from the Kronberg Castle. Fraser asked him if he had ever been in any trouble with the police. Carlton responded that in 1939 he had been arrested in Fairfield, Illinois, for being drunk. Later, under oath, Carlton told a quite different story. He stated that a German and not he had found the hidden spot in the basement and had notified him. As the German dug, he, Carlton, went to get Nash. After the German dug up the valuables, he and the German helped Captain Nash take the wrapped valuables to her room, and he never knew what was recovered until he read about it in the paper. The two investigators now knew that either Carlton was lying or everyone else was, including the two Germans who had helped remove the valuables from the subcellar.

Still under oath, Carlton was questioned as to when he had last seen Nash. The two agents were astonished when Carlton replied, "As I recall, it was the fifth of April last. They said they were going to New Mexico and had been to Little Rock, so they stopped off here." The agent then asked who were "they"? And only then did they find out that Durant had been traveling with Nash. Carlton told about their conversation concerning sending Durant's two boys to school in New Mexico. When asked about Durant and Nash's relationship in Germany, Carlton replied that "from my point of view they were going steady."

During the interrogation, Carlton admitted that he had taken items from the castle but not from the cache in the basement. As Carlton told it, "I picked up the silverware in the dining room of the castle and sent it to the States by mail, addressed to my wife, as a souvenir. I got the gold watch out of the silver room of the castle and sent it back by mail to my wife, too. The clock was given to me as a present by the old lady who was secretary to the castle. I sent it back by mail as a gift to my wife."

Following this questioning of Carlton, Agent Phil Fraser seized the following items: six sterling silver dinner forks, six sterling silver knives, eight sterling silver salad forks, and one sterling silver sherbet server (all of these bearing the raised emblem of the crown on their handles); one small gold ladies' watch with hunting case and with engraved enamel emblem of the crown and the monogram "MM"; one gold watch chain, set with pearls; and one large bronze clock with figurines cast from pewter.

The agents decided not to arrest Carlton for the minor offense of evading a customs declaration on a small amount because they wanted him to testify for the government and did not want to antagonize him and decrease his value as a witness. He was thus asked if he would be willing to appear as a witness for the United States and offer testimony in the case against Captain Nash, Colonel Durant, and others. Carlton immediately indicated his willingness to do this anywhere in the United States, but expressed deep concern about having to return overseas. His chief objection was that boat travel made him violently ill. The agents assured him that air transport would be arranged. Carlton then asked for a chance to discuss it with his family, saying that he would give them a firm answer the next day.

After talking to his family, Carlton decided to approach Fred Erisman, a lawyer in nearby Longview, Texas. After a thorough discussion with Carlton and the two agents, Erisman agreed that in order to protect his own interests against the accusations being made by others, it would be much better for Carlton to be present as a witness than to remain at home silent.

Carlton then gave his word that at no time would he leave his home for any extended period unless he left word with his family and local police authorities as to where he could be reached. Erisman further vouched that any time anyone wanted to reach Carlton, either for the purpose of testimony or to obtain additional information, he would see that Carlton was made available. Erisman added that he had known Carlton and his family for many years and that there was no danger whatsoever that Carlton would try to leave town. A little later Carlton insisted that his lawyer be permitted to travel to Germany at Carlton's expense and be present during his testimony at the court-martial.

On June 17, 1946, Colonel Durant and Captain Nash, accompanied by Lieutenant Colonel Pierce and Sergeant Elizabeth DeYoung, flew from Washington to Bermuda, then on to the Azores and from there to Orly Field, Paris, a twenty-seven-hour trip and a typical route to Europe in those days. After an overnight layover in Paris, they changed planes and flew the remaining two-hour trip to Frankfurt, Germany. There they were placed in the custody of Headquarters Command, U.S. Forces, European Theater, and were held under armed guard at the plush military-requisitioned Carlton Hotel in Frankfurt, where Nash and Durant were assigned to separate rooms, even though they were now man and wife. The rooms were guarded, and all meals were served in the rooms. They were kept incommunicado.

That same day, at seven in the morning, the safe containing the jewels was opened in the Pentagon and the jewels transferred by Major Salb to two field safes. The field safes were then securely locked and sealed on the outside with several blobs of sealing wax into which Major Salb pressed his thumb while the wax was still warm. The safes were then loaded into a truck and, accompanied by a jeep filled with guards, driven to the train station. The valuables departed Washington in a B & O drawing-room car named *Maspero*, accompanied by Salb and twelve enlisted men. Upon arrival in Staten Island, the safes were placed in a specially prepared vault aboard the *Willard A. Holbrook*. The ship departed Staten Island the following day and arrived in Bremerhaven on June 28. From there they were sent by train to Frankfurt, Germany, and immediately taken to the Reichsbank and placed in the vault.

On July 8 the recovered jewels were taken out of the bank vault in Frankfurt under tight security to the I. G. Farben building, which was now used as headquarters for the U.S. European Command. During the day, the jewels were unwrapped and arranged for display. Under guard they remained that night in the building, and the following day Her Royal Highness the seventy-four-year-old Landgrafin Margarethe von Hesse, the eldest living member of the house of Hesse; Princess Sophia of Hesse, widow of Prince Christoph of Hesse; Prince Richard von Hesse, son of Margarethe; Prince Wolfgang von Hessen, son of Margarethe; Heinrich Lange; Mrs. Marga von Bochmann; and Dr. Bleibaum were escorted separately through the exhibit and shown the recovered Hesse jewels.

As the Landgrafin moved slowly among the diamonds, rubies, emeralds, and sapphires, she observed that at least half of the jewels were missing, including nine diamond-studded tiaras. To show how some of the missing pieces looked, the Landgrafin hauled out several photographs of members of the house of Hesse. One of the four portraits showed her daughter-in-law, the late Princess Mafalda of Italy, wearing a tiara of diamonds and pearls and a necklace with diamonds that looked like pendants of a chandelier. The Landgrafin and her family members were told by U.S. Army officials that they could not discuss the missing valuables with the press or with each other.

After several hours the royal family was dismissed and the press allowed in to ask questions and photograph the valuables. No one outside of the royal family and the investigators of the crime yet knew that the most valuable jewels, half of the collection, were still missing. Neither were they told that the jewels had been dismantled and were now worth only a fraction of their original value.

Meanwhile, the army was trying to recover many of the items that had been distributed throughout the United States. Their first investigation centered around Gladys B. Madison, sister of Kathleen Nash. The mail clerk in Germany had remembered Madison's name and mailing address in Hollywood. The investigators then set out to talk with Mrs. Madison at 7570 De Longpre Avenue, Hollywood. Much to their desappointment, they found out that she had taken a plane to Minneapolis. They decided to continue on to Hudson, Wisconsin.

The U.S. Army provost marshal's office was notified in St. Paul. Captain Aaron Clarno contacted Mrs. Madison by phone and arranged to meet her at the office of the city attorney on the night of June 17. She met Clarno at the appointed time and was immediately told that the military was not interested in prosecuting her but wanted merely to obtain information regarding certain jewels. Madison refused to be questioned except in the presence of her attorney. When pressed, she absolutely refused to make a statement. Captain Clarno then asked about the sale of two gems to the Slavick Jewelry Company. After a brief hesitation, and unaware that the diamonds had been recovered, she grew jittery. She finally agreed to meet with Clarno in his office the following day at 2:00 P.M., adding that "in the meanwhile I'll contact my attorney."

The following day she called and advised Clarno that her attorney, Mr. Neeb in Los Angeles, advised her not to keep her appointment. She said that she was on her way to the north woods by car for a rest and would not disclose her destination. She said that she would be available at her home in ten days to two weeks.

But in a surprise move she mailed to the proper army authorities in Washington a very beautiful bracelet with eighteen diamonds in it, a magnificenct men's watch, and an antique watch and chain with a little matchbox attached to it that was made of gold and blue enamel. Upon receipt of the items, the army contacted Madison, who admitted that the items had been sent to her by her sister, Captain Nash. She tried hard to give the impression that she was honest and aboveboard, but the army did buy her act; they had a hunch that she had more. And she did.

In the meantime, Eldon O. Haldane, an investigator in Los Angeles, was busy chatting with Mrs. Madison's coworkers at the United Rexall drugstore in Hollywood. The two clerks admitted that Madison had shown them a large leather purse and had said that her sister had sent her the bag, with two unmounted old mine-cut diamonds concealed inside. It was true: Madison had received a letter from Nash promising her a handbag for Christmas. The bag arrived a bit late for the holiday, but inside was a plain white envelope containing the two gems.

Haldane began checking with jewelry stores in the area and soon learned that Mrs. Madison had sold the diamonds to the Slavick Jewelry Company in Los Angeles for five hundred dollars on March 7, 1946, claiming that they were family jewels that had recently been mailed to her. According to the jewelry salesman, Mrs. Madison appeared at ease, well poised, and well groomed. She did nothing to arouse suspicion.

Later, to increase their value, the jewelry store recut the 1.29- and 1.42-carat stones to modern shapes and proportions. The finished weights of the stones were .82 and .95 carats. The investigators confiscated the stones from the Slavicks and set out to talk with Mrs. Madison at her home in Hollywood. But by this time she was either in Minneapolis or nearby Hudson, Wisconsin.

Following Mrs. Madison's return from Wisconsin, the army met with the provost marshal's office in Los Angeles and continued the investigation. On July 3 they arranged a meeting with Madison and U.S. Customs. At the customs office, applying pressure, the authorities presented the typed statements of the two Rexall employees. Madison was not aware that the two diamonds had been recovered from the Slavick Jewelry Company. They talked on and on, but Mrs. Madison would not budge. She huffily stated that she did not have any remaining valuables and denied the army's request to search her house. Everyone knew that she still had the handbag.

As the army recorded it:

> The thing that really riles us up on it is because she held out on us and pretended to be so fair and aboveboard and all the time she had this knowledge of other stones which she had sold and now she won't say anything about them. She has put us off,

she's given us every dodge, and snuck away from the Provost Marshal, the Treasury, and the U.S. Attorney's office.

In other words, lacking clear-cut authorization because she was nonmilitary, there was nothing the army could do to continue its investigation of Mrs. Madison. This was unfortunate, as we shall see later.

The same conditions applied to Durant's civilian brother James. Durant's investigators knew that James had leased and/or had access to a large deposit box at the National Savings and Trust Company, Fifteenth Street and New York Avenue, N.W., in Washington. On May 13, 1946, Colonel Durant had emptied the box and had had in his possession a large quantity of stolen jewels.

All banks in Washington, Chicago, and Richmond had been checked for safe deposit boxes that might have been used by Durant and his brother, but none was located other than the now empty box at the National Savings and Trust Company.

James Durant had previously waived his constitutional rights and permitted a search of his house, but he refused to waive such rights when it came to opening the deposit box for representatives of the U. S. government, in spite of the fact that he executed a sworn statement to the effect that none of the property in the box was his property and that anything that might be inside was the property of his brother. The army was prohibited by civilian law from completing the search.

On August 3, 1946, the army agreed to turn Durant's prized Hudson over to James. Unable to travel to Chicago, Durant made arrangements for Mr. Foster W. Gallagher to pick up the automobile. Gallagher arrived on August 23 and, in addition to getting the Hudson, signed for an Eastman Kodak, a Zenith long-distance radio, and miscellaneous travel bags and clothing, which in turn were handed over to James Durant.

During the investigation, Julius H. Buchman wrote General Dwight D. Eisenhower a letter which contained the following two paragraphs:

> Consequently, I have carefully read and analyzed the varying newspaper accounts which are not to my knowledge completely accurate.
> I feel that this is the proper time to re-examine other similar incidents which came to my attention during the period I

served as MFA&A Specialist Officer of the Frankfurt Military
Government Detachment with jurisdiction in the SHAEF
enclave and later in the security zone of United States Forces
European Theater (USFET).

All Buchman received was a kindly thank-you letter. Buchman
would later testify at Durant's trial, however. The publicity generated by
newspapers prompted more than a few persons to write the army. One
of the more sympathetic letters was from Rita L. McCarron of
Cheyenne, Wyoming, who wrote that from the photograph in the
Denver Rocky Mountain News she believed that it was Kathleen Nash
Durant who had stolen her mink coat on March 2, 1944. She wrote, "I
want the coat back as it was a gift of my son who died in the Pacific."
The army responded by saying that based on the available evidence,
Nash was not a suspect in the theft of the fur, at least. There were
several letters like the one from Jack Werst, residing in the Waldorf-
Astoria Hotel in New York. Mr. Werst had cabled Landgräfin Margarethe with an offer to pay top dollar for the recovered jewels. He
further cabled the army: "My syndicate, which can furnish finest
United States bank references, ready to pay cash immediately. If
interested, please communicate with Provost Marshal General, Frankfurt area, authorizing him to contact me through military channels here
for permission to examine jewels." Apparently the army ignored Mr.
Werst's request.

16

The Trials

Most critical in the trial of Durant was the testimony of his brother James Durant and the testimony of Durant's former girlfriend Martha Lucille Orwig. In the beginning, both had agreed to travel to Germany at the army's expense and testify against Durant. Both asked the army not to publicize their involvement in the case, but shortly after, a reference to Orwig was made in *Newsweek* magazine. The article stated that "a beautiful young darkheaded girl" had unwittingly brought some of the gems from England to the United States for Durant. Angered by the story, Orwig stated that she would no longer cooperate with the army in the court-martial. After another article appeared under the headline "Beauty Used as Dupe for Gem Transfer," Orwig absolutely refused to travel to Germany.

The army tried tracking down the leaked stories. Only General Lucius Clay and his staff in Berlin were aware that the original leak to *Newsweek* was made by Captains Edith Standen and Everett P. Lesley. Army officials believed that the present leaks were not from the same source and tracked them to Miss Vada Ward. Ward was an American civilian employed by the U.S. Army in Europe and had attended a football game the previous fall with Colonel Durant. Colonel Owen Summers wrote to the investigators, "You may wish to check into this matter and if she is representing *Newsweek*, get her off our payroll and onto *Newsweek*'s or the *Times Herald* in Washington."

The army tracked Ward to her sister's home in Oswego, Oregon, and sent a radiogram to the commanding general in San Francisco directing his office to interview her as soon as possible. The radiogram suggested that the general should obtain a sworn statement from Miss Ward concerning her acquaintance with Nash, Durant, Watson, and Carlton: "If Miss Ward is uncooperative and if there is any indication whatever that she may be or may have been in possession of any of the Kronberg property, it is recommended that you request the assistance of the local customs collector in procuring from her all information she may have."

The army had no reason to believe that Ward knew any of the particulars of the case, but wanted to harass her and let her know that leaking information to the press was a no-no. The radiogram made mention that she had formerly worked for the *Washington Times-Herald*. There was also a previous memo that erroneously linked Miss Ward with the leaked *Newsweek* article.

Ward was interviewed in Oswego and told investigators that she was escorted to several functions by General Robert Q. Brown, Colonel Durant, and once by Major Watson. She continued that Durant had confided in her more than once that he did not like General Brown and that furthermore, Brown, or "Qunnie," as she called him, had told her that he was disliked by Captain Nash. She claimed to know nothing of the Kronberg theft except what she had read in the papers. She did admit knowing a good friend of Nash's, Major Jack Cunningham, a dental officer from Bar Harbor, Maine.

The investigator, John Quigg, suddenly got more than he had hoped for as he continued his interrogation of Miss Ward. The investigation report states the following:

> Miss Ward was somewhat reticent concerning the activities of Major Cunningham as having been on apparent good terms with Captain Kathleen B. Nash. Although she did not wish to include specific information concerning him in her affidavit, she did furnish additional data during the interrogation. She stated that Major Cunningham had told her that he had sent home numerous souvenirs items and during her visit to his office he had in his possession what appeared to be a Dresden china vase of value of approximately $500, which he said he intended to send home. She said that the services of Major Cunningham were greatly in demand and that it was her belief that many of the items gathered by him were donations from

other U.S. personnel who were grateful for the dental treatment received. She secured her appointment with Major Cunningham through the intercession of General Brown. Miss Ward stated that Major Cunningham was having difficulty packing his numerous belongings when he was preparing to return permanently to the United States, presumably because of the quantity of souvenirs in his possession.

Miss Ward had little respect for Captain Nash and was unable to understand what Colonel Durant saw in her.

Miss Ward was fully cooperative with Quigg and expressed her disgust with the thriving black market and other illegal activities of American personnel in Germany. She categorically denied any knowledge of the removal of jewels or any valuables from the Kronberg Castle. She denied bringing or having made arrangements to bring any illegal items into the United States. Although the army could not tie Ward to the case, they had sent a strong message to her that she was not out of their reach.

The army continued to battle the press and tried to play down the investigation, but on August 1, 1946, the *Washington Times-Herald* ran the following story:

Landgrafin Margarethe of Hesse said today that at least half of the crown jewels of her royal house, including nine diamond-studded tiaras, were still missing after being in the hands of the U.S. Army. The most valuable items have not been found, as we know. The largest stones were not among those we inventoried at Frankfurt, recently. I am afraid that at least half the value of the collection is still missing. There are nine large tiaras and heaps of brooches, earrings, pins and bracelets that have not been found. The jewels they showed us in some cases were just heaps of stones. She said the surprising thing was that dozens of items she identified at army headquarters were personal trinkets—silver pieces from her writing desk and napkin rings— that had not been buried in the Kronberg Castle subcellar where the American soldiers found the more valuable jewelry.

Needless to say, the army was distressed over this story and received an avalanche of inquiries as to whether a search was being continued for the missing jewels. Officials had no comment. Military authorities issued a directive that the army must not enter into any controversy with the press or with the Landgrafin's implication that the army had not recovered her large diamond tiaras.

During this time, the army was desperately trying to locate Captain Leola F. Birmingham; they wanted her statement as evidence against Durant and Nash. By July 12 they had tracked her to Dallas and ordered her to report back to active duty immediately, to Fort Sam Houston, Texas. She complied and from Fort Sam was sent to Chicago and given a polygraph test by the now-in-demand Keeler. She endured five sessions. During the fifth examination, Birmingham continued to react negatively to questions pertaining to her having taken "some objects" not revealed, but she did not respond guiltily to questions concerning the Hesse robbery itself.

The army was seeking information concerning Nash, Watson, and Durant and were most astonished when Birmingham implicated Major General James M. Bevans in the theft of valuables from the Kronberg Castle and other places. Because of his general's rank, however, the army did not follow up on Mrs. Birmingham's leads. From Chicago, Birmingham returned to Fort Sam Houston by Braniff Airways. Once there, she was to remain on active duty, pending instructions from U.S. Forces, European Theater (USFET).

Back in Texas, she requested a leave, claiming that she had urgent personal business involving the sale of a house and divorce proceedings, beginning on August 1. The army asked permission to transfer her to temporary duty in Dallas for several days to take care of these affairs. As their request was being turned down, USFET wired a message to Fort Sam Houston that further retention of Birmingham was not necessary. Based on that message, she returned to civilian status, still on terminal leave. USFET feared Birmingham's testimony concerning a respected general officer.

The U.S. Army judge advocate's procedure for trial was to draw up charges against Nash immediately and proceed at the earliest possible date, since they had the best case against her, in view of her signed confession. The judge advocate also reasoned that while Watson's testimony against Nash was not needed, her testimony against the major was necessary to obtain a conviction against him. With Nash convicted, she had nothing to lose by testifying against her former superior. Charges were also drawn up against Watson, and he was to be tried following Nash. Durant was to be tried following Watson, and as in the case of Nash, Watson, if convicted, would also have nothing to lose by testifying against Durant. To complete the cycle, the judge advocate further felt that if both Nash and Watson were convicted, the process would create an advantageous psychological atmosphere for nailing Durant. They also reasoned that by scheduling Durant's trial last, they would allow more time for the army to gather evidence against the wily colonel.

Thus, the three accused—Durant, Nash, and Watson—were tried by three separate general courts-martial in the newly renovated Headquarters Command Community Center, 17 Finkenhof Strasse, in Frankfurt. The trials would last for more than a year. Early in the process, in mid-October, the ten colonels who comprised the jury received their whiskey ration allotment. They were ready now for the long haul, if need be.

Still wary of the publicity created by the press, the military authorities knew that the trial would draw a large group of spectators. In order to prevent crowding, jostling, and disorder in the court, they printed up 150 tickets, equaling the number of seats in the courtroom. As a spectator entered the building on the lower floor, an MP would issue the ticket. The holder of the coveted ticket would then proceed upstairs to the courtroom, and another MP would appropriate the ticket. Of course, once the 150 tickets were issued, the court would be full, and no one else would be allowed to the second floor. As might be expected, certain distinguished visitors would get in touch with trial officials and send their driver around to pick up the ticket for the day that they desired to attend. Thus, the number of tickets issued to the MPs would be reduced by that number; anyone with a ticket was assured of a seat.

The first to be tried was Captain Kathleen B. Nash Durant. She was charged with larceny, conspiracy, embezzlement, and being AWOL. A week prior to her trial, Nash made the following statement: "The charges of my stealing the $1,500,000 House of Hesse crown jewels are baseless. If the court says that I have committed any of the criminal acts alleged, then thousands of people in this theater of war and in the United States are as guilty as I and have unclean hands."

Her trial began on Monday, August 19, 1946, at 9:00 A.M. in Frankfurt. During the opening arguments, the court overruled a defense motion that the purported confessions had been made under duress, and that she had been questioned without sleep following her arrest—which was true. The court ignored this plea and permitted her written confession to be introduced. In her opening statement, Nash named the participants in the jewel theft: Jack Durant, David Watson, and Roy C. Carlton. She further stated that she had been promised her freedom if she helped the army recover the jewels. She said that she was told by the authorities that the army wanted to keep the theft quiet and was only interested in getting the jewels back, not in prosecuting anyone.

As they would do later during the trials of Watson and Durant, the Hesse family members testified as to the identity of the stolen property. The Landgrafin Margarethe von Hessen introduced herself as such, and the defense counsel immediately objected to the flaunting of a meaningless title in a manner prejudicial to the interest of an American citizen. However, that was her name, and after considerable debate the court agreed that she should be addressed as such. As the court looked down on the seventy-four-year-old, keen-witted, soft-voiced little bird of a woman in a modest black coat, the defense sought to bar her from testifying on the grounds that as an evil Nazi, she had sworn an oath of fidelity and allegiance to Hitler and not God, and that because of this fealty could not be believed. The judge ruled that her membership in the Nazi party did not disqualify her from testifying against an American.

Other members of the Hesse family testified, and their testimony as reported in the *Chicago Tribune Press Service* follows:

> Prince August Wilhelm, a skinny long, bent figure in baggy tweeds, goose-stepped into court with the awkwardness of a Borzoi product of canine breeding. He lifted his feet without coordination, as if he was dragging a ball and chain in his present political confinement....Princess Sophia testified in English with a British accent....The hefty princess identified items which had been buried in the basement of the Kronberg Castle....Another of the Landgrafin's sons, Prince Wolfgang, bald and with the upturned nose and bags under his eyes of his royal British relatives, was recalled to the stand for further identification of the gems.

This was unabashed German bashing, but was what the general public understandably thought of their former enemy, which had been responsible for two terrible world wars.

Carlton left Washington on August 13, and Erisman departed on August 15. In Frankfurt, both men stayed at the army-requisitioned

Carlton Hotel. Attorney Erisman had come all this way at Carlton's expense. The army had taken the precaution of running a background check on Erisman and found out that he was one of the leading lawyers in Texas. For a number of years, Erisman had been state chairman of the Committee on Criminal Law. He was judged absolutely reputable and trustworthy by the army investigator Lindley Beckworth. Based on his investigation the army approved Carlton's request to allow the Texan to accompany him to Germany. They had further extended VIP treatment to Erisman, since they felt that he could be beneficial to the prosecution, particularly in convincing Carlton that the full story must be told.

On August 24, 1946, Carlton, a steamfitter in civilian life, testified for less than thirty minutes. His complete testimomy centered around the removal of valuables from the Kronberg Castle subcellar. Knowing that he was the center of attention for a few brief minutes, he suddenly turned cocky, evasive, and downright "smart-assed," as he placed complete blame on an unidentified German for the discovery of the box of valuables. When asked how the jewels were dug up, for example, Carlton sneeringly answered, "Well, we had to buzz through about an inch and a half of concrete." By his brash attitude, it was evident that Carlton knew he had beaten the system. He was quickly excused and returned to Texas with Erisman. One cannot help wondering why a lawyer would take this much time off to listen to the babble of a steamfitter. Could Carlton have had the goods on some person or persons unknown? Where did Carlton get the necessary funds for Erisman's expensive trip?

Nash's trial lasted six weeks and ended on September, 30, 1946. In his closing appeal for mercy, Nash's lawyer pleaded that the WAAC captain was being made the scapegoat for all the looting done by American soldiers in occupied Germany. Thousands of others, he said, had done the same thing. It was unjust, he added, to point the finger at one woman and say, "You will now pay the penalty for something that the whole world knows that many, many people have done with immunity." His plea fell on deaf military ears, however, and Kathleen B. Nash was sentenced to penal servitude for five years and began her imprisonment in the Federal Reformatory for Women at Anderson, West Virginia. But once in prison the tenacious woman quickly filed a writ of habeas corpus, not pleading innocence, but claiming that the army had lacked jurisdiction to try her at all, since she had been a civilian at the time of her arrest.

Albert J. Watson, the major's father, had arrived in Germany on

June 17. He movingly reported: "My visit to Frankfurt to see my son, Major D. F. Watson, held in connection with the Hessian Jewel Case, is simply to satisfy the desire of any father to be with his son so he can share his anxieties, help dissipate his fears and help him in selection of counsel."

The senior Watson remained in Germany and spent his time finding the best legal counsel he could acquire within the limitations of a court-martial.

Watson's trial followed on October 15 and lasted less than two weeks. Watson had stated to the news media that during his trial he would disclose the names of several generals who had been involved in the Hesse affair. His defense lawyers, John Harlan Amen and Smith Brookhart, tried to subpoena Generals Robert Q. Brown, James M. Bevans, and Harold Roe "Pinky" Bull. The army absolutely refused to have the generals subpoenaed. During the war the softspoken Bull had served as Eisenhower's operations officer. He had been a highly competent staff officer and one of General Omar Bradley's closest friends. Brown also had been a member of Eisenhower's SHAEF staff.

Brown had already been identified by one witness as having prior knowledge of the Hesse robbery, and although he was threatened with a polygraph test, the general never took one. Leola Birmingham had made a transcript in which she outlined some of the involvement of Brown in acquiring looted objects.

But in the most unusual turn of all, someone fingered General Bull, whose Frankfurt home was searched by the CID. Unfortunately for Bull, the CID found his garage crammed with jewelry and other valuables. Immediately both Generals Brown and Bull were returned to the United States, and during the process Brown was demoted to a colonel. Bull in turn filed a sworn statement on October 7, 1946, denying any knowledge of the valuables found in his garage. The defense attorneys, Amen and Brookhart, only had what Watson had told them to go on. They were not aware of Colonel Durant's polygraph test and of CID investigations of the generals' activities, and the prosecution worked hard to keep it that way.

General B. M. Bryan, provost marshal general, went so far as to rule that the candor of the investigative reports—candor normally accepted as an essential element of good reporting—"resulted in their containing much derogatory material and sometimes scandalous information which had no relation to the case whatever." Bryan further wrote that "to make the criminal investigation reports available to the defense would serve no useful purpose and would be detrimental to the Army's criminal investigation activities." Bryan's ruling was later approved by Kenneth C. Royall, undersecretary of war.

At the beginning of the trial the army contended that the defense wanted the generals on the stand for a "fishing expedition" or to "embarrass" them. General Bull swore that he had no knowledge of why the valuables were in his garage and saw no reason to return to Germany for Watson's trial. Bull took his case directly to Royall, who supported Bull and stated that he did not desire for Bull to be made available for trial. Neither Brown nor Bevans was required to testify during Watson's trial.

The last person to testify at Watson's trial was his father, Albert J. Watson, who took the stand hoping to influence the court. The standard first question concerning name, address, and occupation was only partially responded to by the elder Watson. He gave his name and address but declined to mention his occupation. He did not want it recorded that he worked for Peat, Marwick, Mitchell, and Company, one of the nation's premier consulting firms. Both the defense and prosecution asked him about his relationship with his son and their anticipated plans after the war to enter the frozen food business. Dismissed after only a few minutes, the senior Watson spontaneously addressed the court and in a last-chance desperate plea stated that during the last war, as a major, he had served on several court-martial boards and he knew that they wanted to know more and that they should let him tell what he knew about someone he had known for thirty-three years. Out of respect, the president of the court asked if there were any questions, but both defense and prosecution declined. After the dejected father stepped down, his son, enticed by the spoils of war, was sentenced to confinement for three years.

During Nash's and Watson's trial, the army had taken the necessary steps to obtain passports, clearances, and inoculations and to secure other arrangements for both Orwig and James Durant to travel to Germany on September 3. But because of publicity from newspapers and magazines, Orwig refused to cooperate with the prosecuting attorney. Simultaneously, James Durant began to entertain doubts about testifying against his brother. A few days later both James Durant and Orwig refused to go voluntarily to Germany and had their lawyer, Frank L. Ball, Jr., notify army officials as to their decisions.

Attorney Ball wrote:

If you are not aware that the manner in which the government has attempted to send Mr. Durant to Germany amounts to coercion, I respectfully suggest that you consult some attorney in the Judge Advocate General's Department. Until he consulted me he had never been told that you could not require him to testify in Germany.

In all the time I was in the Service, much of which time I was connected with Court Martial work, I never saw an occasion which so flagrantly violated the rights of individuals or one in which the government exhibited such a complete disregard for the rights of the individuals concerned.[1]

This decision of James Durant and Martha Orwig not to appear in Germany caused a considerable delay. General B. M. Bryan wrote:

This memorandum sets forth my strong belief that the chances of the conviction of Colonel Durant are greatly lessened without the testimony of these two vital witnesses, one of them the brother James E. Durant and the other his former sweetheart, Martha Orwig. I further am convinced that the possibility that either or both of them can be persuaded or compelled to testify personally in Germany are remote. Unless drastic action is taken to meet these difficulties, it is entirely possible that Colonel Durant will be acquitted for lack of convincing testimony against him.

The army, alarmed, had to rethink case strategy: Durant's trial would end up being considerably longer, lasting from December 11, 1946, to April 30, 1947. Captain Glenn Brumbaugh from Los Angeles was the defense counsel for both Nash and Durant. Durant stood mute as all charges and specifications were read, and the trial proceeded as though he had pleaded not guilty. The prosecuting attorney was a former New Yorker, Major Joseph S. Robinson. The forty-year-old Robinson, a graduate of Fordham University, was a competent lawyer and exceptionally qualified for this kind of case.

The first witnesses to take the stand were members of the Hesse family, and for the third time they told their story and identified their stolen property. Their testimony lasted until December 30.

On January 7, 1947, Major Watson took the stand and from the beginning declined to answer any questions, stating that his answers might tend to incriminate him. Infuriated, Robinson, responded, "It couldn't possibly incriminate him. This man was already tried and convicted for his participation in this Kronberg jewelry theft. I have a grant of immunity over this man granting immunity from any further possible prosecution.

Regardless, Watson continued pleading on the grounds of the twenty-fourth Article of War—that he would not answer anything that might tend to incriminate him. Under considerable pressure from the court, Watson stood his ground and did not answer any questions detrimental to Colonel Durant. When asked if he knew Angela Hardie or Peggy Harvey, his two girlfriends, Watson pleaded the twenty-fourth Article of War. In court, Watson suddenly appeared to be an astute, educated, articulate businessman and not the effete Mommie-I-love-you-so-much individual he had seemed to be in his letter to Peggy Harvey.

The following day, Kathleen Nash took the stand, and it was immediately pointed out that a wife and husband may testify in favor of each other, but unless both consent, neither wife nor husband can be a competent witness against the other. At that, Nash was asked, "Do you consent to testify against the accused in this case?" She darted back with a quick "No" and was instantly removed from the stand.

The army had anticipated Kathleen Nash's response and had done everything in its power to prevent her refusal. Investigators had looked into the legality of each of her and Durant's divorces and could find nothing untoward. Then they investigated the couple's marriage in Chicago. At first the army thought that the marriage-in-one-day had violated blood-test-results laws, but they were then informed that the "quickie" practice had begun during the war to expedite military marriages and was proper. They then challenged the fact that Nash had claimed in writing to be thirty-three, and not her true age of forty-three. This point was dismissed when the state of Illinois notified them that an adult's age, precise or not, was required only to ensure that the applicant was not under the legal age of sixteen at the time of the marriage. By the time Nash refused to testify against her husband, the defeated investigators were well aware that the marriage and the subsequent divorces were both legitimate.

Because of the refusal of several key witnesses to travel to Germany, the army felt compelled to try to transfer the trial to Washington, D.C. The witnesses were actually within their rights, for at that time witnesses could not be made to testify outside the boundaries of their federal district court areas. Convinced that the testimonies of James

Durant and Martha Orwig were crucial, in February the army went to the trouble and expense of moving this segment of the trial from Frankfurt to the Pentagon. The mountains of recovered jewels were loaded onto six different airplanes and returned to the United States.

One of the first to testify was Martha Orwig, and mindful of her job with the military, she quickly dropped her objections to testifying against Durant and gave testimony favorable to the prosecution.

The Durants would be another story, for on February 27, James Durant's wife, Helen, began her testimony. She told of the five packages they had received from Colonel Durant while he was in Europe. When asked about the cigar-box-size package that she and her husband had made a signed sworn statement about on June 13, 1946, she grew exceedingly nervous and stammered out that she stood on her constitutional right not to testify in incriminating her husband. The court addressed Mrs. Durant and told her that her husband was not on trial and that her answer was not applicable. At that, Mrs. Durant asked if she could be excused for the day, as she did not feel well. The court suggested that she rest for a short while and then come back.

Four days later, on March 3, she was recalled, and when questioned about the cigar-box-size package, Mrs. Durant replied, "I refuse to say." Then she asked for permission to address the court, at which time she read a prepared statement. The full-page typed statement basically said that her husband was suspected to be a full-fleged conspirator in the case and therefore she declined to answer any further questions. She then read the following:

> I had been advised by the assistant trial judge advocate that the court would send a doctor to examine me while I was in bed, ill and under care of a physician. The trial judge advocate stated that if I did not appear here today he would take the necessary steps to bring me here. In my opinion, I am not in the proper health to be here today, but I have gotten out of bed to be present, in view of these threats.

The court president then told Helen Durant that she must respond to the questions. The prosecutor, Major Robinson, continued questioning her for another two hours. Only on one question did she give a genuine answer, with the innocuous "I couldn't say for sure, I am a housewife and I cook the meals." To the remainder of the questions, Mrs. Durant stubbornly responded with "I decline to answer."

As Mrs. Durant was excused and was leaving the courtroom, Frank L. Ball, Jr., introduced himself to the court and stated that he was the attorney for James Durant and that he moved a motion to quash a subpoena commanding the appearance of his client, James Durant, in the case of *United States vs Colonel Jack W. Durant*. Ball continued on with his motion, stating that the military powers in the European Theater did not have authority over a civilian in the United States. As Ball continued trying to discredit the proceedings, he blurted out, "Now, on the second matter. If, as a matter of fact, that is true—if records have been lost—" At that moment, Ball was immediately interrupted by the court, and one of the members said threateningly, "I suggest that you leave that out." The truth was that the court absolutely did not want it transcribed in the court records that a lieutenant colonel, whom they refused to identify, had destroyed court records containing the testimony of two Washington jewelers. A colonel had taken the stenotyping machine and destroyed the notes in it, raising the question of whom he was trying to protect.

Ball continued for three more hours his denunciation concerning the unlawfulness of the subpoena. At the end of Ball's exhausting argument, the court made only one comment: "The plea is denied."

Then James Durant took the witness stand and, after identifying himself, read a prepared statement that he—like his nervous wife—declined to answer any further questions. The court president then told him the same thing he had told Mrs. Durant, that he must respond to the questions. Major Robinson continued questioning him along the same lines as he had the wife, except he asked detailed questions about the twenty-eight thousand dollars. For more than four hours, James Durant, like his wife before him, responded to each question with an "I decline to answer."

During the trial, the army was trying to follow the money trail resulting from the sale of the missing jewels. In doing this, they examined James Durant's home mortgage to see if it had been paid off or the balance substantially reduced. Both Jack and James Durant's banking accounts were examined to show deposits and withdrawals for 1945 and 1946. The army also made discreet inquiries into how much Frank L. Ball, Jr., had been paid and by whom. The army also wrote the Internal Revenue Service and notified them that the brothers had acquired new wealth since the Hesse jewel theft and that they should include these gains in their IRS calculations.

A few weeks later James Durant was fired from his job in the

General Accounting Office and acquired a job as a tax assessor with the City of Falls Church. During this period the jewels and the court officials made the tiring trip back to Frankfurt for the completion of Jack Durant's trial.

After a stormy trial on both sides of the Atlantic, on April 30, 1947, in Frankfurt, Germany, the prosecutor, Major Joseph S. Robinson, summed up by describing Durant as "the mastermind behind the whole piece of thievery." Robinson wrote, "The honor of the United States is at stake. It is our obligation to see to it that private property in enemy territory which we occupy be respected, and that any interference with such private property for personal gains be justly punished."

As Kathleen Nash looked on, her slim husband, Colonel Jack W. Durant, was found guilty on eight counts and was sentenced to fifteen years of hard labor and dismissed from the army.

That afternoon, under the watchful eyes of guards Captain Edythe S. Cobbe and Tech-4 John Seaquist, Nash left by plane en route to New York for further confinement in the Federal Reformatory for Women in Alderson, West Virginia. Durant remained confined in Germany pending various appeals; he, too, filed the same habeas corpus as had his wife. Watson returned to the United States on May 8 and began serving out his three-year sentence on Governors Island, New York.

Durant returned to the United States in August to begin serving time in Atlanta.

One month later a U.S. district judge ruled in Nash's favor in the petition for the habeas corpus that she had filed. She was released from prison on September 4, 1947. Jack Durant felt sure that he would be released on the same grounds in just a few months. Justice prevailed, however, and on May 4, 1948, the U.S. Fourth Circuit Court of Appeals in Richmond, Virginia, reversed the earlier decision, and Nash was ordered back to federal prison to complete her five-year sentence. This reversal ended Durant's chances for an early release.

During the time of the trials, the Bureau of Customs informed the army that a criminal case report had been prepared by agents of the customs service and forwarded to the U.S. Attorney charging Durant, Nash, Watson, and Carlton and several others with violations of the customs revenue laws and conspiracy to violate these laws. Customs then requested that the jewels be returned to the United States and be available as evidence only and that there would be no attempt to confiscate them. It was further agreed by all parties that within seventy-two hours upon the completion of the civil action, the jewels would be returned to the army for prompt shipment through military channels to U.S. authorities in Germany for return to the rightful owners.

Amazingly, again the jewels were given a plane ride from Frankfurt. On July 24, 1947, two safes containing the jewels were received from prosecutor Robinson and turned over to customs, where they were then retained pending criminal proceedings against various civilians. Apparently, no charges were ever filed, and a trial concerning civilians involved in the Hesse jewel robbery would never take place.

After various appeals, Major David F. Watson ceased to be an officer on July 28, 1947, and on July 30, 1947, was confined to the U.S. Disciplinary Barracks, Greenhaven, New York, for three years. During the appeals process, Albert Watson, now an executive manager for Peat, Marwick, Mitchell, and Company in Kansas City, prepared for retirement in northern California and started a write-in campaign, managing to get 276 letters from military personnel, congressmen, senators, and civilians, all urging clemency for Watson or attesting to his prior good record. There was one exception, a letter from Watson's minister, Sidney H. Buchman. The contents of the letter are unknown, but the army did try to get references concerning Reverend Buchman's character. The remaining letters all contained Watson's officer number and basically were composed in the same rhetoric, as if copied from a master. A typical letter follows:

> It was a great shock to me when I read in the paper that his name was connected with this case for I know of the high ideals he possesses and I felt for sure there was some mistake.
>
> However, if he was implicated, I am sure it must have been the undue influence of his superior military officers who in all probability caught him at a time he was going through a slight weakness, which we all exhibit at times. This war was not sought by the young men of our country, and those who saw service overseas were under terrific strain and tension so it would not be surprising if there was a lapse in judgement. I do know, however, that Major Watson is honest and should not be treated as a criminal. He is too fine a young man for that.

The writers made no mention at that time that the U.S. occupation forces were prosecuting some German war criminals by international tribunals and military commissions for offenses almost identical in nature to those of Nash, Durant, and Watson. It would have been a breach of faith on the part of the American government to, on the one hand, castigate the Germans for such transgressions and, on the other, impose an extremely light sentence upon Major Watson. The shifty trio were, after all, criminals—not merely individuals acting in good faith but somehow naively misapprehending the law.

Watson was experienced in the operation of chain stores, having worked for Safeway, and he and his father had planned to establish a chain of frozen food stores in their community of Piedmont, California. He had made arrangements to build a plant, and during the past two years his father had been sending Watson literature relative to handling frozen food and could hardly wait for him to get out of the army so they could get on with the project. Watson's court-martial and imprisonment put a stop to these plans, but in 1948, Watson, through his father's influence, obtained an excellent high-paying job with Handy-Spot Company of Northern California. As late as December 1955, Watson and his influential friends, including congressmen and senators, were petitioning the army and various other organizations for a presidential pardon. Watson wrote:

> I have lost the privilege of being a citizen of the United States, the privilege to vote, the privilege to participate in local and national political affairs, the privilege to serve my community and my country in Civil Defense and Boy Scout work and the release from the oppression of fear from censorship of my community.

Even though under great pressure, the army refused to yield and recommend a presidential pardon for Watson. As late as March 1956, General Eugene M. Caffey wrote:

> Mr. Watson's principal basis for requesting a pardon lies in the fact that he has apparently been quite successful in the business world. His file has been re-examined, and I am of the opinion that under the foregoing criteria Mr. Watson does not qualify for a favorable recommendation from the Army. The crime for which he was convicted was one of the most notorious of World War II and wrought irreparable injury throughout the world to the United States Army's prestige and reputation for integrity. The Army owes this man nothing. He

is no different than thousands of other former servicemen who have been convicted of crimes and the mere fact that he is living a good life and has influential friends should not be considered sufficient grounds to warrant the Department of the Army giving him a favorable recommendation on his pardon application.

In January 1948 the law firm of G. Vernon Brumbaugh, Durant's defense lawyer and now a civilian, filed in behalf of Jack Durant for the return to him of twenty-eight thousand dollars, a ball of gold wire, one silver stein, and the 106 diamonds that had been seized from the Customs Bureau in Chicago.

Also, in 1949, James Durant hired the services of attorney William J. Hughes, Jr., and filed a claim for the twenty-eight thousand dollars that he had turned over to the army after it had been taken from the mason jar on June 19, 1946. James maintained that his brother had given him the money. The Hesse family had also filed claim for the money, which had been stored in the U.S. Treasury vaults in Washington; the army had turned the money over to the court system to be awarded in accordance with the proper judicial decision. The fate of the twenty-eight thousand dollars is today unknown.

Shortly after the trials, U.S. military authorities investigated two superfluous reports regarding the looting of the Hesse jewels. Although the accounts were mostly centered around domestic disagreements, they are worthy of examination.

On May 29, 1948, Gordon Smith, a former city commissioner in Phoenix, Arizona, met with army CID agent Donald McClellan. Smith stated that he was acquainted with a person by the name of Mary Ping Bell, who was in partnership with a Claudia Ogden. According to Smith the partners had had a recent disagreement, and as a result Bell was bitter toward Ogden to the extent that she alleged to Smith that Ogden had in her possession two of the jewels that were once part of the loot possessed by Jack Durant and Kathleen Nash. Smith went on to say that the jewels were either in a safe deposit box or were being held as security by Del Webb, a prominent contractor in Arizona who was interested in Claudia Ogden. Agent McClellan listened to the story but did not investigate because of the hearsay nature of the escapade. Nothing further happened in the hometown of Kathleen Nash, and the rift involving the joint ownership of a bar continued between Claudia Ogden and Mary Ping Bell.

A month later Sergeant Meyers of the U.S. Army recruiting station in Phoenix received an anonymous phone call that Claudia Ogden was in possession of two large gems that had belonged to the Hesse crown jewel collection. The caller went on to say that the jewels had been obtained from a man by the name of Madison, who owned a used-car lot in Glendale, Arizona, and who was also the brother-in-law of Kathleen Nash. Although the caller would not identify herself, the sergeant could hear the informant telling someone in the room, "Kenny, be quiet," and, "Kenny, don't do that." Meyers, the father of four small children, deduced from the sound of the voice that the caller was talking to a boy between four and six years old.

Sergeant Meyers wrote a letter regarding the phone call and mailed it to the Criminal Investigation Division, headquartered at Fort McArthur, California. Upon receipt of the letter, CID agent Joe O. Barker traveled to Phoenix and interviewed the local CID agent, Donald McClellan. McClellan told Barker about his conversation with Smith, and Barker read McClellan's report. Both agents then interviewed Gordon Smith, who declined to name his source but promised to reveal the identity if it became necessary.

The two agents then went to see Mary Ping Bell, who had purchased a half interest in a cocktail bar and as a result had become a partner with Claudia Ogden. The partnership had continued smoothly until May 1, 1948, when a conflict had arisen between herself and Ogden. Bell said that she had telephoned Ogden's former partner Lee Madison at the Glendale Ford Agency in Glendale. Bell wanted to ask Madison about Ogden's actions during the time they had been business together. During the phone conversation, Madison asked Bell if Ogden had ever spoken of any jewels. When Bell answered affirmatively, Madison snapped, "Well, she had better keep her damn mouth shut or she will get them taken away from her. In fact, she stole them from me!" The informative Bell went on to say that Ogden had referred to the jewels as "museum pieces" and went on to say that she had had the jewels appraised by an expert in Los Angeles by the name of Shipley.

A few days later Robert Shipley, the president of the Gemological Institute of America, Los Angeles, was interviewed and claimed that in February of 1947, Ogden had telephoned him and told him that she was sending him two jewels to be examined. Later, Lee Madison arrived with two jewels, a perfect ten-carat emerald and a five-carat pink diamond. Shipley remembered both stones as being of excellent quality. He did not remember the value of the jewels and stated that no records were kept by his firm.

The army CID investigators questioned Kathleen Nash, now a federal prisoner, about the Hesse jewels and her former brother-in-law's involvement with the gems. But, as might be expected, Nash refused to give any information whatsoever respecting the disposition of the jewels stolen by her and Durant.

Because the suspects involved were civilians, the army, still smarting from the unwanted publicity fallout surrounding the Durant-Nash case, dropped the investigation and turned over their records to the Bureau of Customs. The bureau followed up with interviews of Robert Shipley and Gladys Madison. On June 8, 1949, the Nogales, Arizona, bureau chief wrote, "It is the opinion of this office that further investigation will only net negative results and since we are not in possession of anything concrete or positive the matter should be closed with this writing."

And it was.

The Ogden case was closed, but during the time the army had been investigating the case in Arizona, a disgruntled wife living in Massachusetts had written to the FBI and told them that her now disloyal husband had been involved with the Hesse robbery.

On March 1, 1946, Lieutenant Colonel William L. Saunders arrived at Camp Kilmer, New York, from the European Theater. After an overnight stay at Camp Kilmer, Saunders took the train to Boston and met his wife at the Back Bay Station. The next day, Sunday, March 3, he explained to his wife that he had to report to Washington, D.C., the following day and insisted that she go with him. Mrs. Saunders did not have the money for the train fare, so she borrowed the funds from her brother and gave the money to Saunders, who purchased his wife's ticket. The couple, who had been married since March 14, 1925, arrived in Washington on Monday morning and checked in at the Statler Hotel.

A few days later Saunders obtained a fifteen-day leave, and the couple departed for Atlantic City, there meeting some friends from Bedford, Massachusetts. In the course of conversing with these friends, Saunders told them about some pictures of Queen Victoria done when she was fourteen years old by Thomas Gainsborough and which he had looted from the Kronberg Castle. He further told them that they were worth between fifty thousand and sixty thousand dollars.

From Atlantic City, the Saunderses went on to Boston and stayed at the home of Mrs. Saunders's sister. While there, Saunders was looking through a current magazine and came across an article written on the Apostle Spoons. He brought the magazine to his wife and asked her if she had ever seen any Apostle Spoons. She told Saunders that she had not, and he said that Mildred Louise Boie, a Red Cross worker attached to the XXI Corps, had liberated twenty of them from Kronberg Castle and that they were worth in the vicinity of four thousand to five thousand dollars each. Mrs. Saunders expressed surprise and asked him if that wasn't serious. He scoffed and said it was nothing, confessing that he had locked the library door and that Miss Boie had backed a car up to the French windows and filled the vehicle with priceless first editions, explaining that she was a writer and knew and understood the value of such things. He then told how "Kathy Nash" had allowed him and Miss Boie to enter a room that no one was supposed to enter and that was "sort of a museum where clothes that had been worn by royalty on state occasions were stored." He went on to explain how Boie had cut pieces of priceless embroidery from the garments to make table runners and bell pulls.

After the fifteen-day leave, Saunders returned to Washington, while his wife remained in Boston with relatives. Mrs. Saunders had noticed that her husband had been rather restless and nervous. A month or so later he told his wife that he needed some rest and suggested that the two of them go to Virginia Beach to get some sunshine. After one day there, Saunders told his wife that he wanted a separation and told her about his love for Mildred Louise Boie. On the same day, Mrs. Saunders's sister phoned and told Lieutenant Colonel Saunders that she had received notice from the Port of New York that the boxes Miss Boie had sent from Germany had arrived. Saunders went on to active duty at Fort Bragg, and his wife returned to Boston.

All of this took place prior to Kathleen Nash's arrest for her part in the looting of the Kronberg Castle. After the arrest of Nash and Durant, Mrs. Saunders read the stories in all the papers, then got in touch with her husband and pleaded with him to give back what he had taken, but he laughed at her, bragging that "no dumb cop would ever get him and that she would never get anywhere in this world because she was too damned honest."

Apparently realizing that a reconciliation with her husband was not going to materialize, Mrs. Saunders, on February 24, 1947, wrote the FBI a letter describing the events recounted to her by her husband over the preceding year. The FBI turned the accusation over to the U.S. Army. On April 9, 1947, at Fort Bragg, William Saunders read his wife's allegation as written to the FBI. Saunders then composed his own sworn statement, in which he acknowledged that he had been the assistant G-5 of the XXI Corps from December 1944 to September 1945. Saunders admitted that he spent practically every weekend at the Kronberg Castle, but he denied any involvement in any thefts at the castle or anywhere else in Europe. Saunders wrote, "The allegations made by Mrs. Saunders are untrue and have no doubt been made in an attempt to embarrass me. Mrs. Saunders and I are currently living apart."

Saunders's sworn statement as "an officer and gentleman" was sufficient to end the investigation.

The FBI did, however, find and photograph several pieces of silverware as a result of Mrs. Saunders's statements. The photographs were sent to Lieutenant Colonel Ralph W. Pierce, chief of the Criminal Investigations and Apprehensions Branch, in Washington. Afterward, they were sent by air mail to Germany. The photographs were shown to the members of the Hesse family, but they were unable to furnish detailed information regarding the pictures. The FBI files were closed and they remain closed to this day.[2]

The already bizarre goings-on now took another ironic turn, best described in a June 26, 1956, report written by the Kurhessische Haus Foundation:

> After the trials against the perpetrators, the American Major Robinson, the attorney in the last of three trials, explained that the recovered jewels could not be returned to the rightful owners from the Occupying Forces. He (Robinson) had been given the assignment of taking the jewels back to America. He in his civilian life was a lawyer and would resign from the military and could offer his help. A lawyer mandate would be recommended, because he in his official duty had to bring the jewels back to America, and he has all the papers and transcripts and by the delivery of the jewels to the proper authorities, he could obtain a receipt. He could obtain the proper security and see that the jewels would not get lost. As a lawyer he could work for the return of the jewels. Prince Wolfgang von Hessen, working on the whole jewel affair in the name of the members,

took Mr. Robinson's offer and retained him as the lawyer and expert in the case.

Ironically, Robinson, as the report states, was retained as the attorney for the Hesse family. He was to seek the return of the jewels that had been turned over to the U.S. government. In 1948, Robinson wrote to the Army:

> It is the family's desire that the jewels and all the other property be turned over to me. They do not have banking facilities in Germany where they may be kept and, in any event, they wish to dispose of certain parts thereof upon the payment of import duties.[3]

The army replied that the jewels and other valuables would be returned to the U.S. military authorities in Germany for return to the rightful owners.

On May 20, 1949, Robinson wrote again:

> In my opinion, no useful purpose can be served by the United States holding the property any longer. The Landgrafin of Hesse is seventy-eight years old. She is in need of at least part of her property to pay for necessaries for herself and family. She is the granddaughter of Queen Victoria of England, and a sister of the last German Kaiser. Her standard of living has been substantially reduced because of a lack of funds to pay for necessaries. She now lives in part of a small cottage near the Kronberg Castle in very reduced circumstances. She has at best a few years to live and some consideration ought to be extended to her. It is, therefore, that I ask you to please take the matter up with army officials with a view towards securing an early return of the property.

Most noteworthy, less than six months later, on November 23, 1949, the *Washington Post* ran the following article:

> District Judge Henry A. Schweinhaut yesterday gave attorney Joseph S. Robinson of New York 30 days to file a new suit to retain the famous Hesse crown jewels in the United States and indicated that unless the new action had a better legal basis than the old he would dismiss it. The action centers

around Robinson's attempts to keep the jewels in this country so he can impress his attorney lien against them for his fees.

What was Robinson up to? Surely the Hesse family had suffered enough at the hands of the occupying forces. Did Robinson remember his closing statement at Durant's trial on April 30, 1947, when he insisted that "any interference with such private property for personal gains be justly punished"?

Finally, on August 1, 1951, in a brief ceremony in Frankfurt, Germany, General Claude B. Michelwait, judge advocate general of the army, representing the United States, released custody of the jewels to Joseph Robinson. The owners of the jewels were present: Margarethe, Landgrafin of Hesse; Wolfgang, prince of Hesse; Philip, prince of Hesse; Richard, prince of Hesse; and Sophia, princess of Hanover. After the return of the valuables, it was confirmed that because of the disassembly and destruction of the jewelry, they now had only *one-tenth* their previous value.

On July 30, 1954, Howard W. Elkinton, executive director of the Carl Schurz Foundation, wrote the Honorable Hugh Scott the following:

> While at the Salem School in February of this year, I was informed by the Princess Sophia of Hanover that complete restoration of the jewels has not been made, that they recovered hardly three-fourths of the treasure and that the Colonel and Kathleen Nash Durant hid the balance of the jewels to be used when they emerged from prison. Further, I believe the marriage of these two persons took place in order to escape dual responsibility for the theft.... Members of the House of Hesse engaged an American lawyer who promised to push their claims. Just what he did, I do not know but he presented his bill which forced the family to sell one-third of the recovered jewels in order to pay his fee. Needless to add, this whole episode has not enhanced the good repute of our forces in Europe.

Watson was paroled in December 1947, Durant was released on February 18, 1952, and Nash, after serving her complete term, was paroled on November 6, 1952. After prison, Jack and Kathleen Durant lived on as husband and wife. Jack Durant died in 1984; Kathleen had died a year earlier. All of this occurred preceding the author's research. On October 11, 1991, the author telephoned James Durant, who by now was living in a nursing home. Old and feeble, he would only say that the issue of the Hesse jewels was a closed book.

And closed it remained. James Durant died at the age of eighty-six on November 20, 1991, leaving a $1 million will. One of Jack Durant's two sons was killed while serving his country in Korea; the other, living in Florida, claimed that all he knew about the Hesse affair was what he had read in the papers. He added, however, that near the end of his life his father had been destitute and had lived with him during the last years. The son, now sixty, refuses to discuss the matter further.

The author found the following unsigned, undated note in the National Archives' materials concerning the Hesse affair, but was unable to expound further on it:

> *Page 2013 June 4, 1946*
>
> And that list of cemeteries I gave, I'd at least run that just to be sure, double-check it. And if he actually concealed it in one of them, why then find out which one if he won't break down and get them. Now we want to be sure we get all of them from him? He might break down and give us one batch and then not give us the rest and if we hear anything more from you as to the possible location in a particular cemetery here, why then we will definitely go out and locate it. If he wasn't lying originally and if she wasn't about a cemetery ask the question so that we find out whether it is near a headstone or near the foot or a few little questions of that sort.

In 1946 more than $2 million (1945 value) worth of jewels may have been fenced through the Chicago underworld.

Or they may, even now, sit unclaimed in a safe deposit box in the Windy City or lie buried in a marshy gravesite in northern Virginia.

Miss Evelyn Tucker

You understand of course that if the army were to
see this letter they would burn me at the stake.

—*Evelyn Tucker*

17

The End of the Gold Train Property

THE UNITED STATES EMERGED from World War II as the foremost international power, for it possessed the chief weapon of destruction, the atomic bomb, and the chief weapon of reconstruction—wealth greater than any nation had ever claimed. For most Americans the war had led to neither hardship nor suffering but a better way of life. Unfortunately, this wealth was not to be shared with the devastated enemy, because as a result of the agreements at Yalta in February of 1945, the German people and not the German government were chosen to suffer for the destruction they had wrought upon Europe and North Africa. This was to be accomplished by making the German citizenry pay for the cost of the war. German factories would be dismantled, and badly needed coal and other natural resources would be taken out of the country. This determination was further reinforced at the Potsdam Conference in July 1945, when a proposed U.S. policy, JCS 1067, put a ceiling on the German standard of living at the barest subsistence level—just above disease and starvation.

The principles governing the dwindling of Germany's economy were continued at the Paris Conference on Reparations, convened in the winter of 1945. In addition to reparations agreements, Article 8 earmarked certain assets for the rehabilitation and resettlement of displaced persons who had been victims of Nazi persecution. These assets were to be released to the Inter-Governmental Committee for Refugees (IGCR). The Allies were to develop, by mutual agreement and in consultation with the IGCR, a plan to accomplish this humanitarian goal.

The United States took the lead by making $25 million secured from the liquidation of German assets in Sweden, Spain, and Switzerland available for the resettlement process. All of the property from SS loot was to be turned over to the IGCR, excluding Jewish books and manuscripts, ritual tapestries, clothes, Jewish ceremonial regalia, currencies and securities, furniture and personal belongings of small intrinsic value, gold bullion, gold coins, and silver coins. The IGCR discovered that large amounts of this plundered wealth existed in the Property Control Warehouse in Salzburg.

On June 4 and July 13, 1946, General Mark Clark sent telegrams to the War Department and Department of State. The message in both was that "the property now contained at the United States Military Government Warehouse, Salzburg, is of unknown origin and ownership." In an apparent attempt to clarify the situation, on August 23, 1946, the U.S. Department of State issued a telegram (WARX 98112) to General Clark. Its intent was to clarify the terms of the Final Act of the Paris Conference, Article 8D. It clearly stated that property could not be returned if determination of national origin was impractical and that property could not be restored to the lawful owners if they had died or ceased to exist without legal successors. It also stated that property could be disbursed to the IGCR if determination of individual ownership was impractical. Regardless of the claims in the telegram, the truth is that the property in the Property Control Warehouse was known as to its national origins and in many cases was still identifiable as to individual ownership. The telegram further expressed that property turned over to the IGCR must be removed from Austria and Germany and sold in acceptable foreign currency outside these two countries.

This directive greatly distressed Father Flaherty, a major and the 42d Division chaplain, because a considerable quantity of the loose clothing in the warehouse, such as coats, dresses, scarves, gloves, shoes, and so on, had been separated into two groups: poorer-quality clothing and linens and finer-quality clothing. The items were collected in forty boxes about six feet square each. Flaherty was made aware of this and requested that the poorer-quality clothing be distributed to DPs. The chaplain had visited the many dismal displacement camps in the area and had firsthand knowledge of the miserable living conditions of the inhabitants.

These DPs had taken to the roads soon after liberation by the advancing Americans. On bicycles, in wagons, and on foot, DPs streamed away from rural districts, towns, and cities; many Poles, Hungarians, and Russians headed for no place in particular. Unable to provide for themselves, they became the responsibility of the UN Relief and Rehabilitation Administration. Homeless, without jobs, knowing neither German or English, elated at being free but uncertain about their future, they created problems that went beyond the need for food and housing: murder, rape, and robbery flourished. Many had returned to their homelands after the war, but the DP camps in the immediate area of Salzburg still contained over ten thousand victims, and Father Flaherty thought he could help a little by distributing the clothing to them. He requested that the garments be turned over to him. His charitable request was denied.

Hungarian officials were aware that the Property Control Warehouse had not been guarded adequately and that large-scale looting had further decimated the valuables stored within. Hungarian museum objects and religious relics were displayed openly in Salzburg merchants' windows. The black market for items was so lucrative that the Hungarian government protested the lack of security and stressed that while Austria had not won the war with the Allies, it apparently was sharing in the war booty. More valuable items were burglarized from the Property Control Warehouse in Salzburg than in any other one place in occupied Europe.

On December 5, 1946, representatives of the Hungarian Restitution Delegation visited the warehouse. The Hungarian government requested an inventory of all items and demanded that Hungarian experts be allowed to examine the objects to determine which items belonged to Hungarian citizens. During the subsequent visit the Hungarians discovered the valuable Kisfaludi collection of crockery and four cases of tobacco seeds. For some inexplicable reason the tobacco seeds were handed over to the Hungarian Ministry of Agriculture, the only property returned by the U.S. Army to the Hungarian government.

The Hungarian Restitution Ministry then filed a claim for the Kisfaludi collection and wrote for permission to inventory the warehouse for additional Hungarian claims. The Hungarian secretary of finance, Mr. Nyardi, insisted that all of the train's contents be returned to his native land for the benefit of the 100,000 remaining Hungarian Jews. Nyardi was informed that because of the terms of the Final Act of the Paris Conference, Article 8D, signed by the United States, England, and France, Hungarian Jews would not receive their confiscated property and that it would be sold for the benefit of Jewish victims from Germany and Austria. Despite protests from Hungary, the valuables from the Budapest train would not be returned.

Based on the previous unsubstantiated telegrams from Mark Clark that asserted a lack of proof of ownership, Captain Howard Mackenzie was notified that all previous instructions concerning the Hungarian valuables were superseded by cable number WX-85682. This cable, sent on November 16, 1946, from the Joint Chiefs of Staff, stated that all valuables in the Property Control Warehouse, with the exception of Jewish items of cultural or religious significance, would be turned over to the IGCR. Again this directive underscored the fact that national origin or identification of ownership of the property was impractical. Again, this was simply untrue—still remaining in the warehouse and unopened were 2,732 boxes, trunks, suitcases, and other containers of valuables. Proof of ownership lay in Captain Mackenzie's testimony as a witness for the prosecution during the court-martial proceedings of enlisted men on September 27, 1946. The testimony follows:

> COURT-MARTIAL MEMBERS: Small objects of high value for their size, was there any effort to lock them in boxes or safes to make them secure from people walking through there?
> CAPTAIN MACKENZIE: They were kept in the original containers because it was felt if they were removed the means of identification would be lost. A great deal of material the ownership of which has never been determined is in there....Most of the valuable material is nailed into boxes. Some of the most valuable material is still in the original suitcases and baskets and trunks in which they were found.

Because of such proof, the Hungarian government was positive that the items would be returned. After all, they had recouped from the Americans their gold and silver reserves, and the French had returned most of the gold bars that had been removed from the train during its backtracking through the Tyrol. The Hungarians were also aware that the Americans had in their possession the sacred Hungarian Crown of Saint Stephen. Because of its historical prominence they had no doubt about its immediate return.

But neither the U.S. Army nor the Hungarians expected the order of November 16, 1946. This order instructed Mackenzie to open the containers and sort the items into categories according to type of merchandise and value. After the sorting process, the determination of individual property would be impractical, and the property could be turned over to the IGCR.

The property control officer at Salzburg was delighted by this unexpected turn of events. The army had been investigating the rapid disappearance of property from the warehouse, and many officers had returned to the United States with filched property. Additionally, two suitcases of gold dust had disappeared from a vault that contained many valuables from the Hungarian Gold Train. In spite of thorough investigations, no progress was made in the recovery of the gold dust or in identifying the location of property removed from the warehouse. By mixing up the property and rendering it unidentifiable as to ownership, the U.S. Army could be held blameless. Without an adequate inventory list, an owner, even if he or she recovered some items, would have no recourse in claiming that more property was due him or her.

Thus the unproductive investigations of previous missing property fizzled out as large quantities of gold, jewelry and watches, silver, and numismatic coins were separated from thousands of hand-woven Persian rugs and thousands of mink, muskrat, rabbit, lamb, and seal coats. As the Army Corps of Engineers opened, sorted, and repacked the Gold Train valuables during the summer and fall of 1947, additional gold, silver, currency, and diamonds were found hidden in the clothing of the former owners. Several five-hundred-dollar bills were found sewn into the cuffs of dress shirts. This method of hiding money and jewels by concentration camp victims was a common and pitiable practice. Identification of ownership was fast becoming impossible.

During the sorting of the material, Count Josef V. Markovits and his wife and son obtained the necessary travel permits and traveled from Feldkirch to the Property Control Warehouse. Markovits contacted Captain Mackenzie, and the captain reluctantly allowed him to enter the warehouse in search of his property. In the various groups of clothing, Markovits was able to locate four sacks and four boxes of his possesions. The enclosed clothing contained his initials, and only because of this was some property handed over to him. He could not locate his gold watches, gold rings, or other valuable heirlooms.

Because he had to return to Feldkirch, Count Markovits gave the power of attorney to his friend Francis Scheuch for securing the remainder of his property. Scheuch was a native of Salzburg and could intercede with local American authorities for a basket of toy dolls, toy trains and cars, shoes, utensils, canned food, sugar, and other items owned by the Markovits family. Shamefully, during this time of cold and hunger in Europe, these much-needed and coveted items never were returned to the count.

On May 19, 1947, the IGCR team appeared at the Property Control Warehouse. This IGCR staff consisted of four people: Robert Gold, the field supervisor, and George Wenzel, Edward Staffe, and Patricia Van Delden, Wenzel's assistants. The team was completely understaffed and remarkably unqualified to inventory, classify, and appraise the valuable Hungarian property and transfer it from Austria to the United States. Furthermore, the Department of State was anxious to have the items shipped to the States as quickly as possible, because the Hungarian Restitution Ministry was anxiously trying to block removal of the valuables from Europe. The U.S. Army was equally as anxious, since a transfer would cover its irregular activities.

Administrative authority was the responsibility of the IGCR, but they had requested assistance from the army. Captain Mackenzie assigned an American civilian, William W. Schwartzmann, to lend a hand to the operation. The first items to be appraised were the vast collections of diamond jewelry. The IGCR immediately sent Emile Klipper, an IGCR appraiser, to Salzburg. It took Klipper ten days to inventory the diamonds; while thus engaged, he appraised several Meissen, Dresden, and Chinese figurines.

On June 3, Mackenzie turned over sixty large individual pieces of jewelry to Robert Gold and Patricia Van Delden. Two of the sixty inventoried items were listed as follows:

1. One pendant, platinum with one center stone, approximately 1.5 carat, and several smaller stones.
2. One platinum brooch with diamonds, center stone approximately 3/4 carat, plus smaller diamonds.

The diamonds were sent to the Foreign Exchange Depository in Frankfurt as Shipment Number One and were mixed with jewelry that had been taken from various concentration camps.

In the warehouse the IGCR was busy appraising much of the Hungarian property. The remaining gold and silver jewelry was grouped as bulk scrap and appraised on the basis of weight times market prices. The IGCR considered this necessary to avoid having their four "experts" perform endless months of appraisal work. Five trunks of stamps were appraised by George Wenzel. The army agreed to accept his overall assessment of the stamps, in spite of the fact that they were never assigned a dollar value. The Persian rugs were separated by size into three piles and counted. A shockingly low value was assigned to each pile—$10 each for the small size, $20 for the medium size, and $30 for the large-size rugs! Complete sets of silverware were valued at $100 per chest; 28 boxes of furs, containing about 100 furs each, were appraised at the value of $100 or about $1 per fur; china and glassware was assessed at $2.50 per pound; and 500 boxes of bulk silver, including bowls, dishes, and vases, were given the absurd value of $7.50 a pound. A Gimbel's department store representative from New York stated later that it would have taken the entire Gimbel's staff seven years to examine, itemize, and appraise the bulk silver alone.

It was agreed that other classifications of inventory would be appraised on an analogous basis in agreement with Robert Gold. The army only disagreed with one appraisal price, the value of bulk silver. In a capricious compromise decision, all parties immediately agreed to raise the price to $10 a pound. After the above prices were established, the army gave full approval for the removal of all property from the Hungarian Gold Train. (Later, the 28 boxes of furs were further reduced to $800 for the complete lot!)

The IGCR agreed to pay the army in American dollars to help with the loading and shipping of the valuables. The Army Corps of Engineers was assigned the task of building large wooden shipping crates and also helped in packing the booty. In the process, they used 880 pounds of two-inch nails just to build the crates.

During the packing operation, tons of valuable metals had been discovered. Much of this was gold- and silver-plated jewelry, often encrusted with diamonds and other valuable gems. These valuables and an additional 60 chests of inventoried jewelry and 10,011 ounces of silver that had been deposited for safekeeping with the U.S. Currency Control Section in Salzburg, along with an additional 844 ounces of silver coins, were sent to the Foreign Exchange Depository in Frankfurt. The 893 pounds, designated Shipment Number Two, was smelted into gold and silver bars.

In tracking the progress of these first two transfers of valuables from Salzburg to Frankfurt, the reparations director of the IGCR, Abba P. Schwartz, headquartered in Geneva, Switzerland, could not locate the receipts and records for the shipments. All of the inventory records were inexplicably lost. Because of this, a deep-seated animosity now existed between Robert Gold and Abba Schwartz. The IGCR staff could not fully understand the hostility, but as a result an atmosphere of cynicism began to surround the operation in Salzburg.

During the first week of July, a sack of gold dust was found by William Schwartzmann in a pile of trash on the second floor of the warehouse. This bag was identical with other bags of gold dust that had been found during the sorting of material. Schwartzmann theorized that the bag of gold had been dumped accidentally in the trash or that it was put there deliberately by someone for the express purpose of removing it later. In their naïveté, Schwartzmann and his IGCR staff agreed to leave the gold there and wait to see if anyone tried to recover it. The cache was kept under close scrutiny, but within twenty-four hours the bag was removed undetected.

After the theft the U.S. Military Criminal Investigation Division was notified and directed to check into the matter. During the ensuing investigation, one civilian was found with diamonds in the cuff of his trousers. The suspect said that the diamonds had fallen into the cuff accidentally. Mr. Gold alleged that another civilian representative of the IGCR had pilfered the gold dust, jewelry, watches, and other valuable items from the warehouse. No indictments were handed down, but it was the majority opinion that the IGCR staff members were not qualified to work on this type of project. As a result, however, Gold himself was fired and, almost simultaneously, Patricia Van Delden resigned from the IGCR.[1] Schwartzmann was reassigned to a new project.

George Wenzel was now appointed field supervisor of the IGCR staff, and Captain Charles Langer assumed responsibilities for the day-to-day operations at the warehouse. One of his first duties was to substantiate the contents and value of the first two shipments of valuables sent to the Foreign Exchange Depository in Frankfort. Without inventory records, one could only speculate about what might have been stolen by the large number of personnel who had access to the treasures. The first two shipments contained over half a million dollars' worth of jewelry and five $1,000 bills. Langer determined that Schwartzmann had the receipts for the shipments, but he was unable to locate them.[2] After this inauspicious beginning, Langer decided to design a proper receipt form to be used for the release of property to the IGCR. It is interesting to note, also, that the redesigned receipt stipulated that future claims against the released property were not the responsibility of the IGCR.

The first news release of the transfer of the SS loot from the Foreign Exchange Depository and the Property Control Warehouse to the IGCR was published by most newspapers and was given considerable publicity by the U.S. Army and the IGCR. This news was the first evidence that many victims had received that the U.S. Army had recovered a considerable amount of SS loot. The number of letters and claims received and the number of people attempting to visit the depository after these newspaper revelations was extraordinary. The following letter was typical of the mail received:

Henri Berger
Neuvecelle sur Evian
(Haute-Savoie)
France

Neuvecelle, September 8th, 1947

My Colonel,

By Mr. Edwin Harbich's contribution to the *New York Herald-Tribune*, European Edition, yesterday's issue, I learned of your statement concerning Gestapo loot in torture camps. I should be very obligated to you, if you could tell me of any possibility to get back, eventually, the wedding rings of my parents, killed at Auschwitz camp in October 1944. They are engraved: Josef, 11.6-1924 and Suzanne or Suzi 11.6-1924. If necessary, I can prove the death of my parents by a statement of the International Association of Internes.

Thanking you by advance, agree My Colonel, My respectful salutations.

Henri Berger

After the first two shipments, the IGCR team at Salzburg arranged for the shipment of an immense cargo of ten flatbed railroad cars and three truckloads of silver and jewelry. This mind-boggling amount of treasure was discovered during the packing of the large crates, and again Mr. Klipper returned to Salzburg and commenced inspecting the valuables prior to their shipment to Frankfurt for smelting and processing. As arrangements were being made to ship the huge wooden boxes, it became evident that they were too large to fit into freight cars, so it was arranged for the IGCR to borrow thirty tarpaulins from the army and ship the valuables on flatbed cars. This shipment left the Property Control Warehouse on November 14, 1947, and the boxes containing stamps, china, silverware, and rugs were sent on a through shipment to the German port of Bremerhaven. The shipment's final destination was New York City. The United States already had a number of offers from reliable firms to purchase the property.

The shipments continued being sent in this manner until the tenth and last shipment was made on February 16, 1948. This last load was small, consisting of 244 pieces of table silver and two silver cigarette cases. The mission of the IGCR at the Property Control Warehouse was thus concluded.

The army also transferred to the IGCR two additional properties not taken from the Gold Train. The first was a lead-sealed canvas bag taken from the safe of SS officer R. Pischl in Telfs, in the Tyrol in Austria. The bag contained a large collection of historic silver coins. The second property was recovered from SS Hlinka Guardsmen of the Czechoslovakian army. The Hlinka Guards were stationed in a refugee camp in the small village of Aurolzmunster, located north of Salzburg, within twenty miles of the German border. On November 19, 1945, thirty-five Czech Hlinka Guards were returning to Czechoslovakia on a refugee pass but were ordered to return to Aurolzmunster because they had an excessive amount of food and clothing in their possession. A subsequent investigation disclosed a large cache of food, clothing, and tobacco in the possession of the Czechs in the refugee camp. Food and clothing were under the control of a Czech ration board, and the amounts were deemed excessive for the number of people involved. Further investigations revealed a large deposit of valuables that had been comandeered by the Hlinka Guards. The valuables were placed into a safe deposit box in the Ried branch of the Salzburg Bank and consisted of four boxes of gold, silver, jewelry, and coins. The items were then confiscated by the U.S. Army. Because of the number of gold teeth and wedding rings scattered throughout the collection, it was suspected that the grisly cache had war implications.

In early 1948, three years after World War II, the refugee camps received the first shipment of items from the original massive quantities of the Hungarian Gold Train. U.S. Army officers in Austria had first choice in selecting valuable objects for their personal use: There followed more unchecked theft and looting by U.S. military personnel. The IGCR was then allowed to pick through the contents of the train. Only then were the remaining practically worthless items turned over to the victims in the refugee camps. Included was clothing in fair condition, empty battered suitcases, and porcelain and glassware of very poor quality and from broken-up sets. In a rare instance of respect, the proprietors of the warehouse treasury did turn over to the archbishop of Salzburg seven chalices, five silver crucifixes, and a standing crucifix. It had been stipulated that these religious articles were to be given to bombed-out parishes that had suffered the most destruction.

During the sorting, packing, and shipping of the items, a huge pile of Judaic religious writings and sacred objects had been accumulated in one section of the warehouse. In January 1948, Captain Oscar M. Lifshutz recommended that these items of great spiritual significance be distributed to European synagogues. The now scarce pieces could be used to restore, rejuvenate, and rehabilitate Jewish religious life in Europe. The Jewish religion in Europe, which Nazi savagery had attempted to obliterate, was sorely in need of spiritual symbols that the survivors of the Holocaust could look to for a least a modicum of solace. The sacred items included Hanukkah menorahs, Torah breastplates and crowns, scroll pointers, and kaddish cups. The collected pieces were estimated to weigh six thousand pounds.

Captain Lifshutz insisted that these articles be distributed to the Jewish communities established since the end of World War II and to the DP camps where there were many Jews:

> In my opinion, the turning over of these items to one organization would not result in a proper and adequate coverage. It would only give ground for controversy and ill will. The items belong to the Jewish synagogue, and the synagogue or those people representing it can best decide where the religious requirements demand their use. It would place the entire problem on a plane beyond reproach or argumentation. A religious guidance would be an equitable one.

On May 19, 1948, instructions came from Washington to have the Jewish religious works transferred to the U.S. Archival Depot in Offenbach near Frankfurt. On May 28, sixty boxes of Judaic items were loaded into a freight car and shipped to Offenbach. They were then stored in a warehouse with more than 2 million books that had been assembled from Jewish libraries throughout Europe. At the end of World War II, part of this vast collection had been discovered in a bombed-out home in Frankfurt, and the remainder was found in a repository north of Frankfurt in Hungen. The books had been removed from their hiding places and stored in the depot. After the establishment of Israel, most of this inventory was shipped to Jerusalem in one large shipment.

As the last valuables were being shipped from the Property Control Warehouse to the IGCR, after much deliberation and legal battles, the Fuschl Castle was closed as a U.S. Army officers' club and returned to Baroness von Remitz on October 15, 1947. After nine years of dispossession, she thought to reclaim the castle and surrounding property. Through some good fortune, the baroness had managed to attract an investor and excellent manager and converted the castle into a hotel. To attract tourists, she established a special bus route from Salzburg to operate from July 1 to September 15. The baroness and her two children hoped to live on the revenues from this commercial endeavor.

Herr Loe Knoll, the manager, was most upset in June 1948, when U.S. Army officers told him that they intended to remove all the furniture and fixtures from the castle. The hotel had opened on May 15 and was solidly booked with guests. These facts and legal briefs were presented to the army, notwithstanding that the Remitz family was told that the furniture would be removed by the U.S. Army on Friday, July 2, 1948. The army reasoned that many of the belongings in the castle bore the monograms "v. R." and must be the property of Nazi foreign minister Joachim von Ribbentrop. Despite Mrs. von Remitz's pleas, the army refused to acknowledge that "v. R." stood for von Remitz.

On the assigned date the U.S. Army showed up in force and removed all furniture and fixtures from the castle and surrounding buildings. This included all beds, linen, refrigerators, tableware, kitchen utensils, chests, cupboards, and office equipment. James Garrison, chief, Reparations Division, wrote, "The furniture is not of high quality nor is in the best condition, but could be utilized by U.S. Civil Affairs personnel to a good advantage."

The "liberated" haul was stored in the Property Control Warehouse and found its way into various American households through requisitions from the warehouse. Somehow, even under these stressful and intimidating conditions of occupation, Fuschl Castle continued to operate as a tourist stop and today is listed in the publication *Leading Hotels of the World.*

18

Austria—1947

IN JULY OF 1947, Captain Howard A. Mackenzie was transferred to the Linz Depot and turned administrative responsibilities of the Property Control Warehouse over to Mr. Veron Kennedy. During the transfer, Captain Mackenzie became Mr. Mackenzie, by a process in the military known then as being "civilianized." Veron Kennedy was aware that he had inherited an insufficient staff in the claims section. The Allied nations were making vigorous demands for the return of art objects that they strongly suspected were secreted in Austria. The Dutch, for example, went so far as to track several of their great works to the salt mine of Alt Aussee. The war had been over for two years, and countries that had remained patient during a period of gratitude for liberation from Nazi tyranny now began to assert that they would no longer accept delays for restitution of their rightful possessions and complained that works of art were being integrated into the general Austrian art collection. As a result of this pressure the position of MFA&A officer was reestablished.

Miss Evelyn Tucker acquired this position in August 1947 and was assigned to the Vienna staff. Although she lived in Vienna, her main responsibility lay in the provinces of Upper Austria and Salzburg, and she would spend most of her time there. Tucker would travel to both destinations via the Mozart, a first-class military train. While in Salzburg she would stay at the Bristol Hotel, or Osterreichischer Hof; while in Upper Austria she would stay in Linz at the Wolfsteiner Gasthof or Linzerhof; and while in Munich, the Excelsior Hotel—all top-rate military hotels administered by the U.S. Army. Miss Tucker's primary responsibility was to investigate and return missing art. The job fascinated her, taking her as it did to many stately old castles, remote monasteries, and deep salt mines. In the process she met blue-blooded aristocrats and high-ranking clergymen in prominent positions within the Catholic church. Tucker's position as a representative of the U.S. occupying force stationed in Vienna gave her entry into these privileged circles. It also gave her, it would appear, something of a superiority complex, a common result of being suddenly elevated in status. She spent the first few days reviewing the files of the past two years' activities and familiarizing herself with the removal of valuables from Austria in 1945 and the subsequent storage in Munich.

The Allies had demanded that the United States transfer the remaining art stored in the salt mine at Alt Aussee to Munich and that it be properly identified by personnel of the Munich Collection Center. Handling these requests from Belgium, France, England, and Holland was one of Tucker's first assignments, and her actions brought a storm of protest from the Austrian Bundesdenkmalamt (Austrian Monuments and Fine Arts Division). Their protest was leveled at James A. Garrison, chief of Reparations and Restitution, and Major Richard P. Weeber. The Austrians adamantly insisted that the transfer document signed in 1946 had given Austria total responsibility for the art contained in Alt Aussee. Garrison stood his ground and emphasized that the document merely constituted a guardianship arrangement and that the U.S. Army had access to the mine at any time. Garrison represented a conquering force, and thus the Austrians had little choice. Miss Tucker's first assignment was to inspect the contents of the Alt Aussee mine.

During the first week of August 1947, Tucker made the necessary arrangements for Mr. Herbert Stewart Leonard to travel from Munich to Alt Aussee. Leonard was the chief MFA&A officer at the Munich Collection Center. During hostilities, the thirty-seven-year-old army officer had served with George Patton's Third Army as a bomb-disposal officer. At the end of the war he was one of the first MFA&A officers to enter Berlin, and he stayed there until July 1947, when he was transferred to Munich and in the process became civilianized. In his capacity as an army officer, Leonard had been the last person to interrogate Göring, Ribbentrop, Frank, Seyss-Inquart, and Rosenberg, just before the Nazi bigwigs met their deaths at Nuremberg. Leonard, enjoying a moment of vengeance, took delight in informing the rapacious Göring, who had less than twenty-four hours to live, that his most valued Vermeer was a fake. Leonard felt a great sense of pleasure in seeing how the information upset Göring.[1]

On the morning of August 26, 1947, Evelyn Tucker met Leonard, Dr. Gottfried Kreutz, representative of the Bundesdenkmalamt, and Max Eder, the mine administrator, at the entrance to the Alt Aussee mine. For the previous two years the Austrians had consolidated art objects into the two large chambers known as the Springerwerke and Kammergrafwerke. From the Steinberg Haus the party walked more than a mile in the mountains to the Springerwerke chamber. Tucker noticed that the Springerwerke's entrance was guarded by a locked iron door. The chamber itself was fifty by forty yards in size and was lighted by electricity; it had wooden floors and contained sturdy wooden racks on which the paintings and other objects of art were arranged neatly. Many of them were in their original packing cases with posted notices of their contents. Tucker and the other officials then visited the Kammergrafwerke. It was approximately seventy-five by seventy-five yards, with electricity and wooden floors, but it was comprised of two levels. After the party entered the top level, they gained entrance to the lower level by a long, wide wooden staircase.

As the team began to check the Bundesdenkmalamt inventory list against the actual items, they began to uncover many discrepancies. Items shown as having been Austrian and removed by them were still in the chambers and were clearly Dutch. Inexplicably, Rothschild markings were noted on many of the objects. There was a great quantity of property in packing cases labeled French, Dutch, and Belgian. Many items were labeled as having been owned by Jews. One unrecognized masterpiece was a painting by Hans Makart (Austrian, 1840–84) called *Caterina Cornaro*. It was owned by the National Art Gallery of Berlin, inventory number 2075. Located in the Springerwerke chamber, the painting was wrapped around a fifteen-to-twenty-foot roll and was too large to be removed from the chamber.

Also, according to Max Eder's inventory, many items had recently been removed from the mine by Americans and sent to Salzburg and Linz without being reported to the Bundesdenkmalamt.

On the way out of the mine, the group passed a sightseeing tour group. They stopped, and Eder spoke with them for a few minutes, then gave his key to the leader of the group. As the group departed, Tucker and Leonard, concerned, asked Eder who the people were and what right they had to view the treasures. Eder said although he did not personally like the idea, he had to "follow orders"; the tour leader was

Albrecht Gaiswinkler, a member of the Austrian Parliament. Tucker was alarmed. She had reason to be—Gaiswinkler had been arrested by the Austrians in the Karolyi case, which involved the stealing of American, Dutch, and Swiss currency in May 1945. It remains a mystery as to why Gaiswinkler and his party were allowed in the mine.

Tucker and her team left the mine at 5:00 P.M., and on the way out Tucker noticed a great quantity of property in packing cases in a room to the right. The cases were labeled French, Dutch, and Belgian. When she mentioned this new find, Eder told Tucker that several months ago he had removed pieces from the larger chambers and packed them for shipping, on orders from Linz. Lying uncrated on top of one of the cases was a life-size wooden baroque statue, a *Madonna With Child*. The rarity had been situated in its present location for months and was suffering damage from exposure.

Dr. Kreutz was puzzled by this and the other inconsistencies, and Leonard was convinced that the art must be sent to the Munich Collection Center. Kreutz agreed that the non-Austrian property should be moved to Munich and, unexpectedly, claimed that upon many occasions he had reported to the Bundesdenkmalamt in Vienna that the majority of the art at Alt Aussee was unidentifiable and that origin and ownership should be cleared up. He claimed to have had many fights with Vienna over the situation at the mine, but had been unable to convince authorities of the seriousness of the problem.

Eder then stated that he would require an estimated fifty liters of gasoline and two liters of motor oil for his gasoline-powered train to bring the valuables out of the mine. He said that upon delivery of the gasoline, he would proceed at once to bring the property out. Under great protest from the Austrians, beginning on August 28, 1947, the art was shipped in eleven trucks from Alt Aussee to Munich. Because of its size the Hans Makart painting remained in the mine.

James Garrison reiterated that the purpose of the transfer was to establish the origins of the art and that it was imperative that no damage arise from the removal, because the art that could not be identified by experts would be returned to Austria. Garrison also insisted that this would include the unidentified art that had been shipped in 1945.

Also shipped under these orders from Alt Aussee was the art collection of Adolf Hitler, purchases made by SS General Kajetan Mühlmann. Most of these paintings had been purchased by the general's staff in Holland from private collections. In addition, part of the Hitler library, stored at the Villa Castiglione in Upper Austria, was packed and shipped to Munich.

Miss Tucker had never visited the Property Control Warehouse while it contained the bulk of the Hungarian valuables, but during the packing and removal of the items from the Hungarian Gold Train, it was reported to her that about two hundred "junk" paintings, eleven boxes of silver and china, and twenty-seven "decent" Hungarian paintings had been found and stored in a small corner room on the second floor of the large warehouse. Tucker, reviewing an inventory list, could not help noticing the similarities between this property and items described on an inventory list submitted by Baroness Edith Weiss of the Manfred Weiss family of Hungary.

The baroness had traveled several times to Salzburg and met with Tucker to discuss the Weiss art collection, which had disappeared from their many residences in Hungary. She did not have an exact listing because the Weiss family, through coercion and bribery, had purchased their freedom and escaped from Hungary packing little more than their toothbrushes. This flight was a result of the extermination horror of 1944 brought about by Adolf Eichmann and his henchmen. Large stocks of Manfred Weiss machine tools had been located throughout postwar Austria, the larger of which had been used by the Danube Airplane Works, Budapest, to build new weapons of destruction, the Messerschmitt jet fighters. Because of the nature of these tools, all of the Weisses' property had been blocked from being returned by the U.S. Department of State, and this would include—illogically—their art collections.

Unaware of this blocking order, Evelyn Tucker had the matching eleven boxes of silver and china, plus the twenty-seven Hungarian paintings, removed from the remaining cache of valuables and stored on the second floor of the Property Control Warehouse. They had been moved to the second floor to keep Baroness Weiss from seeing the enormous accumulation of wealth still stored on the main floor. Using a side entrance that led straight upstairs, Captain Langer, the baroness, and Miss Tucker viewed the separated property. The baroness did not identify any of the property as belonging to her family, but she did recognize many of the paintings, even revealing the owners' names.

After several phone calls, Tucker established that the two hundred junk paintings had been accumulating in the small room for the past two years and that no inventory existed for them, though Captain Langer had placed a value of ten dollars on the complete lot. On

November 6, 1947, Miss Tucker and Langer went to the warehouse expecting to see a tawdry collection of virtually worthless paintings. Upon opening the door to the small room, both were astounded at what they saw. The room was stuffed to the ceiling with hundreds of paintings. They immediately assigned a team to count the paintings and were astonished to find that the total was 1,181 paintings.

Miss Tucker transferred the paintings to the Carabinierisaal in the Residenz Palace, Salzburg. This palace had been the former home of Prince Archbishop Andreas Rohracher of the Roman Catholic church. Now part of it was used as a holding area for fine art found in the Salzburg area. The Carabinierisaal was a huge room with a stone floor, high ceiling, and as the researchers soon discovered, no heat. Chilled to the bone, Tucker found it impossible to work there for more than an hour at a time. Nevertheless, it was here that Tucker inventoried the 1,181 paintings. She immediately realized that the paintings were not "junk" at all, but from a variety of valuable collections. She found, for instance, a van Ruysdael seascape and a small etching by Rembrandt dated 1639. Although the room contained many valuable paintings, it was still referred to as the "Art Dump."

Tucker returned to the Property Control Warehouse and began a search for paperwork on the paintings. She found a folder with a Final Report dated July 10, 1946, which stipulated that fifty-eight Hungarian paintings had been removed from Fischhorn Castle and combined with the property from the Hungarian Gold Train. The report also suggested that the Fischhorn be checked occasionally for other art works. Tucker made a mental note of this suggestion. Later, while signing a receipt for the paintings, she was told that a small painting, *Madonna With Child and Angel*, was in a safe in the Property Control Section. She removed the painting; written on the back was "Fischhorn—no. 250." She stored this work along with the others at the Carabinierisaal. Tucker resolved to visit Fischhorn Castle on her next trip to the area, which was scheduled for the spring.

19

The Austrian Monasteries

DURING THE FALL AND WINTER, things went well for Tucker as she traveled throughout Upper Austria inspecting art depositories. It was at the St. Florian Monastery that she would begin to question the legality of her duties concerning the transfer of art and other valuables to her employer, the U.S. occupation forces of Austria.

On October 30, 1947, she arrived at Linz, the capital of Upper Austria, on the Mozart train and settled into a room at the Linzerhof, the 42d Infantry Division Hotel for staff officers. The following morning she met with Dr. Kreutz, and they were chauffeured to the St. Florian Monastery, located in the village of St. Florian, about a ten-minute drive from Enns. The monastery, owned by the St. Augustine order, was completed in 1740 and is considered one of the finest examples of baroque architecture in Austria. The magnificent buildings and grounds showcased good taste combined with great wealth. During the war the monastery was appropriated by the German Rundfunk Broadcasting Company. Twenty freight cars of heavy antique furniture, large baroque mirrors, antique musical instruments, large paintings, and a library of five thousand volumes on music, art, and literature were brought to the monastery by Rundfunk and were used to refurnish the monastery as a broadcasting center. The Nazis employed musicians to play the antique instruments in broadcasting music by Bach, Mozart, and Beethoven.

While the army driver waited in the car, Tucker and Kreutz knocked at the gate and asked for the attendant. They were told that the

235

custodian of the treasure room was in Linz with the key. Not satisfied with his answer, Tucker asked to see the abbot. The man reluctantly took them upstairs to the abbot's luxurious quarters. The abbot was most gracious but kept repeating that he did not know if the Germans had left anything behind and insisted that the keys were with the custodian in Linz. Finally, Tucker interrupted this repetitive dialogue and explained that she represented the American headquarters in Vienna and that the Americans had claims for the antique furniture, paintings, and musical instruments that the Germans had brought there and that she was under an obligation to return the property to the Allied countries. Furthermore, she added, the abbot was obstructing her investigation. The abbot pondered this for a moment and said that he could show them two rooms of property, but that the key for the main property room really was still in Linz.

The abbot escorted Tucker and Dr. Kreutz down several hallways and stairways, each blocked off by a huge baroque iron grillwork gate. At each of the gates the Abbot produced a key, until they came to a large hall approximately three hundred feet long and fifteen feet wide. The hall was packed with large, heavy antique furniture and paintings. Some of it was readily identifiable as French and Dutch. In this one hall was enough looted art to fill ten freight cars. Tucker told the abbot that she would notify Property Control and have the valuables identified from various claims and removed. Grumbling, he mumbled something in a Swabian German dialect that Miss Tucker could not understand about "the looting Amis."

Back in the car, Tucker questioned Kruetz about this comment of the abbot's concerning the "Amis," which she knew was slang for Americans. Kreutz told her that the local Austrian police had documented the removal, in late 1945, by the U.S. 83d Infantry Division of five truckloads of the best items from the St. Florian Monastery and that these were used in Upper Austria to furnish the homes of the ranking American officers. There were no receipts signed, nor was permission given to remove the furniture, rugs, and household goods. In spite of the protests lodged by the local police, this major ransacking was never investigated, even though the plundered property included French and Dutch items. This greatly distressed Tucker, and she began to question the whole operation.

On the way back to Linz, Tucker's party stopped by the Ennsegg Castle, located on the river in Enns, which had been the residence of Archduke Francis Ferdinand. The archduke and his wife, Countess

Sophie Chotek, had been assassinated at Sarajevo in 1914, triggering the First World War. Half of the castle was used as a residence for two elderly countesses, and, to Tucker's surprise, the other half was used for the manufacture of washing machines. In this manufacturing half were several rooms used by the Bundesdenkmalamt as a storage area.

Deposited in this area were twenty-five cases of numismatic coins that had been sent to Austria from the Munich Collection Center. There were also thirty-six large paintings that had not been listed on any inventory sheets. Kreutz told Tucker that the paintings were in transit by the SS when the transport was bombed at St. Agatha. Retrieved from the wreckage, the paintings were moved to the safety of the castle. What he did not tell Tucker was that the paintings were actually from Hitler's personal collection and were being shipped from the Thuerntal Castle, now in the Russian Zone, to the Ennsegg Castle. Tucker thought that three of the paintings appeared to have belonged to the Bondi, Rothschild, and Hass collections. She made a note to have the paintings removed, but would never get to carry through with this request, and the paintings remained in the castle.

The following day, October 31, Tucker and her team visited the Kremsmünster Monastery near Linz. It is one of the oldest monasteries in Europe, located atop a mountain with the same name, and was founded in 797. The monastery housed a boy's school and was considered a must for boys from the aristocratic families of Austria. The architecture is a mixture of Romanesque, Gothic, and Baroque, and it is owned by the St. Benedictine order. Tucker noticed that the monastery did not possess the magnificence of St. Florian but had a far friendlier atmosphere and exuded the mellowness that comes with great age.

During the war the monastery continued to be utilized by the Nazis as a boys' boarding school, staffed by Nazi teachers. In addition, part of the ancient structure was used for a Gestapo headquarters, and the monks' quarters were used to house several hundred Czechoslovakians and Hungarians. As American troops approached in May 1945, the Gestapo tried unsuccessfully to burn the monastery. On May 5 it was captured by the U.S. XX Corps, and in early June the 26th Infantry Division (Yankee Division) moved in with about a thousand men. The officers were housed in the abbot's rooms, and the enlisted men were quartered in the other rooms. They remained in place until February 1946.

Now, almost two years later, Miss Tucker and her team arrived. As they were parking the car, two monks came up and, speaking English, introduced themselves. Tucker explained their mission and elaborated that past MFA&A documents had stated that the monastery contained two depositories, one containing valuables from Austria and the other unidentified but left undisturbed by the MFA&A officer, Robert Miller. The monks inquired about Miller, and she gave them his New York address, as Miller had sent them a large can of smoking tobacco shortly after the war. The two monks were more than willing to show Dr. Kreutz and Miss Tucker around. They were most friendly and told Miss Tucker that at the end of the war the Americans had found and returned their extensive collection of fine art and their baroque library. While walking to the first storage area, the two monks said that Robert Miller and the Americans had earned their undying gratitude for the zeal and speed with which the restoration was made.

They did not elaborate on the multi-million-dollar coin collection, as its mysterious disappearance involved the prince archbishop of Salzburg and a few of the more valuable coins were still missing. Looted by the Germans and stored in Alt Aussee, the coins had been removed by Dr. Hans Helmuth von Hummel. Afterward, both von Hummel and the coins had disappeared.

This first storage area Tucker visited contained a large marble stove that had been dismantled by the Germans and was from the Rothschilds' palace in Vienna. Tucker saw that the beautiful stove had been ruined forever, and Kreutz added that the Rothschild family was no longer interested in its return. The second area contained more Rothschild valuables, which were in the process of being moved to the art depot of the Austrian government.

As Tucker was preparing to leave, one of the two monks, Brother Willibrod, smiled and said that he must confess to a small wrongdoing. As the monk beamed, he said that during the period that German soldiers had been billeted at Kremsmünster, some of the monks had fled to Switzerland, and two had actually gone on to America. He and several more, however, had been forced into the German army, where he had served as a sergeant in the medical corps. When the Germans fled at war's end, Brother Willibrod returned to the monastery. The American soldiers had now taken over the monastery and allowed Willibrod to stay. After several weeks and as the Americans were preparing to depart, the friar noticed two small locked cases in the hallway. Knowing that the cases could not contain military supplies, he used his foot to push the small cases under his long robe. Shuffling along in what must have been a comic spectacle, he managed to slide the cases into a hidden spot under the stairway. The owner had not left the hallway, but Brother Willibrod's movements went undetected. When the officer/owner reached down to claim his two cases, he was astonished to find that they were missing. As the officer left, he was cursing his fellow officers, exclaiming that he would never have believed that an American would steal from his fellow officer, never suspecting that a holy man was the culprit.

Brother Willibrod had suspected that the cases contained loot from the monastery, and after the Americans left, he opened the cases, surprised to find that they contained twenty-two small paintings by noted German artists. The paintings were oil-on-canvas and oil-on-wood, and mainly done by Bavarians, so it appeared that the American officer had looted from a collection as he made his way through southern Germany. The monk was delighted to turn over the two cases to Tucker, and as she was packing them in her car, he said, "Take care of my beautiful children." The sprightly monk had done his bit for the arts.

Remaining in Salzburg the following week, Tucker checked various U.S. Counter Intelligence offices for single items that had been taken by the military, items such as rugs, paintings, and pieces of sculpture. She examined four wooden cases of Joachim von Ribbentrop's paintings in the Property Control Warehouse and separated several of the more valuable ones from their cases. As she repacked the artworks, she held one toward the light and admired its fragile beauty. It was *White Horse* by Albert Cuyp, about eight inches by eight inches, oil-on-wood. Tucker also inspected a long ermine evening coat which had belonged to the notorious Robert Ley's mistress. Later in the week, she made an inventory list of the twenty-two paintings she had received from Brother Willibrod. After completing the inventory, she read several outstanding Hungarian and Czechoslovakian claims and was surprised to discover that the claims were made for property reported to be in the Kremsmünster Monastery.

The following morning, November 2, Tucker and Kreutz returned to the monastery, and she requested to speak once again to Brother Willibrod. She asked about the Czech paintings, and Willibrod motioned for her to follow him. He led the pair to a small room and pointed at the paintings stacked in the room. Tucker asked the friar why he had not told her about the paintings on the previous visit, and he replied that he had simply forgotten. Tucker then inquired about the four chests of art treasures claimed by the Hungarians. Brother Willibrod questioned several other monks, and they all claimed to have no recollection of the chests; furthermore, they said, only one monk had remained at the monastery during the SS occupation. They then told Tucker that the monk, Brother Mayrhofer, might be able to assist her, but that he had been arrested by the Americans and was still imprisoned in Camp Mooseberg. For the past year, he had served as the Catholic priest at the prison camp. Tucker was determined to find Mayrhofer; but she would never get the opportunity. She and her party returned to Linz, and at five that evening she caught the Mozart to Vienna.

Returning to Salzburg the following week, Evelyn Tucker worked exclusively on the Frederic Wels collection. Wels, prior to the war, was the owner of a rather modest gallery, Wels Gallerie. At the beginning of the war, Wels, a Nazi party member, branched out and was commissioned by the Austrian Nazi party to establish a large art gallery in Salzburg. For this purpose he was directed to purchase mostly from France. Wels was instructed to purchase many of the fine tapestries and paintings that had been looted by Napoleon in 1813, when he thoroughly looted Salzburg. Until Wels began his purchases, the city of Salzburg had no art galleries to speak of. Wels was successful in purchasing many of the items looted by Napoleon, and the thought of returning the art to France made most officials in Salzburg bristle with indignation. Most of Wels's purchases had been collected and returned through the Munich Collection Center. The difficulty in cleaning up some of the loose ends of the vast Wels art collection was beginning to fluster Tucker.

Her first meeting with Wels was in the Oesterreichischer Hof, a grandiosely furnished hotel for ranking American civilians and U.S. officers in Salzburg. While there, Tucker reviewed a rather lengthy inventory of paintings that had been purchased in France by Wels and that had not yet been returned. During the review, she also mentally evaluated Wels and was rather impressed with his proficiency in both English and French. During their conversation, Wels presented his own lengthy list of his personal property looted by the U.S. Army in 1945. The list included books, art, fur coats, his wife's dresses, underwear, and many other household goods. He demanded to know what Tucker was going to do about the missing property. She was aware that his family possessions had been stolen by an American lieutenant and that the investigation was going nowhere.

Although humiliated by this confrontation, Tucker reasoned that she needed additional information from Wels and decided to listen to his complete story in order to remove some of the mystery surrounding him. In gaining his confidence, she listened as he told of his property being looted and his arrest and two years' imprisonment by the Americans at Camp Orr. He, like most former Nazis, was never tried in a court of law and was considered a war criminal by the Americans because he purchased art in France during the war. Wels further stated that upon his release from Camp Orr, he had presented a receipt for personal items such as his watch, wallet, and other belongings. The American captain had torn up the receipt and thrown it in his face. Upon asking the captain how he could get his property without a receipt, the officer replied, "Oh, you want a receipt?" and without another word the captain sat down and filled out a receipt form. Under the section covering personal property the captain wrote "none." Wels claimed that he left the camp without his personal belongings and with the feeling, shared by most Europeans, that the Americans as a whole composed the most immoral army of occupation the world had ever known.

Tucker noticed during the conversation that Wels kept eyeing a large painting hanging at the end of the room. She asked if Wels liked the painting, and he responded, "Not especially, but it is one of mine that I bought in France." Tucker, a little nonplussed, wondered why this painting was still in an American-managed hotel, and the statement about the "looting Amis" by the St. Florian's abbot flashed through her mind. She then asked Wels if he knew the location of more of his missing art. "Sure, in the officers' club at the Klessheim Castle."

The castle had been taken over in 1945 by the U.S. Army but was now vacated by the military, although the adjoining Cavalierhaus was still used by the Americans. The Cavalierhaus Officers' Club in Salzburg was built by the Nazis as a guest house for guests of Castle Klessheim. The club was part of the Klessheim estate and was completely furnished and decorated by the Germans with loot from France and Holland. The Cavalierhaus had been taken over in its entirety by General Harry Collins's officer staff in 1945, and since that time MFA&A personnel had not been allowed in the club to compile an inventory or photograph the collection, although it was common knowledge, for example, that the club contained *Diana and Aetaron* by I. A. Vallin, a painting that was on a claims list filed by the French.

Tucker tried to obtain permission for Wels to visit the Klessheim estate. Permission was granted for the castle, but it was absolutely forbidden for Wels to enter the officers' club. Wels, like most Austrians, had not been allowed into the estate during the American occupation. The pair arrived at the castle on November 21, 1947, at 9:00 A.M., and Wels was most anxious to see the interior, since he had been the one responsible for its renovation in 1939. They toured the castle, but Wels could not identify any of his collection, though he and Miss Tucker suspected that the better pieces of art had been moved from the castle to the officers' club.

Unfortunately for Evelyn Tucker, she began to investigate looted art located in U.S. military clubs and private American residences. This was to be the beginning of her undoing, and it started with a field trip from Linz on December 18, 1947.

She and Dr. Kreutz and a military driver left Linz at 8:00 A.M. There was about one and a half feet of snow, and the roads were icy, so they used a jeep for the trip. Her first call was on the adjutant military governor; she introduced herself and explained her mission of trying to locate and restore missing French fine art. The governor retorted with "But what in the world are the French doing with their fine arts in Austria? Where do they have them—in a museum?" Realizing that he was serious, Tucker requested a list of resorts and officers' clubs in Upper Salzburg. Asked why she wanted the information, she explained that she wanted to make an inventory of the fine art in these places. She was denied this information, however, because the military governor explained that "he was tired of reparations people coming around and wanting to take things out of his clubs." As she left, the officer called patronizingly after her, "Miss Tucker, just stay American, don't turn French or Austrian on us."

She just smiled and departed for the Gmunden Rest Center. While there, she could not help but observe that it contained a large amount of very fine French period furniture, as well as Dutch, French, and Hungarian paintings. Two very handsome fourteenth-century Italian vases, a matching pair, were on display and in her opinion should have been in a museum. Later, back in Linz she checked the real estate inventory, and the two exquisite vases were listed as "2 jugs, value $2."

Continuing her trip into Upper Austria, she revisited the St. Florian Monastery to check on the property she had uncovered two months before. The same abbot received Miss Tucker and her party and took them back to the large hall. The Property Control department had tagged many pieces of furniture and paintings with Dutch claim number 70 identification tags, but the property was still in the hall awaiting removal by Dutch authorities. Tucker was dumbfounded and asked the abbot why the items had not been released to the Dutch trucking firm of Schenker & Company, per her authorization. The abbot told her that an American property control officer had come to the monastery and reviewed the valuables, then told the Dutch to leave and would not release the property. The officer then had several pieces loaded into an army truck and left. The abbot said he was told that the items were taken to the general's villa, the Traunblick Villa (occupied by General Geoffrey Keyes), and the Gugelhaf Officers' Club in Linz and that a large wooden chandelier had been taken into Vienna. Stunned, Tucker knew that the two villas were the homes of the ranking U.S. general in Austria.

Tucker then visited the Gugelhof Officers' Club in Linz and discovered that it was furnished almost completely with property from the Schwarzenberg Castle in Czechoslovakia. During this visit she spotted the *Pastoral Scene* from the school of François Boucher and told the sergeant in charge that she was going to have the painting removed because it was part of a French property claim. During their conversation, Tucker noticed the long mirror hanging on the wall behind the bar and suspected that it had just been placed there from the St. Florian valuables. She inquired about the origin of the mirror and stated that it might belong to the Dutch. At that moment the captain who managed the officers' club came in and said that he did not mind the removal of the picture, but was most unhappy about losing the mirror. After some terse negotiations, Tucker left with the painting. The priceless mirror remained in the club.

Unable to visit either the Traunblick Villa or the general's villa, Tucker was now certain that contained a Van Dyke. Also removed from the St. Florian Monastery and sent to the general's villa was a rococo console table, a Chinese rug, and an Italian rococo mirror. These items were claimed by the Dutch under claim number 70. Inasmuch as Tucker could not tell the Dutch that these three items were in the general's villa in Linz, she wrote the Dutch mission that the property was lost and that she was unable to locate it.

The Traunblick Villa was maintained for General Keys and was filled with much fine art, including a work by the French painter Jean François Millet of the *Angelus* fame. This home was off-limits to Evelyn Tucker.

During the time that Tucker was in Linz, with information supplied by Dr. Otto Demus, she reinvestigated the missing Salzburg coin collection that had been burglarized by American troops in 1945. She investigated Mr. Howard Mackenzie and Captain Bertram M. LeVien, provost marshal; now, in 1948, both men were assigned duties in Linz. Her investigation did not uncover any new evidence, but her actions were becoming an annoyance to the Americans in Austria.

Returning to Vienna, Tucker began to make inquiries about the loot in the military establishments in Upper Austria. At this time she was totally unaware of how much had been looted by the Americans in the Salzburg Province.

20

The Salzburg Province

Miss Tucker continued various trips to Linz and Upper Austria, but during the spring she returned to Salzburg. On May 6, 1948, she and Baron Pretis, an MFA&A Austrian employee, left the Bristol Hotel and traveled to the area of Zell am See. At 10:00 A.M. they arrived at the Mittersill Castle, a famous gathering place for European nobility. The Mittersill was an international sporting club where, before hostilities, Princess Julianna of Holland spent her honeymoon and the duke of Windsor was a frequent guest. The castle was taken over for the Ahnenerbe, an organization established by Himmler that was comprised of over fifty different research associations. One of the branches of the Ahnenerbe had been established to carry out deplorable medical experiments, using concentration camp inmates as human guinea pigs. Mittersill was not used for this type of sadistic experiment, but for the Sven Hedin Institute. Hedin, a Swedish explorer and pro-Nazi, had traveled extensively in Tibet and Mongolia. The castle housed a large Tibetan collection that had been acquired by Hedin on an expedition to Tibet in 1943.

Tucker knew the history of the castle and was aware that the recent looting of it was completely shrouded in accusations and counteraccusations. On December 13, 1945, the Tibetan collection had been removed from the castle and taken to the Property Control Warehouse. From the warehouse, some of the furniture had been removed and was being used in American housing. Dr. Müller, an Austrian custodian of the castle, had been caught by the American military in the act of stealing

245

truckloads of furniture. He was selling the furniture and depositing the proceeds in his private bank account in Switzerland. Arrested, he jumped bond and fled to Switzerland. After Müller, Mrs. Nijinsky, wife of the famous Russian dancer, was appointed custodian of the castle. She stole and sold enough valuables to finance a trip to England, where she remained. It also had been reported that a Lieutenant Colonel Smith had removed large quantities of furniture and had taken it to the Fischhorn Castle.

Tucker dwelled on this sad history as she inspected the filthy interior of the castle. Other than built-in furniture, all that remained behind were a few framed photographs of Mongol warriors, Tibetan masks, and about two hundred scientific books scattered about on the floor. She knew that at the time of the arrival of the American army, the castle had contained a mixture of comfortable old castle furnishings and modern equipment brought in by the SS. Now it was a looted, filthy, uninhabitable wreck.

After three hours of inspecting the Mittersill Castle and depressed by the theft and disorder, Tucker and her associates left and arrived at the Fischhorn Castle in late afternoon. Unaware of the previous activity at the Fischhorn, Tucker ignored the Off Limits to All Military and Civilian Personnel sign posted at the entrance to the property by order of General Ralph H. Tate. She knocked on the castle door, and a maid answered. Miss Tucker introduced herself and stated that she was there to check some fine art in the castle and would also like to talk to Mrs. Gildemeister. The maid said this was not possible. Mrs. Gildemeister's sister was very sick, and additionally, everything in the castle belonged to the Gildemeister family. They had been talking through a small window in the main door, so Tucker asked her to open it and let them speak with someone else. "No," said the maid. "It is forbidden." Again, Tucker insisted on seeing someone in authority. The maid opened the door, came out, and pointing up a small hill toward a house in the distance, said, "Perhaps the business manager of the castle will show you around." As the maid stepped back inside, Tucker followed, but the maid turned around and started to push her back outside. Tucker gave the maid a strong shove and forced herself inside the courtyard of the castle. Meanwhile, Baron Pretis had gone up the hill to see the manager, Mr. Zillich.

Tucker sat just inside the door and waited for Pretis to return. After a half hour, Pretis returned and said that the manager flatly refused to come to the castle and show them anything. Tucker, now more adamant than ever, absolutely refused to leave until she had inspected the castle. In a loud voice she repeated that she had an important position with the U.S. Occupation Forces and also she had come all the way from Vienna to check the fine art and intended to do so before leaving.

At that moment the doctor attending the sick sister came into the courtyard and inquired as to what the ruckus was all about. Tucker repeated her mission, and the doctor brusquely ordered the maid to "stop this nonsense. Can't you see that she is determined to check the paintings and the sooner she checks them the sooner she will leave?" The party gained entry, and Tucker made an inventory of seventeen suspected paintings, sixty modern Swedish chairs, and several rugs in the castle.

When she returned to Salzburg on May 10, Tucker reported to Mr. Veron R. Kennedy, property control officer, regarding the furniture at the Fischhorn. She had concluded that the chairs and rugs were SS loot and should be confiscated for American dependent families. At the Property Control Office, she was told that the army was leasing the Fishhorn Castle and had given the "inmates" until May 17 to evacuate the castle—telling them to remove any paintings or objects of value. Tucker immediately advised Kennedy to remove the inventoried items. Simultaneously, Miss Evelyn Tucker returned to the Fischhorn and removed four of the most valuable paintings: two sixteenth-century paintings, *Lady With Neck Frill* and *Cleopatra With Slave* and Lucas Cranach's *Madonna With the Child and Grape*. These three valuable works were taken to the Property Control Warehouse. The fourth painting, *The Doge's Palace in Venice* by Rudolf von Alt, was taken personally to Vienna by Miss Tucker and released to Dr. Otto Demus, president of the Bundesdenkmalamt. Tucker wrote: "I wanted him to be sure and see it. Alt's usual medium was watercolors, but this was a very nice oil, of which he painted only a few."

The members of the Gildemeister family, several servants, and members of the American Quaker Relief program had lived in the castle for two years, and about 50 percent of their property had been returned through the assistance of General Tate. In May 1948, Lieutenant John B. Leonard went to inspect the Fischhorn. He was the officer who had taken Gildemeister's desk two years earlier. The army contended that the Gildemeister family had pulled a fast one. Leonard had no written orders and was not allowed entry into the castle. General Collins's staff would even the score. By now they had fabricated a story that the desk had been looted by the SS in Holland and was worth ten thousand dollars. It had taken two years, but on May 15, 1948, Mr. Zillich was notified to evacuate the castle by May 19. Mr. Zillich asked for an extension, first with a humanitarian explanation, saying that Mrs. Gildemeister's sister was dying, and second, demanding proof in writing for the requisition of the castle. The Americans would not extend the departure date or relinquish their claim on the Fischhorn and informed the manager that the castle had been rented at the request of General Harry J. Collins and that the act had been approved by the Real Estate Office, U.S. Forces, Austria, Vienna Headquarters.

Mr. Gildemeister immediately wrote a letter of protest to the Department of State in Washington. He was informed that his estate had been leased by the Austrian government to U.S. forces to provide housing for U.S. officers and their dependents. A military School for Standards had been located at Zell am See, and housing was needed for the families of military officers who would be teaching at the school. The castle would be inhabited by four families, and four of the bathrooms would be turned into kitchens, and the families would then accommodate themselves as they desired. The reported SS chairs and rugs remained in the Fischhorn for their use. James A. Garrison, chief of the Reparations Division, further wrote, "Mr. Gildemeister, therefore, who has been dependent upon information received mostly from Austrian peasants has a warped impression of the entire matter."[1]

Gildemeister was further informed that any future complaints he had would have to be directed by him to the Austrian government. Of course, this was not true. Austria was occupied by Allied forces and subject to Occupation Agreement, Article 1a, which stated, The Austrian Government and all subordinate Austrian Authorities shall carry out such directions as they may receive from the Allied Commission."

Mr. Gildemeister acknowledged:

I would not say anything if a military necessity existed for the requisition of the castle. I can only explain the whole procedure as an act of bad feelings on the part of General Harry Collins, caused by events years ago. Perhaps it is likely to happen to men left too many years in the same post of occupation.[2]

In May, Maria Luisa Gildemeister went to Salzburg and delivered sworn testimony and receipts for three of the paintings. During this time, Miss Tucker presented the paintings to Polish art experts for further inspection. The paintings were photographed by the Polish, who relinquished claims to *Cleopatra With Slave* and Lucas Cranach's *Madonna With the Child and Grape*. The paintings were returned to the Gildemeister family. In February 1949 the Polish government notified Tucker that their mission had dropped all claims for *Lady With Neck Frill*. The painting was returned to Mrs. Gildemeister, but it had suffered considerable damage since its seizure by Tucker. There were six long scratches across the surface. Maria Gildemeister noted the damage on the signed receipt. The remaining thirteen paintings that had been inventoried by Miss Tucker were released to the Polish mission and sent to Warsaw.

21

The Munich Collection Center

IN 1948 THE VALUABLES in the Munich and Wiesbaden collection centers were under the direction of Mr. O. R. McJunkins, from Jacksonville, Florida, chief of the Reparations and Restitution Branch. The greatest problem at the end of the war in connection with European cultural objects was collecting, sorting, and returning to the proper country the works of art, archives, and libraries displaced as a direct result of World War II. To provide a means to collect and process objects of art, the United States established three main collection points in the U.S. Zone of Germany.

The Wiesbaden Collection Center held mostly German artworks, primarily from former state museums, plus a certain amount of loot taken from German Nazis. The Wiesbaden Collection Center contained about 700,000 objects. The Offenbach Archival Depot was reserved for archival material, books, precious scrolls, and primarily Jewish looted collections. Offenbach contained a grand total of 1,841,310 items. The Munich Collection Center specialized in art objects seized from museums and art seized from individuals. Munich contained over one million objects. These collection points contained approximately one-fifth of the artwork of the world. By 1948 most of the art had been returned from the Munich and Wiesbaden collection centers to their country of origin.

Now the plan was to turn over what remained in the two collection centers to the local German governments of Bavaria and Hesse. McJunkins was given the order "to cut all red tape" and return the remaining controversial items located in Munich to their country of origin. All Jewish property was to be sent from both collection points to Offenbach. Abiding by this last request, a frustrated U.S. official wrote, "I feel sure that fellows more sapient than I can look at a painting and say that it was last owned by a Jew who lost it after January 1, 1933. I am at a loss."

A far more serious problem was faced by McJunkins. The Department of State had made the decision to return to Italy the items acquired by Germany at the time they were Axis partners. The Germans and their staunch admirer Herbert Stewart Leonard, director of the Munich Collection Center, protested adamantly the return of the collection. Leonard wrote:

> Among the claims for such works of art of national value are portraits by Waldmüller and Amerling who were, all their lives, rather fashionable portrait painters in Vienna. The Italians are, of course, pressing their advantage.... You can't guess the sharpness of army venom when its resentment is aroused over the emergence of truth!"[1]

On the Italian restitution, Mr. Richard F. Howard, MFA&A chief for OMGUS, wrote:

> Of course there was not only consultation and concurrence from the State Department; but if I remember correctly, there was a cable from Washington which specifically directed that the Military Government return to Italy objects which were illegally removed. There was some of the usual double-talk in expressing what was meant by illegally removed. Anyone who implies that there was any lack of validation, concurrence, agreement or legality within the Military Government, with the sole exception of Leonard who in the process violated security measures and disobeyed the direct orders of the Military Government, is imbued with the same Germanophile prejudice which permitted Leonard to go off his rocker.[2]

Into this discord entered Miss Evelyn Tucker to protect the art claimed by Austria. During her brief stays in Vienna, Tucker spent considerable time with Dr. Demus, the president of the Bundesdenkmalamt. Demus used his time wisely with Tucker and maneuvered her into promoting the Austrian cause in the restoration of art. His goal was to retain all of the looted art currently in Austria and also return to Austria the art found in the Austrian depositories that had been taken into Germany at the close of the war. Tucker, distraught by the looting of the Americans, in her naïveté would unwillingly accommodate the best professionals in looting—the Austrian government. After all, they had hundreds of years of experience; the Americans were rank novices.

In 1945, Andrew C. Ritchie of the Albright Art Gallery in Buffalo, New York, acting in the role of MFA&A officer, had returned the crown jewels and regalia of the Holy Roman Empire in a C-47 transport plane along with the prominent Czernin family's Vermeer, *The Artist in His Studio*. Additionally, the Munich Collection Center had shipped to Austria fifteen shipments of Austrian art, but Dr. Demus had received the impression from his two staff members working at Munich that the U.S. Army was not going to return the unidentified art seized from Austria territory at the end of hostilities, nor was it going to return the art purchased in Austria during the German occupation. Demus and his staff began indoctrinating Miss Tucker with the following established procedures regarding the looted art.

The Joint Chiefs of Staff had sent a directive, WARX 99226, dated March 4, 1946, specifying that "all fine art removed from Austria during the period of March 13, 1938, to May 18, 1945, even through acquisition, purchase or any method purporting to be a legal transaction shall be returned to Austria." Furthermore, U.S. Forces in Germany (OMGUS) and U.S. Forces in Austria (USFA) agreed that all fine art found in the U.S. Zone of Austria and removed to the Munich Collection Center for processing remained under the jurisdiction of the commanding general, USFA. In the spring of 1946, to avoid unnecessary travel, it was agreed by USFA and OMGUS to empower the director of the Munich Collection Center to sign receipts on behalf of the commanding general, USFA, thereby giving the director a dual capacity.

With this knowledge, Tucker and Dr. Demus traveled to the Munich Collection Center in Tucker's new Ford, which had just been delivered to Vienna by rail. At the collection center they were met by Herbert Stewart Leonard and Edgar Breitenbach, the chief investigator. During their tour they were told that the center had a German staff of 160 employees. Tucker noticed that it was closely guarded and elaborately equipped. The art had been separated into various types such as sculpture, paintings, antiques, furniture, tapestries, and so on, and each category was handled by individual specialists in the particular field. Tucker was dismayed that the property taken from Austria had not been kept separate from the other valuables.

At the center were 2,500 unidentified items that were referred to as the "Hitler collection" and, in fact, were items of art that had been intended for the future Linz Art Museum. Leonard and Dr. Erika Hamfstaengl, his assistant and chief German representative, were most proud that they had managed to reassemble the collection. This attitude worried both Tucker and Demus. As Demus looked through the Hitler collection, Tucker discussed with Leonard two sixteenth-century gold pendants belonging to the Rothschild collection that had been stolen from the Munich Collection Center. The pendants were part of a great deal of antique jewelry that had been assembled for shipment to Austria. When Tucker pushed the issue and stipulated that the staff should be more careful in the handling of small items with a high value, Leonard responded that the pendant had been turned over to the Austrian curator, that no one knew of the existence of this particular jewelry except the two Austrian employees, and that it was lost due to their carelessness. Tucker dropped the issue at this point, for she had no way of knowing that she was being lied to. The jewelry had actually been stolen by a German guard, and Leonard was aware of the fact.

During Demus's investigation of the Hitler collection, he noticed that the paintings were ones that had been removed from Alt Aussee, but both Tucker and Demus noticed that the prevailing attitude was that Austria did not have a claim to these items or any other items in the collection center, unless it could prove that they were confiscated or sold under duress. The German staff said that this was "occupation policy."

Tucker again approached Leonard with the question of returning art to Austria. Leonard claimed that OMGUS had issued an order to turn over to the Bavarian state government all unidentified art that was presently in the Munich Collection Center. She then reminded Leonard that he had a dual role, one working for OMGUS and the other working for USFA, and that by taking this position he was only representing OMGUS. They looked at each other wordlessly for a long moment; then Leonard shrugged his shoulders and said, "Eve, my chief is in Berlin." He then produced a telegram from General Lucius Clay, supreme commander of Germany, stating that the center and all unidentifiable property there would be turned over to Bavaria by August 31, 1948. Leonard added that Bavaria had borne the complete expense of operating the Munich Collection Center and deserved the millions of dollars' worth of remaining unidentified loot. He further claimed that the German government had ceded all of Hitler's personal possessions to Bavaria because the state of Bavaria was the last permanent residence of the Führer. Stunned by this logic, Tucker stated that OMGUS could not terminate a treaty with USFA without as much as notifying them. She further insisted that Washington had announced to the world that it considered the *Anschluss* of Austria the first act of German aggression and that the return of the unidentified art taken from Austria was based on that assumption. A dazed Miss Tucker and Dr. Demus returned to Vienna. It was time to reevaluate their position.

After considerable research and work with the Austrians and with no support or direction from her superiors, Miss Tucker returned to Munich on August 4, 1948. Neither James Garrison in Vienna, Veron Kennedy in Salzburg, nor Colonel McKee, Miss Tucker's immediate supervisor, had the slightest intention of jeopardizing their careers by defending Austria's claim to World War II loot. They could not reconcile themselves personally to the idea that Austria—Germanic in history, blood, and speech, which had fought side by side with Germany, killing American soldiers—had been exploited by German aggression and now needed our help. Regardless of the directives issued after the war, most Americans working in Europe were not buying these politically motivated Department of State policies.

On the other side of the coin, Leonard had been in Germany during the war and remained there afterward. After three years of working with a largely German staff, he had somehow become enamored of things German and took it upon himself to represent Germany in foreign affairs. In this self-imposed role, Leonard would disregard direct orders by the Military Government of the United States.

These two strong-willed Americans, Leonard and Tucker, self-appointed ambassadors for Germany and Austria, met again in early August. Tucker had arranged to meet Leonard three days prior to a scheduled showdown meeting. She had hoped to settle the main dispute of the art claimed by Austria prior to the meeting. Nothing was accomplished, and Leonard never backed off from his original statement, saying, "Eve, USFA had no jurisdiction over anything in the Munich Collection Center, and I think that it is too silly for words for you to continue to talk about it." Tucker's comeback was that the art removed from Austria was under the jurisdiction of the commanding general of Austria and he would not give it up simply because a civilian thought it "silly." Nothing was accomplished in their preliminary discussion, and Tucker left a prepared paper with Leonard for his review during the weekend.

The following Monday, August 9, 1948, Richard F. Howard, chief, MFA&A, OMGUS; O. R. McJunkins, chief, Restitution, and Reparations OMGUS; and Tucker met in Leonard's office to discuss the controversial issue of turning the center over to the Germans. With the help of Demus, president of the Bundesdenkmalamt, Evelyn Tucker had prepared a straightforward paper that contained a request that the art be separated into the following categories before turning the collection center over to the Germans:

Category I. Prewar German fine art to be retained in Munich
Category II. Prewar Austrian fine art to be returned to Austria
Category III. Fine art believed to belong to Allied nations, to be retained in Munich
Category IV. Paintings by Austrian artists, origin unknown, to be returned to Austria.
Category V. Property of unknown origin to be returned to Austria

Tucker's paper was read by the group, and then Leonard presented his views in the form of a written statement. Leonard's paper was full of controversial statements and was intentionally sarcastic and provocative. Leonard was unwilling to discuss anything reasonable, so within half an hour, Howard and McJunkins agreed to Miss Tucker's recommendation of the five categories. Over the objections of Leonard, McJunkins told Howard to handle the details. Because of the time needed to separate the art, it was agreed by all to delay the August 31 turnover to Bavaria.

As Tucker took some time off for vacation, other problems piled up for Leonard and his staff. The Italians had demanded the return of art purchased from Italy during the late 1930s when they and the Germans were on friendly terms. Under orders from the Department of State, Leonard was to return the valuables. Again, acting as an ambassador for Germany instead of as an employee of the occupying forces, Leonard objected, stalled, and actually hid some of the art to keep them from being returned to Italy.[3]

Unaware of this and thinking that the segregation of the art was progressing as expected, Tucker returned to the Munich Collection Center on Monday, September 20. After checking into the Excelsior Hotel, she called Leonard and asked him to meet her at the Haus der Kunst Officers' Club. Over a drink she asked Leonard what procedure he had established for the separation of the five categories. To her surprise, he said that he had thought the problem over and had sent his ideas to Berlin and if his paper was not accepted he would resign. Miss Tucker stated that she doubted that he would resign, but Leonard replied laughingly, "I certainly shall, and what is more I will retire to northern Italy and blow my head off." This statement halted their discussions on business for the night. As Tucker left for her hotel she hoped that the bizarre statement had been the result of the large quantity of alcohol Leonard had consumed.

The following morning, Tucker reported to work, and the conversation of the previous night was not mentioned. At lunch she met Leonard and told him that their work was progressing and that she was pleased with the cooperation between the Germans and the Austrians. Miss Tucker noticed that Leonard's young, single, and attractive assistant, Dr. Erika Hanfstaengl, was absent, and she wondered if she was sick or staying away in protest of the work being done. On all her previous visits, immediately after dinner they had met in Dr. Hanfstaengl's apartment or gone to Leonard's, and he had called her over. At about 5:00 P.M. Leonard asked Tucker to join him at the Haus der Kunst Officers' Club for dinner. Again after dinner Hanfstaengl was conspicuosly absent. Tucker asked if Hanfstaengl was home pouting or sick. Leonard snorted that Hanfstaengl was not the pouting type, and as things at this time seemed to be progressing successfully, Miss Tucker thought no more about it.

On Wednesday morning, Leonard instructed his staff not to help Tucker with her work. She went into his office to demand an explanation. Sitting in his office was Erika Hanfstaengl, and as Leonard talked on the phone, they greeted each other quite pleasantly, and Hanfstaengl remarked that she had fallen off her bicycle three days before and had suffered a slight brain concussion. She was feeling all right now, she said, and was taking it easy. Leonard finally ended his phone conversation, and Tucker asked him if it was correct that he had instructed his staff to discontinue working on the separation. Tucker now felt intuitively that Hanfstaengl was behind the work stoppage. White-faced, Leonard picked up the phone, dialed his boss, and shouted, "I am resigning this minute! You will have my written resignation in two hours!" He then slammed down the receiver and huffed, "I am not discussing the matter anymore." He leaped up from his chair and rushed out of the office. Hanfstaengl had sat quietly throughout the entire performance.

Tucker burst into Dr. Breitenbach's office and demanded, "Edgar, what in the world has happened to Stewart this morning? He is acting like a demented person." Breitenbach replied that he did not think it was just the Austrian art that had upset Leonard, but that he had been terribly upset lately over some Italian restitutions. The following day, Richard Howard, Stefan (Steve) Munsing, Edgar Breitenbach, Leonard, and several of his old friends spent most of the day in Leonard's office as Tucker continued separating the art. At the end of the day, Breitenbach came to take Tucker to catch the train. On the way to the station, Tucker asked what had been discussed concerning Leonard's resignation threats. Breitenbach surprised Miss Tucker when he answered that the resignation was not discussed and that the group had just talked about old times. Stunned, Tucker inquired if Leonard was threatening resignation to intimidate her. Breitenbach reached over and squeezed her hand, saying, "Not you, Eve, but Howard." Later, Richard Howard was to write of this episode with Leonard, "The man was a nervous wreck—unstable from the beginning, unwilling to discuss anything reasonable and unable to stay sober during the period."[4]

During his turbulent time at the collection center, Leonard had written to several U.S. museums regarding the possibility of employment. He returned to the United States and in February 1949 acquired the position of assistant to the director of the City Art Museum of St. Louis. Three years later the forty-one-year-old native of Fargo, North Dakota, would die unexpectedly at his apartment in the Branscome Hotel.

Caught up in the importance of their job, Evelyn Tucker and Demus left Vienna in her Ford at 5:00 A.M. on December 16, 1948. They were returning to the Munich Collection Center in triumph to collaborate the return of the art, as had been previously agreed upon. Upon arriving, they were given a very chilly reception by Steve Munsing, the new director of the collection center, who had taken over the position from Leonard. In an update, Munsing told them that as far as he knew, the separation was continuing, but that not a single painting would leave the center until the legal staff of the Occupation Military Government of Bavaria had received proven evidence from the legal staff of USFA that the property in question belonged to Austria. With Munsing's triumphant look, Tucker's heart sank.

Tucker mentioned that the Austria's actions were based on the Moscow Declaration and USFA restitution directives, which stated that all art removed from Austria after March 13, 1938, would be returned. Munsing countered that Washington did not tell him how to handle the situation, that instead he told Washington what should be done and if necessary he would pick up the phone and call President Harry Truman, whom he knew personally. Tucker got in a stab by saying that she was happy that she could discuss this controversial subject without his threatening to jump out a window or resigning. His reply: "Oh, no, Eve, nobody is going to bother me. I have not the slightest intention of resigning, and anyone who bothers me will simply be eliminated." Munsing then gave her a condescending smile and said rather plainly that if she was a "good girl" everything would be all right. He then added rather carelessly that Richard Howard was returning to the States. The inference was that the Italian restitution business had cost Howard his job. Tucker could not help wondering if Munsing really had connections in Washington. She considered him a misinformed, childish braggart. She should have taken his threat of "elimination" more seriously.

Miss Tucker and Demus left Munich on December 18 and returned to Vienna. She took leave from her work until the end of the year.

22

Evelyn Tucker's Final Report

While in Austria, Evelyn Tucker made the biggest mistake of her career: the investigation of General Collins's residence and headquarters. She started by trying to inspect the private military guardhouse located adjacent to Villa Warsburg, General Collins's main residence in Salzburg. The German government had filed a claim for the property in the guardhouse, claiming that it included antique furniture, paintings, graphics, and miscellaneous objects belonging to the Germans. Villa Warsburg contained *Harvest in Maxglan* by Anton Doll, *Laufen Near Ischl* by Anton Schiffer, *Bad Gastein and Waterfall* by Thomas Ender, and a French seenteenth-century tapestry and four Louis XV chairs. Hanging on the wall in Collins's personal office was *Portrait of a Man With Neck Frill* by Van Dyke. The Van Dyke had been removed from Residenz Palace in Salzburg along with *Mountain Ridge on Radstaetter Tauern* by Anton Schiffer and six additional valuable paintings of Hungarian origin. Between the time Collins vacated the office and the time it was acquired by General Kendall, the painting by Schiffer disappeared. Kendall was held responsible for the missing painting, and the property was placed under the jurisdiction of the Austrian government. In order to conceal this swindle, Colonel McKee recommended that the receipts to the Austrian government be withdrawn and that they be retained under U.S. custody.

In Vienna, Tucker continued on her hazardous mission by investigating the headquarters of General Mark Clark and his staff. James Garrison's office contained five paintings of Hungarian origin. Veron

Kennedy's office was also decorated with fine art claimed by the Hungarians. Mr. James Langer's apartment was furnished with *Cows in a Stable* by Verboeckhoven from the Wels collection, two Hungarian paintings—*Sunset With Peasant House at a Lake* by Komarum Kanz and *Head of a Man* by an unknown artist—and Rembrandt's *Hendrije Stoffels in Bed*, a portrait of his mistress. Miss Tucker made three trips to Langer's home and finally convinced Mrs. Langer to allow the removal of the most valuable painting, the Rembrandt.

Tucker should have suspected that her investigation was not wanted by the military authorities when she was restricted from residences, clubs, or offices for the inspection of art objects. Because of these restrictions, she recommended that an investigation be made of property removed to Vienna by General Clark, to determine if it included any museum items or loot from Allied nations.

After Christmas vacation, during the first week of January 1949, Miss Tucker was straightway informed by her boss, Lieutenant Colonel E. S. McKee, that she had been fired. Devastated, Tucker defended herself as the only person familiar with the delicate and explosive work and added that she was the only person who could bring the job to a successful conclusion. McKee responded that she had until February 1 to complete her final report, because her contract expired on that date.

McKee added, "You must recognize, Eve, that you are absolutely helpless—the army has you by the neck and you cannot fight it."

Miss Tucker wrote, "For me to have to even listen to this insulting talk, when I have fought so hard to protect so much from petty thievery and grand larceny, was rather galling."

At that time, McKee had in his possession a reddish Persian rug six by ten feet, requisitioned from the Property Control Warehouse on June 2, 1948; Howard Mackenzie, now a civilian working in the Collection Depot in Linz, had also retained a large reddish Persian rug, eighteen by ten feet.

On January 6, 1949, in frustration, Miss Tucker wrote Miss Ardelia Hall, Department of State, the following letter:

The negligence of this explosive situation was hardly short of being criminal. There was no control on what American officers sent home. The same man sits in control now in Salzburg, he is Chief of Property Control and Restitution. He is also Deputy Chief of Military Government. As such in his first capacity he is custodian of the Property Control Warehouse in Salzburg which he uses as a requisition dump for officers' homes and clubs. He is of course a great favorite with the generals, being among other things a good poker player. Efforts on my part to protect the property from these inroads have been without avail. This man's name is Veron R. Kennedy. He was formerly in labor circles in California and then with the Inter-Governmental Committee for Refugees. There is French looted fine art in the general's villa in Salzburg, Dutch fine art in the general's villa in Linz, French looted paintings in the officers' club in Salzburg. All identified and included on claims filed by these countries, but I have not been allowed to reveal that I have found them. A Lieutenant Colonel returned to the States recently from Salzburg, taking with him 26 Oriental and Hungarian rugs. My Chief, Lieutenant Colonel E. S. McKee, refused to let me write the Provost Marshal to investigate. Several truckloads of fine art were taken from the Klessheim Castle in Salzburg to Vienna by General Mark W. Clark for his quarters. While under protection of U.S. military personnel, a Rubens, Van Dyke, and five more paintings were stolen from the Lauffen Mine and seven paintings including four Dürers were stolen by U.S. Personnel from Alt Aussee. There has been no investigation, but all is carefully documented by the Austrian Government.

Miss Tucker's final report contained the following:

Lieutenant Colonel R. C. Raleigh, Foreign Liaison Officer, signed for 26 Hungarian Oriental rugs which he failed to turn in before he returned to Fort McClellan, Alabama. These rugs had been requested by the Hungarians under claim number 234.

The property of the late Dr. Alphons de Rothschild disappeared from the Alt Aussee Saltmine in Austria, sometime between spring 1945 and spring 1946. Some of the six paintings were offered on the black market at Frankfurt. These drawings are Dürer's four engravings, *Knight, Death and Devil, Madonna With Grasshopper, Adam and Eve, Hubertus and Rowlandson,* and two pen drawings, *The Man Sick With Palsy,* and *Unexpected Visit.*

The following paintings disappeared from the Lauffen

Mine, Austria, while under U.S. Army control: *Landscape* by Berchem, *Faith* by Heemskerck, *Hope* by Heemskerck, *Female Portrait* by Rubens, *Portrait of a Gentleman* by Van Dyke, *Sketch for a Ceiling of the Venetian School*, and *Christ* by Antonello de Messina.

After Evelyn Tucker's contract with the army expired, she toured Europe, then returned to the United States and opened a small art shop in Miami Beach. On her last day she reported the theft of Albert Cuyp's *White Horse*, the eight-by-eight-inch oil-on-wood painting that she had held toward the light and admired in the warehouse. In spite of a thorough investigation, not one clue concerning the missing painting has ever turned up. One can only hope it was taken by Miss Tucker. Her report's closing comments were prophetic: "The gigantic search for their lost heritage which the nations of Europe have been conducting for the last three years will probably continue for the next fifty."

23

The Looting of the
Munich Collection Center

E VELYN TUCKER HAD BEEN UNAWARE that from 1945 onward
various art objects would surface for sale and their origin could be
traced to the Munich Collection Center. During her previous visit, for
instance, Herbert Stewart Leonard had known that the Rothschild
jewelry had been stolen, but kept the information from her. Then, as
now, the most popular place for the sale of looted art was Switzerland.
In 1948, Wilhelm Leibl's painting *Boy's Head With Hat* was purchased
by Dr. Robert Nathan from a banking house in Zurich. The painting
had been seized under Military Law 52 and stored in room 128 and was
listed as property number 41017. Nathan owned an art gallery in St.
Gallen, Switzerland. His gallery also contained fourteen Spitzweg
paintings that had been stolen from the Munich Collection Center.
Knowledge of these thefts prompted the staff of the collection center to
review their vast inventory of remaining art objects. As Erika Hanfstaengl, Leonard, and staff members looked through the rooms of art,
they counted more than one hundred empty frames with paintings cut
from them. Also missing was the Rothschild jewelry that Leonard had
lied about to Evelyn Tucker.

The stolen paintings had passed through several hands to arrive at
Nathan's gallery, and he had no intention of returning the looted art,
nor was he required to do so by Swiss law. The embarrassed staff of the
collection center did not have a clue as to who had stolen the missing

items. A thorough search of local art galleries in the area did turn up several art objects, but they were paintings that had been stolen from the Führerbau prior to the arrival of the occupying Americans.

The robberies remained a mystery until early August 1948, when an old woman limped into the Munich police station and told the inspector that she was a distant relative of Mrs. Albert Krinner. She claimed that a sister of Mrs. Krinner had told her that the family was hiding a diamond necklace and that one of the Krinner boys had sold a silver platter. She further stated that the family had received CARE packages from America allegedly in exchange for valuables.

The police, aware that Albert Krinner was a guard at the Munich Collection Center, notified Edgar Breitenbach, MFA&A officer. On August 23 he visited the sister of Mrs. Krinner. The sister was at odds with the Krinner family and enthusiastically confirmed the police report. She further stated that she had learned of the thievery through indiscreet remarks on the part of Gerta, the Krinners' oldest daughter.

Armed with these facts, Breitenbach confronted Albert Krinner and his wife. Mrs. Krinner aknowledged that she had known all along that her husband was involved in thefts at the collection center. During interrogation, Krinner admitted to stealing the sixteenth-century Austrian Rothschild jewelry. Mrs. Krinner stated that her husband had originally picked six pieces of jewelry but had discarded four of them because he did not consider them valuable. After bringing the two valuable pieces home, he did recognize their value and thought they may have been lamp attachments. He further admitted that he had stolen Christian Weber's property consisting of six sets of china. Krinner said that he had a secret hiding place between two columns in the center. He would place items to be stolen in this hiding place and remove them at a later date. He said that he had hidden the complete set of china in this secret area but that when he returned later to recover the objects, someone had removed two of the cups and saucers. He confessed that he had sold the china to an American army captain who worked at the 98th General Hospital in Munich.

During the next few days many astounding facts were uncovered. Mrs. Krinner had an excellent memory for paintings and identified ninety that her husband had stolen since 1945. The silver, china, figurines, jewelry, and other valuables stolen by Albert Krinner were almost beyond estimation. Of course, Krinner was arrested, but he managed to post bail of five thousand reichsmarks by having his wife sell ten pounds of silver that he had previously stolen from the White Russian treasure chest.

When questioned about the care packages from America, Krinner admitted that he had met Dr. Ivan F. Bennett in December 1946 and had sold him valuable stolen objects. Krinner further stated that Bennett knew that he was a guard at the collection center. Edgar Breitenbach wrote Bennett a letter addressed to the Harrisburg State Hospital in Pennsylvania and requested that Bennett return the stolen property. Breitenbach wrote that it was his earnest desire to settle the affair privately.

In a letter written on November 22, 1948, Bennett responded by stating that he had purchased the valuables in good faith. He was led to believe, he said, that the valuables were family heirlooms, and he had been making purchases since 1946. Bennett wrote, "It hardly seems reasonable to assume that he could have begun stealing at that time and not discovered before the summer of '48." It is not clear as to what happened to the items purchased by Dr. Bennett.

The stealing did not stop there, for on May 31, 1949, the Staatliche Münzsammlung München (Bavarian State Coin Collection) in Munich received an intriguing letter from Charles L. Morley. Mr. Morley, a native of New York City, wrote the letter from Florence, Italy. It was addressed to "My Good Sir" and said that he had seen some gems for sale in New York and upon checking a coin catalogue from the Bavarian State Museum believed that the coins might belong to the museum. Morley gave his return address in Paris for the month of June and a Swiss address for July. The director of the museum, Professor Gebhart, immediately wrote Morley a letter to the Paris address. The professor was most excited by Morley's letter and expressed a need for his help. Gebhart even invited Morley to Munich to discuss the coins.

The correspondence continued for six more months. In one of Morley's letters he wrote that the coin dealer had purchased the coins from a young man but was not required to obtain his name. Morley assured Gebhart that this was a proper procedure for the purchase of valuables in the United States. Morley further stated that the coin dealer wanted to remain anonymous, but would sell back the coins to the Bavarian State Museum. Gebhart agreed to the purchase of the coins, but insisted on knowing the name and address of the dealer. At Gebhart's insistence, Morley sent him the name and address: Stack's Coin Dealer, 12 West Forty-sixth Street, New York City.

Professor Gebhart never had any intention of purchasing the coins stolen from the collection. With this name and address he went to see Steve Munsing at the Munich Collection Center and gave him photographs of the coins held by Stack in New York City. Gebhart insisted on the return of the valuables. Munsing promised to take action in regard to restitution. Although Erika Hanfstaengl had received a previous letter from Leonard concerning the stolen gems and coins, Munsing ignored the situation and took no action. A year later, March 5, 1950, Gebhart wrote to the U.S. State Department seeking help in the return:

> Being the head of the State Coins Collection and thus obligated to make every possible endeavor to recover these precious pieces of our collection, I ask you to assist me in this case. I would be very much obligated to you if you would advise me as to the right way I should go and the correct means I might adapt after I have been unsuccessful all the time.

As expected, this letter was ignored also. But the unrelenting Gebhart continued to write.

During this time, Morley had contacted Herbert Steward Leonard, who was now working for the City Art Museum of St. Louis. Morley told Leonard that there were 168 antique gems and coins on the market in New York. Morley stated that since he was a coin dealer, he had taken them home for study and had found some of them in Fürtwangerler's *Antiken Gemmen* as the property of the Bavarian State Museum. At that point, Leonard wrote his friend Erika Hanfstaengl at the Munich Collection Center, and she verified that the coins had been stolen by an American guard. Leonard wrote: "Then this past week I heard from another New York dealer that Stack, a dealer in coins, had purchased the lot, that he had sold them to a man name Berry who seems to be an employee in the Department of State."[1]

Finally, on July 3, 1951, two years after Leonard had written his letter to the Munich Collection Center, Steve Munsing wrote the U.S. Legal Affairs Division the following letter:

> According to information I received today from a reliable source in the U.S. (a visitor who is in Munich at the present) a dealer by the name of Morton Stack (Stacks Coin, W. 46th Street, N.Y.C.) who has an unsavory reputation among certain dealers offered to Charles Morley (of 83rd St. and St. Moritz) another dealer some gems....

Munsing was merely stating what Leonard had written two years earlier. The new source was Robert Hecht, but Munsing was merely covering up for sitting on the situation for two years, while Gebhart pressed the matter, arousing a great deal of interest in Washington, Frankfurt, and Munich.

At this point Miss Ardelia Hall, Department of State, became involved with the missing valuables. After spending considerable time on the project, the U.S. government recovered 159 of the 371 missing coins and gems from Stack. Miss Hall wrote Mr. Burton W. Berry, now the American ambassador in Baghdad, a letter:

> It has been reported by the German Foreign Office which presumably had the information from the dealer, that you had purchased some of the items in the group from Stack's. I enclose a set of 14 photographs of the impressions of the seals and gems. Should it so happen that you purchased some of the other examples, which you can identify from the photographs, would you let me know. If you do not own any of the seals or gems I should be glad to correct the report.

Berry's reply is unknown, and his role concerning the missing valuables is unclear. The missing valuables were returned to the Bavarian State Museum in January 1955.

To add to the mystery and confusion, by now a few of the most valuable of the gems from the Bavarian State Museum had mysteriously made their way into the Metropolitan Museum of Art. And what was the Met's stand on this issue then? It is best described in a 1949 letter that Edith Standen wrote to Herbert Stewart Leonard:

> The daughters of the horse-leech have nothing on the Director and Curator of Paintings at the Metropolitan Museum of Art. Rousseau expressed deep interest in certain important Polish paintings, which, he said with good G-2 mystery, he happened to know were in American hands. Now maybe these should be returned directly to their owners, who are not in Poland, so they could sell them to the Met (unless David Finely got in first) but Rousseau's attitude of grab, grab, grab, irritated me. He actually said apropos of the Germans, "We've done a great deal for those people. We ought to get something out of it." I'm not likely to be offered a job at the Metropolitan or at the National Gallery, I am glad to say.

But Standen did get a job with the Met and today, in her eighties, still goes to work.

In 1957 the unflagging Professor Gebhart found out that the Met had a valuable antique Etruscan gem from the missing collection. He wrote the Met regarding the missing gem, and the Met responded that it had no legal authority to give away any object in its collection. In this case, however, the letter continued, an individual who wished to remain anonymous would be allowed to purchase the gem and return it to the Bavarian State Museum. This offer was made in writing by Christine Alexander, curator of Greek and Roman art. She wrote at the bottom in her own handwritting: "The Trustees, and I personally, are delighted to make this gesture!" The gem was returned within the month, and Dr. Gebhart wrote a most grateful thank-you.

Imagine the surprise of the Met when ten years later it received a letter from the Bavarian National Museum stating that the Met had three more gems from the missing collection. The letter described the gems in detail; there could be no mistake that the Met did indeed have the gems. The letter thanked the Met for their help in 1957. After much correspondence with the new Bavarian director, Dr. Grotemeyer, the Met reluctantly agreed to the return. The Met said that the gems had been donated but would not disclose the name of the donor. Grotemeyer suggested that the Met match its collection against the list of missing gems. The Met subsequently found two more gems that belonged to the collection and went on to say that the gems had been obtained in good faith and asked the Bavarian State Museum to purchase the gems at their appraised value. The museum declined to pay and wrote more letters, including some to the German embassy in New York City.

On October 27, 1966, Dudley T. Easby, Jr., of the Metropolitan Museum of Art wrote the following letter:

I am authorized to inform you that the Trustees of The Metropolitan Museum of Art has authorized the return to the Staatliche Münzsammlung of the five gemstones alleged to have been stolen during World War II. The action was taken under the understanding that at no time is the name of The Metropolitan Museum of Art to be mentioned in connection with the return of these stones.

The gems were returned on January 2, 1967.

24

The Good Fortune of Austria

THE OCCUPATION MILITARY GOVERNMENT UNITED STATES
(OMGUS) in Austria had been vanquished by an American civilian
organization under the direct administration of the Department of
State. The organization, known as the Office of the United States High
Commissioner for Germany (HICOG), made a binding agreement to
turn over all unclaimed art objects to Bavaria. This agreement was
meant to provide a source of funds to Bavaria in order to offset the
enormous financial burden assessed to them because of the General
Claims Act. As a result of this agreement, Bavaria had funded the total
cost of the Munich Collection Center, which included the expense of
collecting, sorting out, and returning to the proper countries the works
of art, archives, and libraries found in Austria. By far the largest amount
of valuables in the Munich Collection Center had been transferred there
by the U.S. Army from the salt mine at Alt Ausee, Austria. To avoid
admitting an error of this magnitude, the senior officials of HICOG
simply stalled and hoped the problem would go away.

The Austrian Government contacted Dean Acheson, secretary of
state, as they continued relentlessly in their quest for the return of their
claimed valuables. The Austrians could understand the reluctance of
OMGUS to return the items. Tucker's former boss, Colonel E. S.
McKee, went so far as to write that Leonard, followed by Munsing,
wanted to keep the Hitler museum collection intact. McKee wrote:
"This speculation is all the more plausible because the principal German
representative stationed at the Munich Collection Point for the past

269

four years is one Dr. Erika Hanfstaengl who was employed during the Nazi Regime as one of the buyers for the Hitler collection."

Steve Munsing insisted that the remaining items in Evelyn Tucker's categories II, IV, and V—property rightfully belonging to Austria— had been thoroughly researched by his German staff and only two hundred items belonged to Austria. He further stated that the identification had been obtained from microfilm recently obtained from the Russians. The film had been taken by the Russians while they occupied Dresden. This city had been the collection center and main office for all loot acquired for the Hitler Art Museum of Linz, and the long and tedious process of identification was supposed to put an end to the bickering, but neither Dr. Wilczek or Dr. Elisabeth Gasselseder, the two Austrians working in the center, were allowed to inspect or validate the microfilm document. They were told that their validation was against new American orders and they must take the word of the Germans. For the Austrians, this logic invalidated the verification process.

In January 1950, for the first time, the Munich Collection Center had a German director, Dr. Bernhard Hoffman. Steve Munsing still maintained an office in the center but now held the position of director of the *Amerika Haus* in Munich. The squabble continued for another year and half, until June 1951. The Munich Collection Center now had 4,608 art objects that were unclaimed and unidentified as to country of origin. By that time the pendulum had swung in the favor of the Austrians, and it was agreed that all objects of which ownership was not established, upon the closing of the Munich Collection Center, would be returned to them.

Of course, the large category V property of unknown origin to be returned to Austria—could be eliminated. Should identification be established, it would not be returned. Maybe there was a way for Bavaria to win after all. S. Lane Faison, former Office of Strategic Services art investigator, had scrutinized and written a large report on the extensive Hitler collection in 1945 while stationed at Alt Aussee. In 1951 he was an art history professor at Williamstown University and was enticed away from Massachusetts for this short assignment of identifying category V items. Reporting directly to Ardelia Hall, Department of State, he began identifying category V art. Why Mr. Faison was able to accomplish this task in a few months using the same staff as the former directors is unclear. But in a relatively short time the items subject to transfer were reduced from 4,608 to 960 paintings— again, without Austrian participation.

Of these 960 unidentified valuable works of art, 394 were from Hitler's Linz Museum collection. None were from Hitler's collection stored in the Poznan Castle, his Eastern European headquarters in Poland. Surprisingly, 91 of the paintings had belonged to the mysterious Martin Bormann, and 7 of the paintings were from the Mittersill Castle in Austria.

In spite of this reduced number, the Germans continued to protest the return of the art objects. They insisted that their taxes had purchased the works of art and that they should remain in Germany. The Austrians countered that they had been good Nazis, too, and paid their taxes and were entitled to their share. The Munich newspaper *Suddeutsche Zeitung* reported that "even in 1951 the restitution of artwork continues to be an exclusive matter of the Americans. They should turn this delicate task over to sincere hands, since no one has a greater interest than Germany itself in making up for what has been done wrong." Regardless of the German protest, the Americans rightly contended that this transfer represented an obligation which the U.S. military in Germany had incurred with the U.S. military in Austria and the transfer of these 960 valuables would accomplish that obligation, which began with 27,000 pieces. The Americans also stated that this was a transfer of the property and in no way anticipated the question of possession and, further, that the Austrians would make another attempt to settle the question of ownership.

But because of newspaper articles and political protest, the valuables remained in the Munich Collection Center until HICOG gave the order on January 20, 1952, and the 960 leftover items were loaded onto two U.S. Army six-ton trucks for the first of two trips to Salzburg. Prior to loading, the objects were photographed and the negatives sent to the Department of State in Washington. On the first trip, one of the trucks could not make it up a steep hill near the border because of icy road conditions. A wrecker had to be used to pull the heavy truck up the hill. On the second day, the two trucks passed the icy spot safely, but soon afterward the engine in one truck broke down. One truck continued its journey and returned without its trailer. The same truck was then hitched to the trailer of the broken vehicle and continued the trip to Salzburg. The Munich newspapers had a field day with the mishaps in an attempt to prove that the U.S. Army was using unsafe and unorthodox shipping methods.

Edgar Breitenbach accompanied the valuables and noticed that some of the tension had eased among Dr. Otto Demus and his small staff of two and the Germans. He turned over to Demus a complete set of property control cards pertaining to the returned art. To the surprise of all, no Americans were present for the transfer of these controversial valuables. Breitenbach had discussed with the Austrians the fact that the objects were still subject to return if the Americans could establish German ownership. Unfortunately, Breitenbach immediately sensed that Demus and his staff were at an utter loss with respect to restitution procedures. Demus knew that he did not have the necessary know-how for restitution and had written, "As I have no comparable set-up [to the Munich Collection Center] I actually dread the thought of being left entirely behind to my own resources when the Americans evacuate Austria.[1]

The 960 art objects were stored in the Carabinierisaal of the Residenz Palace in Salzburg. These valuables were stored with the 1,181 Hungarian paintings that Miss Tucker had placed there, taken originally from the Hungarian Gold Train. Also included in the room were 58 paintings originally removed from the Fischhorn Castle and believed to be entirely German and Austrian; seven seventeenth-century French miniature paintings confiscated by the Austrian police from Georg Schmidt, who purchased them from a German soldier; 28 paintings belonging to the German House of Art, Munich; 6 sixteenth-century Dutch paintings from Alt Aussee; and 300 books from the Sven Heiden collection.

These were not the last items to be turned over to the Austrians. In 1956 it was revealed that a large shipment of silver, rugs, and paintings taken from the Hungarian Gold Train had been shipped to the Quartermaster Depot in Richmond, Virginia. Some of the silver candelabras had the monogram "SZ," and other miscellaneous silver items had the monogram "BJ." One large chest of silverware was marked "Klein M Budapest VII SIP." In keeping with the policy that confiscated property found in Austria would be transferred to the Austrian government, on July 30, 1957, the last valuables from the Hungarian Gold Train were turned over to the Austrian government.

An agreement was worked out between the Allies and Germany to terminate the occupation status of Germany. This contractual agreement was signed on May 26, 1952, and West Germany gained complete sovereignty. Thousands of nonrestitution works of art became the property of the Federal Republic of Germany. For a short time the remainder of the valuables in the Munich Collection Center was in German hands and under the supervision of Dr. Edgar Breitenbach, with the assistance of the able Mr. J. E. G. von Schmidt. The Munich Collection Center contained Jewish property, additional art destined to be returned to Austria, Jewish items belonging to Göring—such as candlesticks, plates, and frames—and the art that had belonged to the high-ranking Nazi officials. The Wiesbaden Collection Center contained items belonging to Germans in the Russian Occupation Zone and Jewish property, with the bulk of the material belonging to the Ettle firm, the largest art firm in Germany. (The Ettle case was being tried by the German courts, and the case had to be settled before final disposition of the art.)

The new Federal Republic of Germany established a restitution office. It was a part of the Division of Cultural Affairs of the German Foreign Office and was headed by Graf Wolf Metternich. The new regime chose to ignore the intelligence and executive ability of Edgar Breitenbach and Mr. von Schmidt, who had been a most valued employee at Wiesbaden. The German members of the old collection point staff, for the most part, were not put on the new payroll, for as time passed, the Germans who had cooperated with U.S. policy became less and less popular with their countrymen.

The excitement surrounding the Austrian shipment did not subside, and additional fuel was added to the newspaper feuds when knowledge was gained about the disposition of other art objects under control of the American military in Austria.

Thus the United States had closed the Foreign Exchange Depository, the Wiesbaden Collection Center, the Munich Collection Center, and the Property Control Warehouse, making further restitution of valuable gold, silver, diamonds, artworks, and other items extremely difficult, if not impossible.

25

Resolution

ALTHOUGH THE ART FROM the Munich Collection Center was returned to Austria because of a treaty between two U.S. Army groups, the Hungarian works of art were not returned to Hungary, because in 1949 the United States transferred the matter of restitution claims affecting alleged Hungarian property located in the U.S. Zone to the Austrian government. U.S. officials reasoned that the transfer of the art objects would bring strong objections from the Austrian government and, further, that the art in the possession of the Austrians would give them an opportunity in strengthening their bargaining position in an expected general property settlement between the two countries.

In 1955 these valuables were sent to a safeguarded, isolated fourteenth-century Carthusian monastery, located a few miles from Vienna in the town of Mauerbach. Here the valuables from the Carabinierisaal of the Residenz Palace in Salzburg, which included the 960 art objects from the Munich Collection Center and the 1,181 Hungarian paintings that Evelyn Tucker had collected, were merged with approximately 6,000 additional paintings, books, manuscripts, coin collections, and other items of great value.

These priceless works of art were handed over to the Austrians in 1955 by U.S. military forces under the Austrian State Treaty, which charged Austria with making every effort to return the art to victims of the Nazi regime. The trouble was that the United States' legal position toward Austria as a liberated country encouraged that country not to recognize any restitution obligations. From 1952 to 1969 the Austrian government made no attempt whatsoever to locate the true owners of the valuables.

On September 2, 1969, the Austrian government published in the limited-circulation *Wiener Zeitung* that 8,423 art objects existed and that claims for the objects should be filed. Surely Austria recognized that it would be most difficult to identify the treasures considering that no one outside of the Austrian government had been allowed into the monastery storehouse. A few claims were indeed processed, but none received since 1973 have been considered. The works of art are described by Austrian officials as "heirless," and they now belong to Austria. They became official possessions as the result of an Austrian law passed in 1969. The statute stipulated that any property not returned to claimants, or any property that remained unclaimed, would belong to Austria.[1] Because of continuing worldwide public pressure, in September 1986 a nine-month period was offered to allow for claims. Nevertheless, as of 1993, 48 years after World War II, only 15 paintings, 100 books and 1 weapon had been returned from Mauerbach to the rightful owners, and the monastery is still off-limits to everyone except Austrian art officials.

The truth is that Austria inherited this large collection of art from the Nazi Party. Among the works, for example, are such priceless works as Vermeer's *The Artist in His Studio*. This painting was to be the centerpiece of Hitler's planned museum in Linz. The Vermeer was sent to Austria in 1946 from the Munich Collection Center, and upon its arrival the Czernin family eagerly went after it, claiming that the purchase by Adolf Hitler was a forced sale. The claim was rejected in civil courts, and in 1952 the highest Austrian court ruled in favor of the state. The judge ruled that the painting belonged to Germany, and in accordance with restitution laws, he considered the property a form of restitution. The painting is today displayed in the Austrian Art Museum in Vienna. It is most difficult to accept that Austrians could receive restitution from Germany, considering that in a 1938 plebiscite, 99.74 percent of its citizens voted in support of the *Anschluss*.

The Artist in His Studio and the several thousand objects of great artistic and monetary value that are still stored today in the fourteenth-century Carthusian monastery in Austria should be properly acknowledged as a gift from Adolf Hitler through the generosity of the occupation government of the United States.

The original 1945 estimate of the value of the Hungarian Gold Train contents was $206,000,000. These valuables were turned over to the Inter-Government Committee for Refugees and sold for only

$1,807,000. There is therefore $204,133,000 in missing property. During the late 1940s, the Hungarian government filed objections concerning the property of Hungarian Jews and of the Museum of Györ and other valuables contained in the Hungarian Gold Train. The Hungarians insisted that the items be returned and then strenuously protested the participation of the IGCR and the subsequent auction of these valuables in New York. Regardless of their persistence, all claims and objections were ignored by the American authorities.

This case remained dormant until 1966. At that time the United States filed a claim against Hungary for war damage and debts for American citizens. Much to the surprise of the United States, the Hungarian government filed a counterclaim against the United States for $206,000,000 for "property carried to the United States by the U.S. Military after World War II." Approximately $47,000,000 worth of these claims were filed on behald of 900 Hungarian citizens. The claim was filed with George W. Spangler, chairman of the United States delegation handling negotiations with Hungary.

The Hungarian claim stated that they had found and identified the property in the U.S. Zone of Austria, prior to expulsion by the U.S. occupation authorities. The claim rightly asserted that after expulsion of the Hungarian representatives, the U.S. occupation authorities permitted the property assembled at shipping points to remain unguarded and that some of it was stolen; permitted part of the property to be stored in uncovered places with the result that it deteriorated and became worthless; used part of the property, and gave or loaned part of the valuables to local residents; sold part at public auctions; and abandoned the remainder.

The Hungarians further contended that the United States was legally obligated to pay compensation because it recognized the property as Hungarian and knew that it had been unlawfully carried away by German forces and consequently that the U.S. occupation forces had the duty under accepted principles of international law to preserve the valuables and permit their return to the rightful owners.

In defense of the claim, the Department of State contended that the liability for the valuables contained in the Hungarian Gold Train rested with the German government. They further contended that the German authorities took the property and because of this the U.S. occupation forces had no legal duty to protect the property from theft or deterioration and that under Article 30 of the peace treaty of the London Declaration of January 5, 1953, and the Quadripartite Procedure for Restitution of Allied Control Authority, dated April 17,

1946, the United States had the right to keep the Hungarian property with no legal obligation to return it. The property was war booty; consequently the U.S. government had an international legal right to keep it. And finally, said the United States, the London Declaration of January 5, 1943, created no liabilities on the part of the United States. The U.S. defense also stated that the department contended that the Hungarian government grossly exaggerated its claim although no evidence had been obtained to support this contention.[1]

The Department of Defense disputed part of the Department of State's defense, for on October 28, 1966, a secret letter was written by them, containing the following: "It appears that very little, if any of the property on the train could be classified as war booty.... Available information indicates that much of the property was susceptible of direct military use and that disposition was made by occupation authorities accordingly."

The defense, using Article 30 of the peace treaty with Hungary, is inconceivable, for section 2 clearly states: "Identifiable property of Hungary and Hungarian nationals removed by force or duress from Hungarian territories to Germany by German forces or authorities after January 20, 1945, shall be eligible for restitution." The valuables on the Hungarian Gold Train clearly fit this description. It is also unbelievable that the U.S. would use the inter-Allied declaration known as the London Declaration as a defense, considering that the intent of the declaration was to secure the right to find null and void any property transfer during the Nazi occupation.

Thousands of art treasures looted in Europe during World War II are still being sought throughout the world. After forty years, government agencies in France, Italy, Germany, Poland, and the Soviet Union are quietly working to track down paintings, tapestries, rare books, and coins worth millions of dollars. Hundreds of art gallery officials, museum directors, and enforcement organizations are watching for the reappearance of art looted during World War II.

The private German collections most thoroughly looted were those of the Krupp family and of Baron Steengracht, lord of Mayland Castle. The Munich State Galleries recovered only 50 of 650 paintings stored in the Führerbau. Also recovered were only 22 of the 262 Schloss paintings acquired for the Linz Museum. These paintings were looted on April 27, 1945, by local Germans, but were traded to American soldiers for butter, eggs, and flour. The majority of the missing German art objects were traded to American occupation troops in late 1945.

Dr. Klaus Goldmann, of the *Museum of Prehistoric and Early History*, in Berlin, is actively in pursuit of the bulk of valuables missing from the Berlin museums. He has stated that many missing valuables from World War II are hidden in the United States.[3] Much of his effort and energy is devoted to researching items in this country. Between 1945 and 1962, 3,978 stolen art objects were recovered in the United States by the Department of State and returned to Europe. The Department of State considered it their responsibility under international law to recover the objects. Not one individual or museum had criminal charges placed against them, but in some cases charges were filed by the country that was victimized.

Why the concern over treasures taken from a nation that plundered the museums, archives, and individual estates of Europe in the first place? The answer is not a simple one.

Historically, at least for many centuries prior to recent ones, the spoils of war belonged to the victors, and not many questioned this convention. In the twentieth-century, however, this notion of reparations and restitution became more firmly entrenched in the Western mind.

The Nazis, or at least some of them, in a sense reverted to the warrior code of a bygone era: whatever was conquered was fair game or booty. They took valuables from every nook and cranny of Europe, as needed or desired.

If irony exists on the American side, it lies in the fact that some U.S. military men, who would outwardly deplore the Nazi mentality, were themselves guilty of plunder and illegal seizure. There is strong evidence that more than a few Americans grew rich as a result of loot seized in Europe at war's end or acquired through long-distance deals.

Like some of our allies in the fight to stamp out the Nazi threat, some Americans and their descendants are living well because of assets that originally belonged to those who met their death in extermination camps, separate executions, or by other horrible means. For these misguided few, the Holocaust was a bargain.

The acquisition and distribution of Nazi loot at the conclusion of World War II, upon which this book barely touches, is a grossly embarrassing chapter in our history. The U.S. government, under a presidential executive order for "national security," is safeguarding the secrets of the disposition of the spoils of that great conflict. Under the guise of national security, our government is protecting those who did such a grave disservice to the millions who perished at Auschwitz, Buchenwald, and Dachau.

Appendix
Partial Inventory of SS Loot

Following are excerpts from 169 typed pages that typify the third inventory turned over to the IGCR from the Foreign Exchange Depository:

1 lot of silver rings and silver wedding rings
and diverse silver objects, total weight about
23 pounds.

1 lot of silver watch cases in bad condition, to-
tal weight about 100 pounds.   value $260

1 lot of metal watches in very bad condition, to-
tal weight 120 pounds   value $34

1 lot 18-carat scrap gold weight 3.5 pounds   value $1,260
5 14-carat gold ladies' watches
1 14-carat gold man's watch   value $ 51

1 lot of rose diamonds	25.52 carats
1 lot of rose diamonds	60.67 carats
1 lot of rose diamonds	22.28 carats
1 lot of rose diamonds	57.50 carats
1 lot crowned rose diamonds	17.02 carats
1 lot of rose diamonds	75.32 carats
1 lot of rose diamonds	277.61 carats
1 lot of rose diamonds	97.12 carats
1 lot of rose diamonds	398.15 carats
1 lot of rose diamonds	80.74 carats
1 lot of rose diamonds	207.26 carats

1 lot of diamonds	10.74 carats
1 lot of rose diamonds with mountings	3.9 grams
1 lot of glass	17.27 carats
421 diamonds	17.95 carats
24 diamonds	4.80 carats
36 diamonds	9.07 carats
360 diamonds	45.45 carats
30 diamonds	10.95 carats
730 diamonds	36.03 carats
140 diamonds	24.60 carats
67 diamonds	20.20 carats
655 diamonds	75.20 carats
177 diamonds	20.23 carats
187 diamonds	21.24 carats
2 emeralds	3.14 carats
11 emeralds	4.32 carats
59 emeralds	24.24 carats
2 cut rubies	1.69 carats
1 polished but uncut ruby	.38 carat
1 sapphire	.56 carat
	value $31,117

1 lot of leather wallets and money purses representing about 176 big pieces and 310 small ones. Total weight 53 pounds. — value $1

1 lot of fountain pens, broken or in poor condition. Some could be used after repair. Representing approximately 1,600 fountain pens. Total weight 54 pounds. — value $1

1 lot of metal knives, forks, spoons cups, cigarette cases, etc. In poor condition, weight 110 pounds. — value $12

Postcards — value $1

2 lottery tickets drawing 17th and 18th May 1944, ticket nos. 615 and 29445 — value $1

23 Red Cross Charity Coupons — value $1

Concentration camp tokens — value $1

12 sundry newspapers — value $1

355 numismatic coins — value $1,700

Acknowledgments

The author is grateful to the many people and institutions that helped with the research and writing of this book. Special thanks are due to the following:

U.S. Army Judiciary, Falls Church, Virginia
Mary B. Dennis, Deputy Clerk of Court

U.S. Army Crime Record Center, Baltimore, Maryland
Wilbur L. Hardy
Larry Ayde

U.S. Army Intelligence and Security Command, Fort Meade, Maryland
Jane Sealock, Chief, Freedom of Information/Privacy Office

National Archives and Record Services, Washington D.C.

John Taylor	Vickie Washington
Rich Boylan	William G Lewis
George G. Chalou	Steve Bern
Frederick W. Pernell	Dale Connelly

I am indebted to Larry Bush of Richmond, Virginia, for his encouragement and skill in the editing of this manuscript.

Last but not least, I pay tribute to my wife, Edda, for her fourteen years of patience during the research and writing of this book. Without that support, the task I undertook in 1980 would have proved impossible. Any success this book attains belongs to her as much as it does to me.

Notes on Sources

The source material used for this book was obtained from thousands of source documents; therefore, the author cannot list all of the documents. Consequently the footnotes are not complete or comprehensive, but do list the main records and publications.

PUBLISHED SOURCES

American Heritage. *World War II*. New York: Simon & Schuster, 1966.
Botting, Douglas. *The Aftermath: Europe*. Virginia: Time-Life, 1982.
Bradley, Omar N. *A Soldier's Story*. New York: Henry Holt & Company, 1951.
_____. *A General's Life*. New York: Simon & Schuster, 1983.
Eisenhower, Dwight D. *Crusade in Europe*. New York: Doubleday & Co., 1948.
Hitler, Adolf. *Mein Kampf*. Germany, 1971. Houghton Mifflin Co.
Hoehne, Heinz. *The Order of the Death's Head*. New York: Ballantine Books, 1969.
Howe, Thomas Carr, Jr. *Salt Mines and Castles*. New York: Bobbs-Merrill Co., 1946.
MacDonald, Charles B. *The Last Offensive*. Washington, D.C.: U.S. Government Printing Office, 1984.
Patton, George C. *War as I Knew It*. Boston: Houghton Mifflin Co., 1947.
Ryan, Cornelius. *The Last Battle*. New York: Simon & Schuster, 1966.
Shirer, William L. *Berlin Diary*. New York: Knopf, 1943.
_____. *The Rise and Fall of the Third Reich*. New York: Simon and Schuster, 1960.
Toland, John. *The Last 100 Days*. New York: Random House, 1965.
_____. *Adolf Hitler*. New York: Doubleday, 1976.
U.S. Department of State. *Foreign Relations of the United States*, Volumes for 1944–46. Washington, D.C.: U.S. Government Printing Office, 1955.
Young, Peter. *The World Almanac Book of World War II*. New Jersey, 1981.
Ziemke, Earl F. *The U.S. Army in the Occupation of Germany*. Washington D.C.: U.S. Government Printing Office, 1975.

Chapter Notes

Introduction

1. Renwick C. Kennedy, "To the Victors the Spoils," *Christian Century*, July 31, 1946.

Chapter 1: Spilling the Beans

1. Everett P. Lesley, Jr., letter to Calvin Hathaway, July 30, 1946.
2. Occupation Military Government United States (OMGUS) message signed by General Clay, July 13, 1946.
3. Everett P. Lesley, Jr., letter of July 30, 1946.
4. Everett P. Lesley, Jr., letter of July 19, 1946.

Chapter 2: The Hungarian Gold Train

1. John F. Back, Report on the Werfen Train, September 17, 1945—National archives.

Chapter 3: The Büdingen Affair

1. L. B. Lafarge, Interim Report, June 29, 1946—Monuments, Fine Art and Archival Agency (MFA&A).
2. J. G. Bonner, Customs Agent, Investigation, November 5, 1945.
3. Jeannene Pouillon, statement, July 16, 1945. 518th U.S. Military Policy Battalion.
4. George W. Harer, statement of Felicitas Ysenburg; June 28, 1945. U.S. Army, Criminal Investigations Division (CID).
5. Doris Schmidt, written statement, July 8, 1945. U.S. Army, CID.
6. Sworn testimony of Rapp: Charles McLean, inspector general (a general military name), August 27, 1945.
7. George W. Harer, statement of Dr. Rapp, July 18, 1945. U.S. Army, CID.
8. George W. Harer, statement of Ysenburg, July 13, 1945. U.S. Army, CID.
9. Examination of witness, inspector general, October 8, 1945, p. 32.

Chapter 4: The Occupation of Berlin

1. Cornelius Ryan, *The Last Battle*, New York: Simon and Schuster, 1966.
2. Ernst, Kühnel, "Statement Concerning the Destruction of the Friederichshan Repository," February 16, 1946. MFA&A.
3. Mason Hammond, "The War and Art Treasurers in Germany," *College Art Journal*, 1946.
4. Lucis Clay, *Decisions in Germany*, Garden City, N.Y.: Doubleday & Company, Inc., 1950.

Chapter 6: The Kaminsky Affair

1. Herta Waschow, Court-martial 270, p. 115, OMGUS.

Chapter 7: Concealing the Nest Eggs

1. Herta Waschow, OMGUS, Court-martial 270, p. 187.

Chapter 8: The General's Kingdom

1. Gilda Thorak, letter to commanding general, October 19, 1954.
2. C. R. Agnew, U.S. Forces Austria memo, March 8, 1946.
3. Walker M. Treece, letter, March 14, 1946.
4. Frazer J. Hayes, U.S. Forces Austraia memo, July 29, 1946.
5. Evelyn Tucker, U.S. Forces Austraia Final Status Report, February 16, 1949.
6. Paul Kubala, Seventh Army Investigation Center Military Intelligence, "Robert Ley Through the Eyes of His Secretary and Mistress," June 1, 1945.

Chapter 9: The Property Control Warehouse

1. Ralph H. Tate, letter to Harry J. Collins, June 3, 1946.

Chapter 10: The Salzburg Coin Collection

1. Howard Mckenzie, taped interview, December 1983.
2. Evelyn Tucker, U.S. Forces Austria investigative interview of Captain LeVien, July 22, 1948.
3. Criminal Investigation Division, 16th Military Police, Fort Dix, N.J. May 20, 1947.

Chapter 11: Robberies in the Property Control Warehouse

1. McGuire Testimony, U.S. Forces Austria, court martial 318499, December 2, 1946.

Chapter 12: Judge James H. McGuire

1. Hilda Radermayer's statement, U.S. Forces Austria, General Court Martial Officer 74 (GCMO74), December 30, 1947.
2. Anneliese Rausch's statement, U.S. Forces Austria, General Court Martial Officer 74, December 22, 1946.
3. Roy N. Walker, certified copy of Philip Bernstein's memo, U.S. Forces Austria, General Court Martial Officer 74, December 23, 1946.

Chapter 13: The Unearthing of the Treasure

1. Captain John W. Nickols, statement, Judge Advocate General Court Martials (JAGCM) 324335, 317327, and 319198, June 17, 1946.
2. Statement of Leola Birmingham, deputy provost marshal, Chicago, July 19, 1946. JAGCM 324335, 317327, and 319198.
3. Leola F. Birmingham, written statement to Leonarde Keller, July 19, 1946. JAGCM 324335, 317327, 319198.
4. Margarete Elizabeth Harvey, statement, September 9, 1946. JAGCM 324335, 317327 and 319198.

5. Martha Lucille Orwig, sworn statement, July 25, 1946. JAGCM 324335, 317327, and 319198.

Chapter 14: Washington D.C.—1946

1. Emma D. Block, statement; July 9, 1946. JAGCM 324335, 317327, and 319198
2. Emma D. Block, statement, July 9, 1946. JAGCM 324335, 317327, and 319198.

Chapter 16: The Trials

1. Frank L. Ball, letter to Colonel Alton C. Miller, April 30, 1946.
2. Extract copy of information contained in Report of Investigation 108th, CIC, August 10, 1948.
3. Joseph S. Robinson, letter to the secretary of army, January 23, 1948.

Chapter 17: The End of the Gold Train Property

1. James A. Barr, Report of Incidents, July 22, 1947.
2. Captain Langer, memo U.S. Forces Austria, Werfen Train, August 22, 1947.

Chapter 18: Austria—1947

1. Herbert S. Leonard, letter to Calvin Hathaway, September 13, 1946.

Chapter 20: The Salzburg Province

1. James A. Garrison, draft reply, U.S. Forces Austria, October 26, 1948.
2. H. E. Gildemeister, letter to the American embassy, Lima, Peru, May 24, 1948.

Chapter 21: The Munich Collection Center

1. Calvin Hathaway, letter to Ardelia Hall, quoting Leonard, August 16, 1948.
2. Richard F. Howard, letter to Calvin Hathaway, August 31, 1951.
3. Richard F. Howard, letter to Calvin Hathaway. August 31, 1951.
4. Richard F. Howard, letter to Calvin Hathaway, August 31, 1951.

Chapter 23: The Looting of the Munich Collection Center

1. Herbert Stewart Leonard, letter to Calvin Hathaway, October 24, 1950.

Chapter 24: The Good Fortune of Austria

1. Otto Demus, letter to James Garrison, February 12, 1948.

Chapter 25: Resolution

1. Andrew Decker, *"A Legacy of Shame," ArtNews*, December 1984.
2. Richard D. Kearney, letter to Benjamin Forman, October 5, 1966.
3. Interviews with Drs. Alfred Kernd'l and Goldmann, July 18, 1987.

Index